This book is published by Pomegranate Communications, Inc., in collaboration with the Oakland Museum of California on the occasion of the exhibition "Squeak Carnwath: Painting Is No Ordinary Object," April 25 through August 23, 2009.

Published by Pomegranate Communications, Inc.
Box 808022, Petaluma CA 94975
800.227.1428 707.782.9000
www.pomegranate.com

Pomegranate Europe Ltd.
Unit 1, Heathcote Business Centre, Hurlbutt Road
Warwick, Warwickshire CV34 6TD, UK
[+44] 0 1926 430111
sales@pomeurope.co.uk

Library of Congress Cataloging-in-Publication Data
Tsujimoto, Karen.
Squeak Carnwath : painting is no ordinary object / Karen Tsujimoto and John Yau.
p. cm.
Catalog of an exhibition at the Oakland Museum of California, Apr. 25-Aug. 23, 2009.
Includes bibliographical references and index.
ISBN 978-0-7649-4888-6
1. Carnwath, Squeak, 1947—Exhibitions. I. Yau, John, 1950- II. Carnwath, Squeak, 1947- III. Oakland Museum of California. IV. Title.
ND237.C2815A4 2009
759.13-dc22
2008036885

Front cover: *A Painting* (detail, plate 74), 2006
Oil and alkyd on canvas over panel, 139.7 x 114.3 cm (55 x 45 in.)
Collection of the artist, courtesy James Harris Gallery, Seattle

Back cover: *In Pursuit of Happiness* (plate 48), 2000
Oil and alkyd on canvas, 195.6 x 195.6 cm (77 x 77 in.)
Collection of Squeak Carnwath and Gary Knecht

Pomegranate Catalog No. A158
Designed by Mark Von Ulrich

Printed in China
18 17 16 15 14 13 12 11 10 09 10 9 8 7 6 5 4 3 2 1

contents

contributors

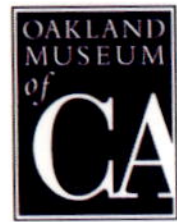

The Oakland Museum of California gratefully acknowledges the following agencies and individuals whose generous support has made the development of this book and exhibition possible.

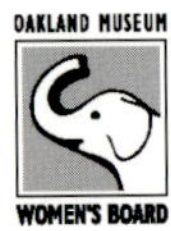

The Oakland Museum Women's Board

Art Guild of the Oakland Museum of California

Sponsors

John and Gretchen Berggruen
Agnes Cowles Bourne and James A. Luebbers
Quinn Delaney and Wayne Jordan
Magnolia Editions, Oakland, California
Nancy and Steven H. Oliver
Jon and Sonja Hoel Perkins
Sharalyn and Garen Kent Staglin

Donors

James Harris Gallery, Seattle
Leslie and George H. Hume
Dorothy F. Knecht
Peter Mendenhall
Katie and Amnon Rodan
Roselyne Chroman Swig

Pomegranate

Please send me information on other books you publish:

NAME: ______

ADDRESS: ______

CITY: ______

STATE: ______

ZIP: ______

The book I purchased was: ______

______

I am interested in the following subjects:

__ American Multicultural
__ Frank Lloyd Wright/Architecture
__ Metaphysical/Fantastic Art
__ Fine Art
__ Maps and Manuscripts
__ Music/Jazz and Blues
__ Travel and Other Cultures
__ Contemporary Lifestyles

BOX 808022 PETALUMA CALIFORNIA 94975-8022
WWW.POMEGRANATE.COM

Squeak Carnwath, 2002. © Marion Brenner.

foreword

When Karen Tsujimoto, senior curator of art at the Oakland Museum of California, is asked, "Why a major exhibition of the work of Squeak Carnwath at this time?" she readily replies, "It's about time!" Indeed, an in-depth examination of the work of Squeak Carnwath, one of the leading California artists of the last thirty years, is certainly timely, if not long overdue. With this midcareer survey, accompanied by the first major publication of the artist's work, the Oakland Museum of California continues its extensive history of presenting large-scale monographic treatments of important California artists; the museum is honored to give full consideration to Carnwath's development and her influence on the art making of our time.

Squeak Carnwath is an artist who, while maintaining a commitment to the traditional medium of painting, has explored both personal issues and grander human concerns with a technique that is at once delicate and bold, luminescent and dense, whimsical and profound. She has been an active artist in the Bay Area since her days as a graduate student at the California College of Arts and Crafts in the 1970s and her first museum presentation at the San Francisco Museum of Modern Art in 1980. She has taught at the University of California, Davis, and at UC Berkeley, and her teaching has influenced generations of young artists. Beloved by collectors both local and national, her work has received critical acclaim over decades. Yet the depth of that work, and her reputation within the broader arts community, are not well known. Sister artists with whom she worked and studied, such as Viola Frey and Jay DeFeo, have achieved major recognition, and it is our hope that through this publication and the exhibition that accompanies it, Squeak Carnwath will be seen as the significant and groundbreaking artist that she is.

The exhibition "Painting Is No Ordinary Object" focuses on Carnwath's work of the past fifteen years, since her first major painting exhibition and the emergence of her mature style. Karen Tsujimoto undertook the exploration of Carnwath's work with characteristic thoroughness and conviction. In the exhibition and in the essays she and John Yau provided for this book, the many layers in Carnwath's work are revealed, from the biographical to the symbolic, from the influence of other artists to the range of artistic production throughout her career. We are fortunate to have a curator of Ms. Tsujimoto's experience and passion for the work of living artists.

The exhibition has been enthusiastically supported by the Oakland Museum Women's Board; the Art Guild of the Oakland Museum of California; John and Gretchen Berggruen; Agnes Cowles Bourne and James A. Luebbers; Quinn Delaney and Wayne Jordan; Magnolia Editions, Oakland; Nancy and Steven H. Oliver; Jon and Sonja Hoel Perkins; Sharalyn and Garen Kent Staglin; James Harris Gallery, Seattle; Leslie and George H. Hume; Dorothy F. Knecht; Peter Mendenhall; Katie and Amnon Rodan; and Roselyne Chroman Swig. Many of these individuals are collectors and longtime friends of Squeak Carnwath, and their funding of this exhibition is really an extension of that personal connection.

We appreciate as well the generosity of the lenders to the exhibition, who are identified in the List of Works Illustrated. For many of these lenders, their "Squeak paintings" are the centerpieces of their living spaces; for several, this is their first museum loan, as many of the paintings in the show have not previously been exhibited in a public institution. We are grateful for them sharing these treasures with us and with our audience.

We also wish to acknowledge the other staff members who have been part of the team that made this project possible. In particular, thanks go to Chief Curator of Art Philip E. Linhares for his support of the original idea of a Squeak Carnwath exhibition; Registrar Joy Tahan; Interim Head Preparator Steven Thornburgh; and Kathy Borgogno, curatorial specialist, for working through every detail on the exhibition and publication.

Finally, and most particularly, we thank Squeak Carnwath and her husband and longtime collaborator, Gary Knecht. They have opened their lives, their histories, and their hearts to this project, and it has been a great pleasure and joy to have shared the experience with them.

Lori Fogarty
Executive Director
Oakland Museum of California

acknowledgments

One of the final pleasures of organizing an exhibition and book of this scope lies in recalling the many individuals who helped to bring the project to fruition. The time and energy expended are negligible compared to the reward of working with so many people of such goodwill and generosity. To all of them, I would like to express my sincere appreciation.

First and foremost I extend my deepest gratitude to Squeak Carnwath and her husband, Gary Knecht, for their tireless cooperation and graciousness in every regard. I have been grateful to have their patience, good humor, and enthusiasm throughout a long and inevitably complicated course of meetings and communications. To work so closely with the artist has been a great privilege and pleasure.

I owe a deep debt of gratitude to Carnwath's studio staff, Tracy Bosworth Bosche and Mary Warden, and to Jim Harris of James Harris Gallery, Seattle. All met my substantial requests for research and other needs with a thoroughness and enthusiasm for which I will always be grateful. The generosity with which they gave of their time, and their unwavering support, were invaluable.

Many individuals, institutions, and foundations share my regard for Squeak Carnwath's work and have expressed this through their generous financial support of this project. My sincere gratitude is extended to these donors, who are listed elsewhere in this book. I would also like to thank the other individuals—family, friends, and colleagues, too numerous to list here—who made valuable contributions honoring Carnwath's achievements. In particular, I thank Era and Don Farnsworth of Magnolia Press, Oakland, for their important and generous work on behalf of our fundraising efforts.

This project would not be possible without the generous cooperation of the many lenders and owners of Carnwath's paintings who have made available their important works for the exhibition and for book reproduction. In communicating with them all, it became very clear how much their paintings mean to them. These openhanded individuals have my gratitude. I trust that the results of this project are just reward for their participation.

With the publication of this book, the first to provide a retrospective view of Carnwath's art to date, I hope that a fuller appreciation of her work can be gained. My sincere thanks to John Yau for the insightful essay that enriches this publication. A noted poet, art writer, and professor at Mason Gross School of the Arts, Rutgers University, The State University of New Jersey, Yau brings to light new ways of understanding the artist's creative process.

It has also been a pleasure to work with Pomegranate Communications. My particular thanks go to Zoe Katherine Burke, publisher; Stephanie King, assistant publisher; James Donnelly, editor; and Mark Von Ulrich, designer, whose combined enthusiasm and expertise helped to bring this book to reality. I thank, as well, the several photographers who have provided reproductions for this book, but especially M. Lee Fatherree, who, with attention to every detail, undertook most of the photography that appears here.

From the inception of this project my colleagues at the Oakland Museum of California have helped, in large and small ways, to sustain its momentum and energy. They all have my heartfelt gratitude. Executive Director Lori Fogarty, Deputy Director Mark Medeiros, and Chief Curator of Art Philip E. Linhares have given their unqualified support to this project from the very beginning. I am grateful for their shared belief in the importance of the artist's work and in fulfilling our museum's mission of honoring the artists of California. My colleagues in the development department—especially Director of Development Maggie R. Pico, former Associate Director of Institutional and Annual Gifts Bernadette Powell, and Grant Writer Ariel Weintraub—undertook extraordinary fundraising efforts. I thank the museum's marketing and communications department, especially Communications Manager Elizabeth Whipple for her enthusiastic work on behalf of the exhibition. For their careful attention to the well-being of the artworks and the exhibition, I thank Registrar Joy Tahan and Interim Head Preparator Steven Thornburgh. Alexandra Franco, initially an intern and then my exhibition research assistant, helped in myriad ways and always with a smile. Art Interpretive Specialist Karen Nelson, with her usual energy, implemented the adjunct educational activities for the exhibition. Finally, my heartfelt appreciation goes to Curatorial Specialist Kathy Borgogno. Her unstinting commitment, attention to detail, and conscientious efforts through all phases of planning for the book and exhibition have been inestimable. She has been an invaluable colleague and constant source of support and counsel.

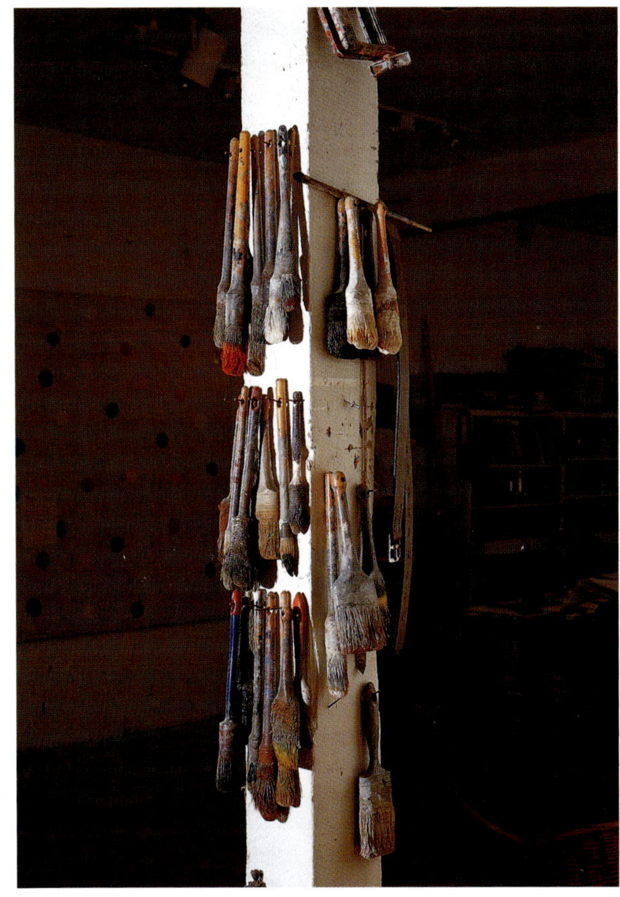

Egghouse studio, Oakland, 2001. © M. Lee Fatherree.

Last, but by no means least, I thank my husband, Bill, and daughter, Carlin, who have patiently and lovingly supported me throughout this project's unfolding.

Karen Tsujimoto
Senior Curator of Art
Oakland Museum of California

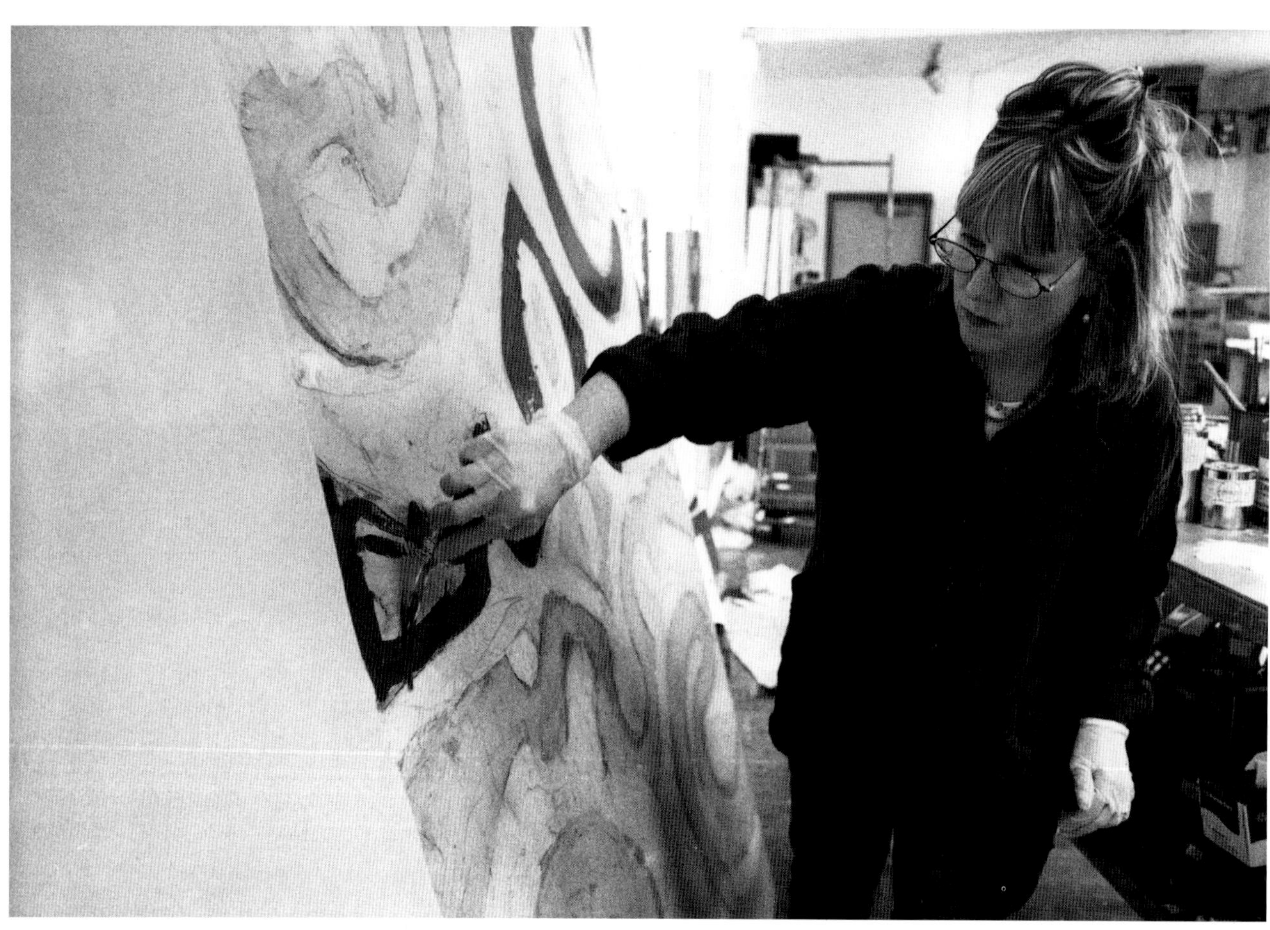

Squeak Carnwath working in Egghouse studio, Oakland, c. 1997–1998.

making art: the practice of life

KAREN TSUJIMOTO

> We make a fiction to understand feelings and emotions. The remarkable thing is that creativity is not a replica of life. But rather a tool for insight. It seems that life chooses our imagining.
> Squeak Carnwath

THESE WORDS CAN BE FOUND written in Squeak Carnwath's painting *Please* (2000; p. 119)—four simple declarations that offer a key to understanding the artist's work. Indeed, if one reads between the lines of her text, it may be said that Carnwath takes as her subject matter nothing less than the meaning of life in all its fragility, gravity, and wonder. Over and over again, throughout the different periods of her paintings, she has pointed toward universal and personal desires, using painting as a talismanic device to try to discover more happiness, more knowledge, more quiet, more peace, more luck, more life. "Painting is a philosophical enterprise," Carnwath explains, "a kind of alchemy, [in which] inert material becomes something else—a document of being, a repository of the human spirit."[1]

In over thirty years of art making, Carnwath has garnered substantial and distinguished critical acclaim. But the critical establishment has largely been occupied with the formalist and painterly aspects of her work, ignoring its iconographic features or addressing them in laundry-list fashion. There is no doubt that Carnwath's painted surfaces are "sensuous," "luscious," "seductive," and "beguiling," as many a critic has observed. Indeed this is what the artist strives for—to create a living membrane of thought, an intimate space that she describes as feeling as close as the warmth of another's skin or the soft breath of someone in a crowded room. The critic Leah Ollman once observed how Carnwath "yearns to grasp the whole, to seize the instinctual equation between hope, faith, and fear that activates humanity . . . If nature is an alchemist, making precious that which seems mundane, then so, too, is the artist, like Carnwath . . . who whispers poems of ecstasy and healing across a paint-encrusted canvas."[2]

But what exactly is one to make of the images, icons, and words that proliferate in Carnwath's paintings? What can be deduced from the symbols—some ancient and archetypal, others personal and enigmatic—in her work? The lack of interpretation of Carnwath's iconography is due, in part, to the artist's own reticence to identify "things," coupled with her generous allowance in letting others interpret her paintings as they might. But threads of understanding can be perceived beneath Carnwath's quiet pauses in conversations and her deflections in interviews. While no one essay is likely to weave a tapestry of understanding that fully explicates her work, small threads of thought are gathered here.

In early childhood, when the mind is untroubled, is when inspiration is most possible. The little child just sitting in the snow.
Agnes Martin

SQUEAK CARNWATH'S FIRST ARTWORK, created at the age of six, was made of cereal flakes and milk on the family kitchen floor. According to Carnwath, the idea of self-expression and being an artist came naturally to her, even at that early age. "It was something that I knew all along. I can't remember not knowing it or not wanting to do it. I can't remember it not being a possibility."[3] As Carnwath observes, her need to make art is as vital to her nature as the need to breathe.

The oldest of six children, Shirley Carnwath Jr. was born prematurely on May 24, 1947, in Abington, Pennsylvania. An incubator baby, she was a tiny pip-squeak of a thing; hence the family nickname that she has retained over the years. Carnwath's was a troubled, nomadic family that thrived on melodrama. Her father, a businessman climbing the corporate ladder, later a general contractor, and ongoing alcoholic, relocated the family up and down the East Coast, and even to Portland, Oregon. Carnwath recalls attending a kindergarten where nuns taught only numbers—no music, art, or even nap time. She lived in no fewer than eight cities before she graduated, in 1966, from Jenkintown High School near Philadelphia.

Despite these dislocations, Carnwath persevered with her art, taking evening art classes in Marblehead, Massachusetts, when she was around nine years old, and attending Saturday art sessions throughout her high school years. The Marblehead years are especially memorable for Carnwath, so much so that she thinks of the town as her emotional birthplace. With her dog running beside her as she biked around or walked the seashore, she could see and imagine anything. "I remember making a treasure map once—actually more than once," Carnwath recalls. "I worked on them for hours using India ink and dipping the paper in tea and then carefully burning the edges for that 'old' effect." She hid the maps around town, slipping them under rocks and in the crevices of old stone walls, her own small secrets as she began learning to navigate in the world.[4]

Given Carnwath's frank acknowledgment that she came from a dysfunctional family, one might guess that making art kept Carnwath afloat in her early years. Indeed, amidst the turbulent waters of her childhood, she seems to have teased out lessons that have helped to direct her creative journey: "I think our culture is like an alcoholic family. It can rob us, make us false." Attentiveness to the details of everyday living can save one from falseness and shallowness. In those details, the artist believes, lie "the kernels of our own majesty."[5]

In a 2001 interview, Carnwath elaborated on how coming from a family with an alcoholic parent has influenced her art practice and her embrace of the "unwatched" and "boring" things of life. "If you live with an alcoholic, you're not supposed to talk about it. It's all melodrama. The alcohol[ic] comes home and you're supposed to ignore [him]. There's this secrecy and melodrama and blow-ups in the family. Now the whole world is like that. Since I grew up in that, I'm not at all interested in promoting that. When it's all melodrama, people aren't sure what they feel . . . This way of being in the world prevents people from accessing their own feelings and how they address their own feelings. So when things are really scary or more violent, or when they are really disgusting—people know negative feelings, but they don't know the subtle variance of just simple pleasures. How color affects them, or something like that."[6]

But Carnwath's father encouraged her interest in art. He bought her paints, papers, brushes, and other art supplies, and at her request, around the end of high school or her first year of college, he took her to Manhattan to see a Jackson Pollock exhibition. Carnwath recalls the experience as "amazing . . . [to see] how other people apply this material [paint] and make visible their reality or their consciousness."[7]

Carnwath's mother had very different concerns, focused on practicality and financial well-being. How would her daughter survive as an artist? Instead, perhaps, Carnwath should go to secretarial school or become a kindergarten teacher. Paradoxically Carnwath's mother had had her own early aspirations; she had wanted to be a writer but was discouraged to pursue her dream. After her mother's death, the artist discovered, hidden in the back corners of closets, her mother's attempts at writing. "They were horrible," she recalls, "because she didn't want to reveal anything about herself—either metaphorically or any other way."

Carnwath came to see her mother as both a victim and "a fabulous negative role model." Ultimately, Carnwath believes "an artist has to be willing to reveal something, and that's the scary part. In some ways you don't have any privacy, but that's also sort of exhilarating. I feel like making any kind of artwork is an act of generosity, so that somebody else can recognize themselves in it."[8]

Despite the mixed messages Carnwath received at home, her commitment to art was clear. "I didn't know whether I would be able to support myself, but I figured that either I would find a way or, since I was raised in this culture as a woman, somebody would take care of me and I would be able to do it," she remarked in a 1986 interview. "The women of today are not going to feel that way. They are going to feel that they have to make their own way. But there's freedom to having been a woman where you can do anything—at least at the time I was born."[9]

Carnwath is part of the first wave of baby boomers, a population that, as it matured, increasingly challenged the status quo and discarded the old order. In 1955, when Carnwath was eight years old, Adlai Stevenson addressed the all-female Smith College graduating class, urging the young women not to define themselves through professional activities, but instead to focus on their roles as wives and mothers.[10] In that same year, Rosa Parks refused to move to the back of the bus in Montgomery, Alabama. Six years later, John F. Kennedy, at Eleanor Roosevelt's urging, established the Presidential Commission on the Status of Women, which evaluated women's progress and made recommendations for action on legal treatment, employment, and tax laws. In 1966, the year Carnwath graduated from high school, the National Organization for Women was organized in response to the federal government's failure to enforce Title VII of the Civil Rights Act, which banned discrimination based on sex. On the opposite coast, in Oakland, the Black Panther Party was founded, advocating for land, food, housing, education, clothing, justice, and peace for all black people and the oppressed.

The older of two girls in a family of six children, Carnwath noticed early on how her brothers were always favored. In grade school, she became aware that teachers were partial to the boys. This eventually taught her to be more aggressive and assertive; later she would address these inequities in her paintings. "I think that any artist's work is a political act, some people's is more overt than others," she has observed. "But if one is really trying to be on their own edge, and take risks at least personally and trying to be generous at the same time and give something back, then I think that one is helping other people's perceptions, opening them up to understand what it is like to be a man or a woman, black or Chinese."[11]

After graduating from high school in 1966, Carnwath moved to Godfrey, Illinois, where she attended the all-female Monticello Junior College for two years. There she continued to study art and developed an interest in ceramics, studying with Hillis Arnold. Surprisingly at that time, Arnold encouraged working with clay as a purely sculptural medium; Carnwath learned to throw pots on a wheel a few years later. In the summer of 1968, Carnwath enrolled in a program at the Aegean School of Fine Arts (now the Aegean Center for the Fine Arts), in Paros, Greece. One of the larger islands of the Cyclades—though no more than thirteen miles long and ten miles wide—Paros is known for its fine white marble. Carnwath remembers Paros as not only a beautiful but a mystical place. It was here that she met Gary Knecht, a native San Franciscan, whom she would marry in 1973.

In 1968 Carnwath and Knecht enrolled at Goddard College, a small liberal arts school in rural Vermont. Goddard stresses individual study, and students create their own curricula. Carnwath pursued her interest in ceramics, learning to throw pots, and also continued to paint, producing images evocative, she would later realize, of Jain tantric paintings. Dating to around the fifth century BCE in India, Jain art and architecture are meant to inspire spiritual values. Carnwath's paintings, since destroyed, prefigured the work to come.

Goddard's educational philosophy, dating to its founding in 1938, emphasizes its students' lives in full, balancing "the intellectual and emotional; thinking and doing; the arts and academics; past, present, and future; making a life and making a living." During Carnwath's brief time there, the campus was a gathering point for politically active students, and Carnwath was exposed to some of the first-wave of feminist thinkers and writers who lectured at the school. Though Carnwath never became a window-smashing radical, she learned the importance of thinking for oneself and forming one's own opinion. A political stance, as she observes, can become a confinement and a stereotype.

> Career advancement can be toxic, Daniel said. A person should do what they love, whatever the status.
> Richard Powers

IN 1969 CARNWATH MOVED TO CALIFORNIA with Knecht as he wanted to return to the Bay Area. She considered enrolling at the San Francisco Art Institute before settling on Oakland's California College of Arts and Crafts (now California College of the Arts), finding the intimate and casual CCAC campus a more comfortable fit. There she met the ceramic artist and teacher Viola Frey, who would become a lifelong friend. Carnwath recalls that it was fate or just dumb luck that brought the two together. Before deciding to register at the Oakland school, Carnwath happened to meet Frey there while she was loading a kiln. Under the impression that Frey was a student, Carnwath talked with her for several hours. By the time Carnwath decided to enroll at CCAC, all of the ceramics classes were filled. Happily, however, and perhaps fatefully, Frey made room in her classes for Carnwath.

Founded in 1907, CCAC had an established reputation for training artists in the practical disciplines of industrial design, applied arts and crafts, and art education. The artist David Ireland recalls that when he attended the school in the 1950s, it was known as a kind of West Coast Bauhaus. During the 1950s and 1960s, the school was a creative incubator for many who have contributed to California's distinguished history of art. Trude Guermonprez set new standards in the field of textiles; Margaret de Patta, in jewelry; Robert Arneson, Marvin Lipofsky, Manuel Neri, and Peter Voulkos in ceramics, glass, and sculpture. By the time Carnwath enrolled at CCAC in 1970, the school was also known for having graduated a small circle of painters, including Robert Bechtle, Ralph Goings, and Richard McLean, who gained national attention for the uncanny realism of their work.

Frey, a CCAC alumna herself, trained as a painter but moved easily between two- and three-dimensional work. When Carnwath met her, she had just joined the CCAC faculty and was creating large ceramic vessels, baroquely embellished with colorfully glazed animal and human forms inspired by bric-a-brac found at flea markets. Later, in vibrantly colored, large-scale figurative ceramic sculptures begun in the 1980s, Frey confronted issues of personal history, masculinity/femininity, power/powerlessness, and what it means to be an artist and a woman—issues not lost on Carnwath.

But Carnwath dropped out in 1971, after three semesters at the school. By her own accounting she had been studying art since she was a child and she simply needed a break to work on her own. Besides, she felt no compelling need to get an undergraduate degree.

At around this time she and Knecht purchased a house in Oakland and started a commune, raising vegetables and chickens in their backyard. Carnwath also participated in a food-buying co-op and went so far as to share with her housemates the money she received from selling her art. She worked at a variety of jobs—retail sales, waitressing, housecleaning, and hauling—after the commune disbanded. She also worked as the shop master in the CCAC ceramics department as she and Knecht took turns financially supporting one another. Carnwath describes this choice of living circumstances as an experiment in "idealism" and a quest to be as different from her parents as she could. Frey, who had also earlier participated in a commune, recalled that Carnwath lived as she did for all the reasons that impelled many young people at the time. Ending war, protecting the environment, and seeking social and economic justice were important issues for Carnwath, as for so many of her peers.[12]

During this period, Carnwath also rented a storefront on Webster Street, near Oakland's Chinatown, and with another local artist, Jessie Russell, opened Roxie and Toots' Salon d'Art, a place where she could exhibit her own work. "My work was never accepted into the [CCAC] juried group shows," she recalled. "I dropped out of school (probably thinking 'I'll show them!'). I began my exhibition career at the salon." Carnwath was then producing what Frey facetiously called "invisible disappearing drawings." They were, as Carnwath elaborated, "self-portraits done with a number nine lead. Very pale. Very light."[13]

Carnwath's plan to gain public exposure for her art was happily successful. She began participating in local and regional shows, including the Richmond Art Center's annual "Designer/Craftsmen" show, then one of California's most important crafts exhibitions. She was also included in the 1974 "California Ceramics & Glass" exhibition, presented by the Oakland Museum (now the Oakland Museum of California). The presentation was one of four open competitive shows then hosted by the museum as a way to survey current developments in California art. Carnwath's porcelain drawing *Island Ladies Get Stuck On* was one of four hundred artworks selected for exhibition from more than two thousand entries. Despite the huge size of the show, Carnwath was in good company exhibiting with among others Laura Andreson, Philip Cornelius, Stephen De Staebler, Michael Frimkess, Richard Moquin, Harrison McIntosh, Ron Nagle, Richard Notkin, and Elsa Rady.

In the mid-1970s Carnwath and Knecht moved to a Victorian house in Alameda, south of downtown Oakland. While focusing on her art, Carnwath also freelanced as a color consultant, selecting paint schemes for other local Victorians. Shortly after purchasing the house she decided to return to CCAC. Her reason was quite practical: now twenty-eight, she felt she needed a master's degree for career advancement and in order to teach. "I wanted to change my work and up the ante—take more risks, have people look at my work more critically," Carnwath recalls.[14] Although she had no undergraduate degree, Frey accepted her into the graduate ceramics program on the strength of her portfolio.

A woman must have money
and a room of her own.
Virginia Woolf

CARNWATH RECEIVED HER MFA in 1977, with high distinction in ceramics. Ironically within a few years, she would decide never to work in clay again. Carnwath remembers a "chauvinistic" attitude toward the medium at the time as Bay Area ceramic artists began working on an increasingly larger scale to validate their art against painting and sculpture. Carnwath eventually came to see clay as an "orphan material," and she didn't want to take on the battle of legitimizing it.[15]

During and after graduate school, Carnwath found inspiration in the work of Virginia Woolf. As with her contemporaries Proust and Joyce—and echoed in Carnwath's paintings—Woolf's principal concern lay in philosophical introspection as she explored her characters' psyches and emotions and the nature of fractured narrative and chronology, especially from a woman's point of view.

Woolf's *To the Lighthouse* (1927) centers around two gatherings—ten years apart, in 1910 and 1920—of family and friends on a Scottish island. One of the novel's themes concerns a houseguest, the painter Lily Briscoe, who struggles in the midst of social and family drama to paint a portrait of her hostess even as another male guest asserts that women can neither paint nor write. *To the Lighthouse* proceeds not through plot-driven action or plot-furthering dialogue but through its characters' private thoughts and observations.

In *A Room of One's Own* (1929), Woolf examined, among other topics, whether women are capable of producing art the equal of that made by men. Her "Judith Shakespeare," an invented sister of William, shows that a woman with Shakespeare's gift would have been thwarted—by dependency or patriarchal mores—in her efforts to express it.

For her 1977 graduate exhibition, Carnwath created a large installation titled *Virginia Woolf's Last Letter*. One of Carnwath's last works made entirely of ceramics, it was composed of small handmade clay river rocks arranged on the floor. Measuring five feet by nine feet, the work is overtly an homage to Woolf, who, at the age of fifty-nine, weighted her pockets with stones and walked into the river near her East Sussex home.

In Woolf's last note to her husband, she wrote: "I feel certain that I am going mad again . . . And I shan't recover this time. I begin to hear voices, and I can't concentrate. So I am doing what seems the best thing to do. You have given me the greatest possible happiness . . . I don't think two people could have been happier than we have been."[16]

Looking carefully at reproductions of Carnwath's early installation, one finds scattered among the gray clay stones some that are cut in half and inscribed with Woolf's words: "You have given me the greatest possible happiness." Seen in retrospect, Carnwath's intimate act of handwriting suggests a watershed moment in her evolving artistic life, for it introduces what eventually become two longstanding preoccupations: the use of words as an integral part of her work and the making of art as a tool in the search for happiness.

Carnwath referred again to Woolf in the 1979 installation *Her Room* (1979; p. 18). This room-sized installation, made of wood, clay, silk, oil paint, wax, and string, among other materials, featured a vertical structure that initially might be read as a tall lifeguard's chair, surrounded on the ground by ghostlike forms huddling near disarrayed campfires. On a second reading, the lifeguard's tower becomes a tall, narrow "room," surrounded by forms representing her five younger siblings, with one of them, a feisty brother, in close proximity to a long spear. As the oldest child in her family, Carnwath undoubtedly often shouldered much responsibility. The vertical structure might then be read as a place of bleak watchfulness or one of wishful escape—like the room she has recalled wanting as a child: a private space, at attic height, where no one could bother her.

Her Room might surprise those who know Carnwath only as a painter. But in her installations, or "fallen paintings," she was "trying things out," learning things that would prove of enduring importance in her art. Carnwath was building up what she calls "cellular memory," an understanding of three-dimensional form as a tool for painting.[17] The installation also reveals her interest in iconography, the representation of one thing by another. The formal elements that appear in *Her Room* will also resurface in Carnwath's mature work. One is the conjunction of opposites: the black and whitish fabric that curtains the "room," the simultaneously vertical and horizontal structure of the piece, the play of transparency and opaqueness; the strong element of autobiography is another. Carnwath also began here to introduce archetypal symbols: handprints, the small crude vessels that sit above the black rectangle of silk. Her handprints reappear in paintings some twenty years later, as in *No More, No More* (1996; p. 59) and *Plaid Lost* (1999; p. 111)—as do the forms of vessels.

Carnwath's experiments with installation art reflect the creative tenor of the national art scene at the time. From the late 1960s throughout the 1970s, installation, conceptual, feminist, and performance art challenged traditional definitions of art. Huge, macho outdoor works, like Robert Smithson's *Spiral Jetty* (1969-1970)—a jetty of earth and stone, spiraling 1,500 feet out into the Great Salt Lake—radically revised the conventional notion of sculpture. Robert Morris sought to explore the awakening of human consciousness in his "scatter" piece installations, activating gallery spaces with randomly strewn pieces of felt, rubber, and aluminum. Judy Chicago established the nation's first feminist art education program at Fresno State College (now California State University, Fresno). The fifteen students in her all-female class built an off-campus studio space where, without defensiveness and male interference, they could evaluate their personal experiences and sense of self-discovery.

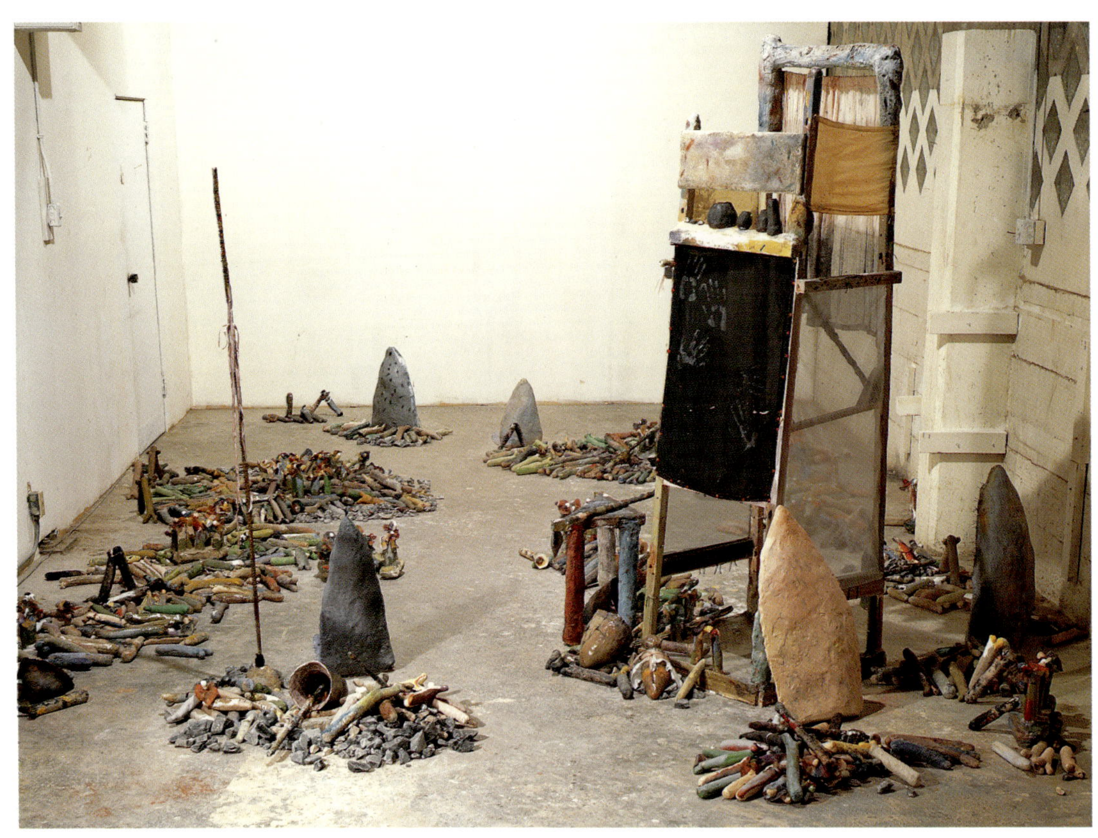

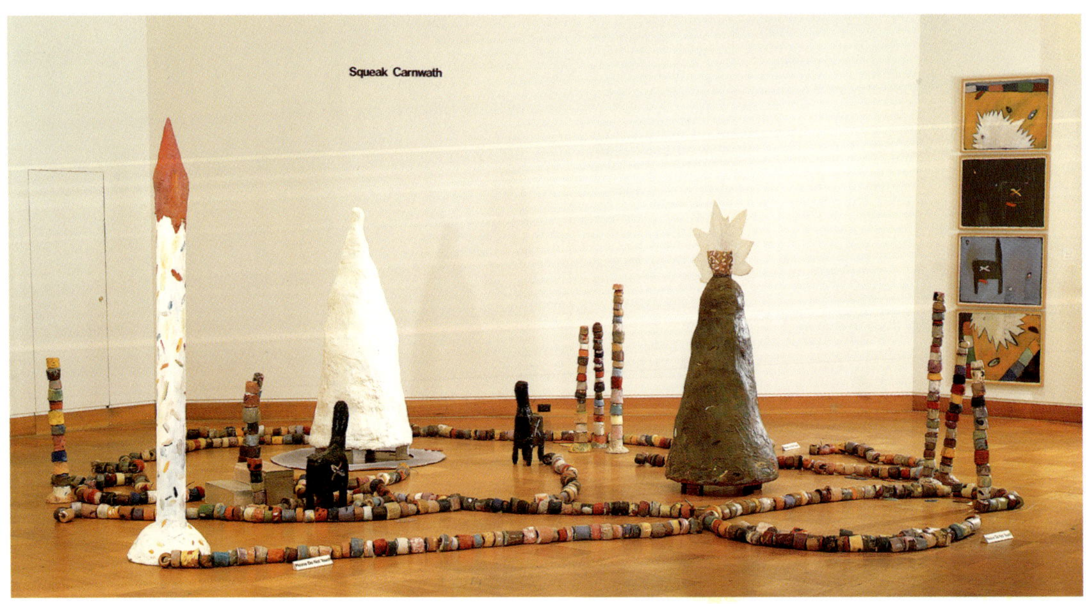

1. **Her Room,** 1979 (above)

4. **My Own Ghost,** 1980 (below)

The rethinking of art was no less radical in the Bay Area. In September 1970, at the Richmond Art Center, Terry Fox lay on a square mound of earth for six hours and attempted to levitate. Fox was seriously ill with Hodgkin's disease at that time, and questions relating to life forces were of uppermost concern in his art. Encircled by a string attached to tubes of "elemental fluids"—blood, milk, water, and urine—his body left a cruciform imprint in the dirt. Entitled *Levitation*, the work was performed privately; the residue, with its psychic charge, was left for visitors to contemplate.

Similarly, Linda Montano's Bay Area performance pieces publicly explored her private life. In a 1974 piece performed at 63 Bluxome Street, a San Francisco alternative artist's space, the artist lay for three hours in a crib, dressed in a nightgown and clutching a baby bottle and doll, while from a tape recorder her mother talked about her birth and childhood. Montano, a former nun who married, was seeking to revisit her roots, looking for clues as to why her life now seemed so unbalanced. Like many female artists of the time, Montano used art as a means of self-exploration, a process of "getting into myself so deeply that I would be able to get out of myself."[18]

In 1980, Carnwath completed *My Own Ghost* (p. 18), another room-sized installation. The piece was significant in two ways: it helped her to gain regional and national attention when it was exhibited at the San Francisco Museum of Modern Art, and it publicly acknowledged a very private moment in her life, the death of her father two years earlier.

As Carnwath was completing the earlier installation *Her Room*, her father was suffering from a terminal illness. Being with him in the last month of his life, Carnwath was moved by the amount of meaningful communication she experienced through minimal use of words. In turn she tried to express her memory and thoughts of loss through essentially nonverbal references in her artwork. Recalling the 1980 piece nearly thirty years later, Carnwath clarified its symbolism: the installation centers around a white "ghost"—her father—and a second, gray ghost with a spiked headdress, "the bride." Two small black animal forms allude to her father's love of dogs, a love Carnwath inherited. A meandering length of what look like colorful, oversized children's toy beads represents the road she drove to visit her father in the hospital, passing red-and-white directional posts that stood as sentries on her daily journey.[19]

The installation also included several paintings and works on paper, among them *My Own Ghost #9* (1979; p. 20). A large work on paper, the piece evokes a sense of an inner light, something that becomes more evident in Carnwath's later paintings; in it, Carnwath also appears to be reflecting on her own mortality. The ghostly form that dominates the work has pubes; a vessel—a universal feminine symbol—sits close to the ghost's heart. Around the border are scrawled the words of the child's prayer "Now I lay me down to sleep." As she would continue to do, Carnwath was converting words into pure graphic signs and relocating these signs into the visual sphere of her art.

Reflecting on compositional elements of this and earlier work, Carnwath explained how, in and after graduate school, she disciplined herself "to think about what things meant and how I was going to make the piece work; and I planned it out more—not how it was going to look, but kind of structurally and metaphorically . . . So I knew more what the work was about when I started it. And now that's not true . . . I want to be frightened again, to not know where I'm going, because it makes it more interesting for me."[20] Carnwath still believes, however, that after all is said and done the artist must be able to "name the experience" to be authentic.

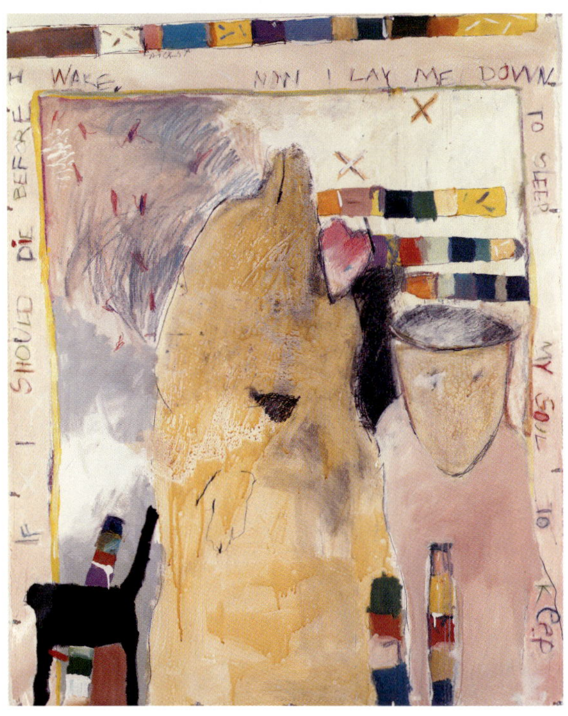

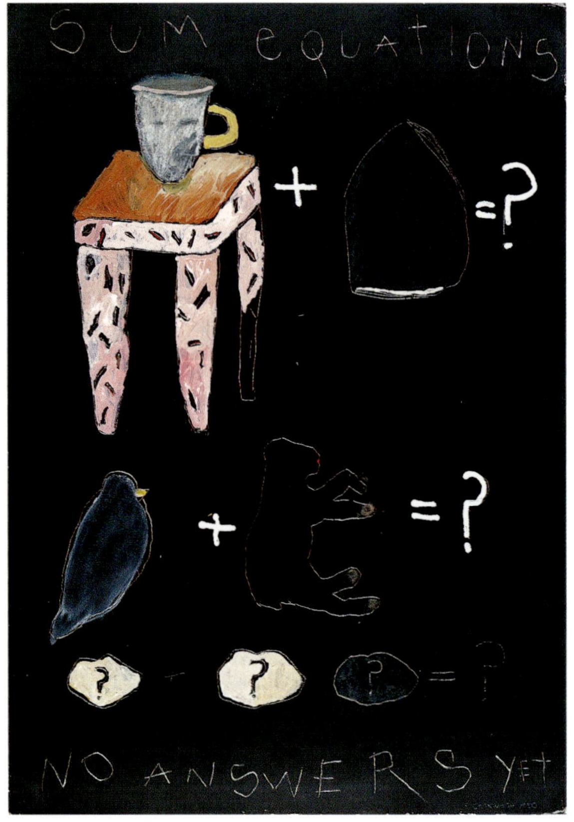

2. **My Own Ghost #9,** 1979 (above)

5. **Sum Equations,** 1980 (below)

Carnwath exhibited the recently completed *My Own Ghost* and related paintings as one of three artists honored by the Society for the Encouragement of Contemporary Art (SECA), an auxiliary of the San Francisco Museum of Modern Art (SFMOMA).[21] SECA's annual exhibition honors significant new Bay Area talent with a cash award and the opportunity for wider recognition.

Reviewing the exhibition in the *Oakland Tribune*, the critic Charles Shere remarked that it should perhaps have been a solo show: to his eye, Carnwath's work clearly stood out among her peers. Shere continued, "I suspect this will turn out to be one of the major contributions of the 70s and 80s, and will particularly stem from the awakened interest in women's sensibilities and awareness. In such hands as Carnwath's it produces strong, vital, universally meaningful results."[22]

Steven Winn observed in a review for *ARTnews* how, at first glance, Carnwath's installation resembled "an exuberant child's messy playroom, with large objects dragged out to the center of the floor and left there, grand projects half completed and abandoned, favorite toys in prime locations, and everywhere spills and unidentifiable litter." But "on closer inspection . . . the lumpy cones made of wood and clay, the plaster doughnuts stacked up on sticks and strung in looping patterns on the floor, even a pair of rudely fashioned jet-black dogs reveal a more complex, carefully worked-out fantasy." Winn concluded, "This is all a child's dream, made of Christmas and toys and ghosts, but a dream that's beginning to go bad in the night."[23]

A painting reveals, covers, and uncovers. It is the archaeology of the mind. It is about the cosmology of the soul.
Squeak Carnwath

EVEN AS THE SECA SHOW attracted attention to her installation work, Carnwath was beginning gradually to return to the practice of painting. At the time she saw painting and sculpture as equal tools for creative expression, as witnessed in *My Old House* (1980; p. 23); *Sum Equations* (1980; p. 20); and *Keepers of Our Culture* (1981; p. 23). But within a year or two Carnwath was focusing exclusively on painting although she has occasionally made small sculptures as a way to explore imagery for her canvases.

These three pieces, all created within a year of one another, point to themes that will resurface throughout Carnwath's later work. First is the issue of autobiography, overt or unstated, that weaves its way throughout Carnwath's art. Second, as represented by *Keepers of Our Culture*, is the artist's search for her place as a good citizen in the world. Finally there is the question, raised in *Sum Equations*, of how the artist is to reconcile these things; in other words, how to deal with life and death. As she points out in *Sum Equations*: "No answers yet."

In *My Old House,* Carnwath seems still to be mourning the loss of her father and what she once knew as home. Reminiscence and self-scrutiny had been growing as driving forces for some years. For example, in 1975, in her first year of graduate school, Carnwath recorded her childhood memories as *The I Stories.* On the tape, she told how as a young girl she got her first whipping, discovered the library, traded clothes with a friend, had her dog taken away, took piano lessons from a kindly man, and discovered the joy of art. Nighttime, she recalled, was an especially fascinating time for her as she lay in bed and imagined, on her bedroom ceiling, paintings in black, white, and gray that ebbed and flowed at her will. When her toes tingled, the ceiling texture would change, while the furniture, banded with bright colors, danced around the room. Carnwath experienced this space with her whole body and recalls being excited and sometimes frightened—feelings she still has when she enters her studio.

These works also foreshadow the crucial roles that symbols would play in the later art. As J. C. Cooper writes, "The study of symbolism is not mere erudition; it concerns man's knowledge of himself."[24] Images of ravens, vessels, windows, and dogs—among many others—can be found frequently in the artist's work. The raven sitting at the window in *My Old House,* once a common symbol in northern Europe for the death-goddess, reappears nearly twenty-five years later in *Four Months* (1994; p. 39). The vessels and vases that proliferate in *My Old House* are among Carnwath's most consistent motifs. The vessel symbolizes the feminine, of course; but also, in alchemical thought, it is the receptacle of opposites, the container of that which is to be transformed. It represents protection, nourishment, and inner values, and is the matrix from which the philosopher's stone is born.[25]

One of Carnwath's last significant sculptural works was a six-foot-high mixed-media piece, *Keepers of Our Culture.* Reflecting on her refocused attention to painting, Carnwath has remarked: "Sculptors will hate me for saying this, but I think [painting] is more complex than sculpture. Painting doesn't displace our physical space. It's an arena where we, as viewers, grant it a reality as if the painting were a 'real thing' or a 'real place.' It's not. Often it's not even a depiction of it. It's an activity that occurs between the painter, the paint and the surface—just this thin film of stuff only millimeters thick. It's really thin, but it's really deep, which is what I love about it. It's something that appears real, but if you were to take it apart, deconstruct it, you find it's just this little layer of dirt, of pigment."[26]

Painting, Carnwath believes, creates a stand-in for the body and the psyche, and as such serves as a crucial tool of self-discovery. For her, the *act* of painting is about making something concrete out of things—thoughts, memories, experiences—that will always be impalpable. For example, the marriage ceremony is an *act* that confirms the intangible: love and commitment. The burial of a loved one is an *act* signifying respect and honor. How do we hold love and loss in our hands? Sengai, the monk and *sumi-e* master, was once accused of wielding his brush to laugh at human frailties. He retorted, "No, I am not. Every stroke of my brush is the overflow of my inmost heart."[27]

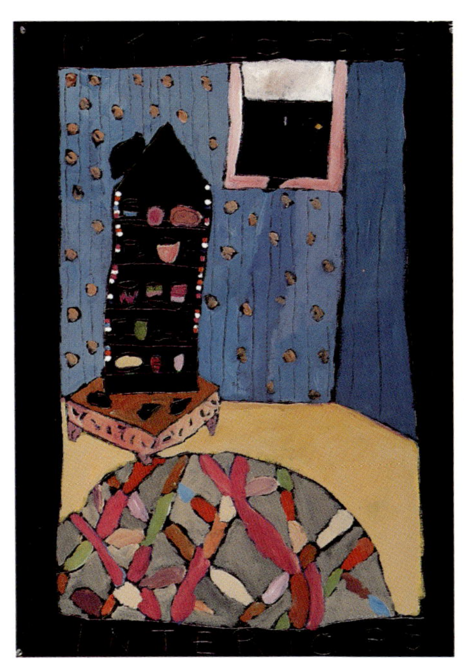

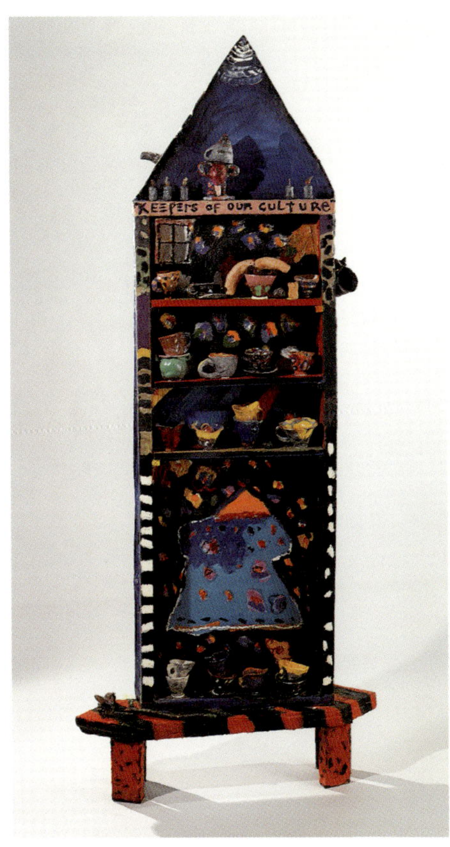

3. **My Old House,** 1980 (above)

7. **Keepers of Our Culture,** 1981 (below)

Mental space is larger than
anyone can think.
Richard Powers

SOON AFTER HER 1980 SECA/SFMOMA exhibition, Carnwath hit a creative wall—as many artists do following major presentations of their work. The canvases *I Must Try Harder To Believe* (1981; p. 25) and *Head Ache* (1983; p. 25) reflect the work that ensued for several years. For a time, as can be seen in *I Must Try Harder To Believe*, Carnwath's paintings became bolder in palette and more simplified and stylized in form—"quasi-primitive," one critic observed—recalling elements of Henri Matisse's figurative cutouts and ancient Cycladic female idols, which Carnwath would have seen during her Aegean travels. The culture that produced these votive figures, most of which were female, was preliterate, thus there are no writings to suggest their purpose. Some archaeologists believe that they portray the Mother Goddess, a symbol of fertility and rejuvenation, although in Carnwath's painting, the figure has only one breast.

I Must Try Harder To Believe might also be perceived as a self-portrait. In place of the face is an oval of black, no doubt representing the dark void of Carnwath's psyche at the time. The pubes' pronounced triangular form contrasts with the phallic forms of the calla lilies, which variously signify rebirth and marriage. The references to breasts and penises will appear in later work such as *Nursery Wall* (1998; p. 60)—though they are rendered more subtly, almost suggestive of graffiti. As Carnwath explains, she likes to tantalize the viewer with a little eroticism and sexuality.[28]

Significantly, the female figure in the 1981 painting appears in a transparent vessel of what one might guess to be *aqua vitae*, the water of life. The partially filled glass reappears years later, in works such as *Water Cake Lily* (1994; p. 38), *Some Same* (1994; p. 38), and *Green Floor* (1996; p. 58). What Carnwath seems to suggest in these paintings is the age-old question: Is the glass half full or half empty?

In 1982 Carnwath exhibited *I Must Try Harder To Believe* and related paintings in her first solo gallery exhibition in San Francisco. The show, at Hansen Fuller Goldeen, was positively reviewed by most critics. But Thomas Albright of the *San Francisco Chronicle* perceived things differently: "The impulse behind these paintings seems authentic enough. One becomes convinced that these image/symbols must mean *something*, to Carnwath at least, through sheer dint of repetition as well as the boldness with which they are executed." Albright asserted that the "formalist structuralism and cryptic narrative content" of Carnwath's paintings appeared as merely "de rigueur" elements for what he saw as the wave of New Imagist paintings then in the national spotlight.[29]

Whether one agrees with Albright's critique or not, he was right to associate paintings such as *I Must Try Harder To Believe* with the New Image paintings that emerged in New York in the mid-1970s. Jennifer Bartlett, Jonathan Borofsky, Neil Jenney, Robert Moskowitz, and Susan Rothenberg were among those identified with this new style. Although each artist's work was highly individual, collectively their paintings pointed to major shifts in the art world: the return to recognizable figurative imagery after a decade of minimalism, and the return to painting on canvas after years of conceptual art. Speaking of her work at the time, which focused on large abstract paintings of horses, Rothenberg, whom Carnwath regards highly, explained: "Most of my work is not run through a rational part of my brain. It comes from a place in me that I don't choose to examine. I just let it come. I don't have any special affection for horses. A terrific cypress will do it for me, too. But I knew that the horse is a powerful, recognizable thing, and that it would take care of my need for an image. Then I did the human heads and hands . . . I connected to [them] because that's what I work with, a head and a hand, and I thought, why not paint [them] . . . What I think the work was starting to talk about is growing, taking journeys."[30]

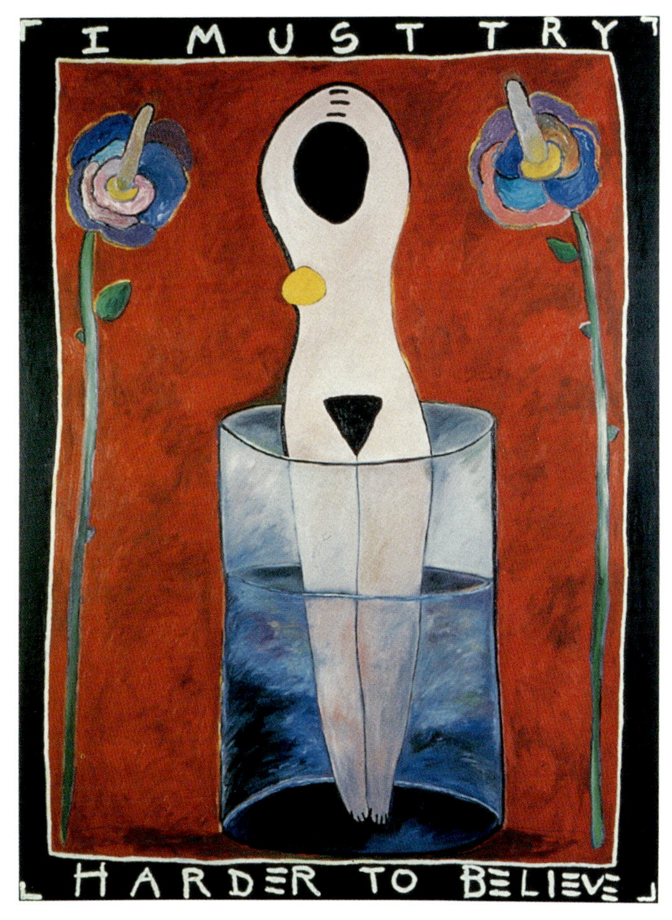

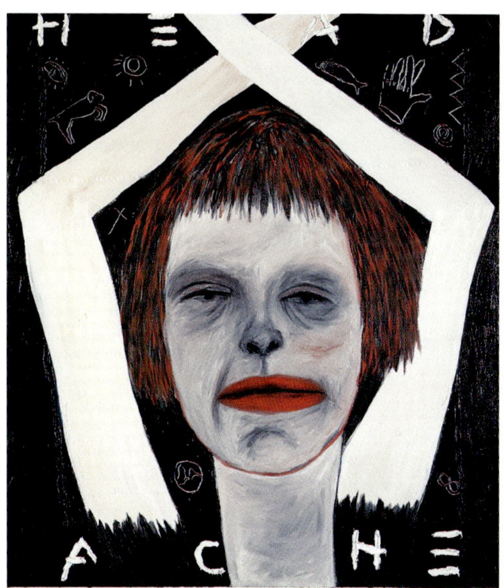

6. **I Must Try Harder To Believe,** 1981 (above)

8. **Head Ache,** 1983 (below)

In 1982, at artist Joan Brown's encouragement, Carnwath took a year-long position teaching drawing at the University of California, Berkeley. Carnwath had little experience with the practice, save for some works dating from graduate school, so she set about teaching herself to draw, working with a model for the first time. Drawing became a preoccupation for the next several years. Writing in her notebook, Carnwath observed how important drawing is for artists and declared that they must learn how to draw "with their own mark, their own sight, their own visions of reality. A line has to be earned by an artist . . . one has to *mean* every inch of the line's existence."[31]

Among the resulting works were several large charcoal drawings, dating from roughly 1984 to 1986 and including *Companion* (1984; p. 27). When they were exhibited for the first time, over a dozen years later, the curator Gay Shelton wrote vividly of how robust and rich they were—the artist's hand dragging thick sticks of charcoal across the paper, feathering laden black lines into mists of gray, creating a sense of luminosity from the white of the paper. Shelton saw these "haptically navigated" drawings as a milestone in the evolution of Carnwath's picture making, where discoveries about line and space, graphic symbolism, and narrative phrasing began to gel for the artist.[32]

But Shelton's brief essay made no mention of the poignancy and symbolism of these dark yet luminous works, which might easily be seen as self-portraits. In *Companion,* Carnwath's Airedale—her lapdog of loneliness—stays faithfully by her side as she weeps. The tears, Carnwath explains, refer to paintings of the martyred St. Sebastian and his arrow-filled, bleeding body; the fish alludes to Picasso's phallic imagery. The spiral symbolizes the water of life; the faintly depicted eyes, seeing and watchfulness. Significantly, the female is nude, as if baring her bleak reality, a haunted one as suggested by the ghostly finger and handprints that seem to be grasping for *something.*

Though we may never know the reasons behind the pathos of the drawing, it is clear that the artist is sharing some pain with us. When asked about the work's content, Carnwath replied, "Those personal things allow me the door of departure or the place to leave from. After that, it is not there anymore, then it's not that personal thing anymore." She elaborated: "I think what it's about is relatedness and a regular loneliness, an existential loneliness; the idea that we have to be culpable for being and how do we negotiate being, which is pretty hard to do. The specifics that occur in the drawing or the weight of the line can add certain emotions or add different layers of meaning to different viewers."[33]

In recent studies, neuroscientists have articulated a phenomenon known as embodied cognition: a breaking down of the distinction between mind and body, perception and thought, thought and action. Put differently, some researchers believe that people think with their bodies, not just with their brains. Pacing, gesturing with the hands, rubbing one's scalp may actually clarify the thought process. In examining how action shapes ideation, some neuroscientists are reconsidering assumptions about thought that date to the seventeenth century and Descartes's well-known statement "Cogito, ergo sum" (I think; therefore I am).

Carnwath lives this idea of embodied cognition in her studio as she coaxes paint across her canvases. "I am concerned with making the surface real and having it be a felt space or place," she explained in 1986. "I really believe in handmade, man-made, person-made, and that we are losing track of that. Part of my job . . . is to preserve that. I want to preserve primary ways of being and perceiving, like making paintings, making sculptures, and doing things with our hands. It reminds me of the fragility of being, like the memento mori. It does not smooth anything out. It is unforgiving in a way that's forgiving."[34]

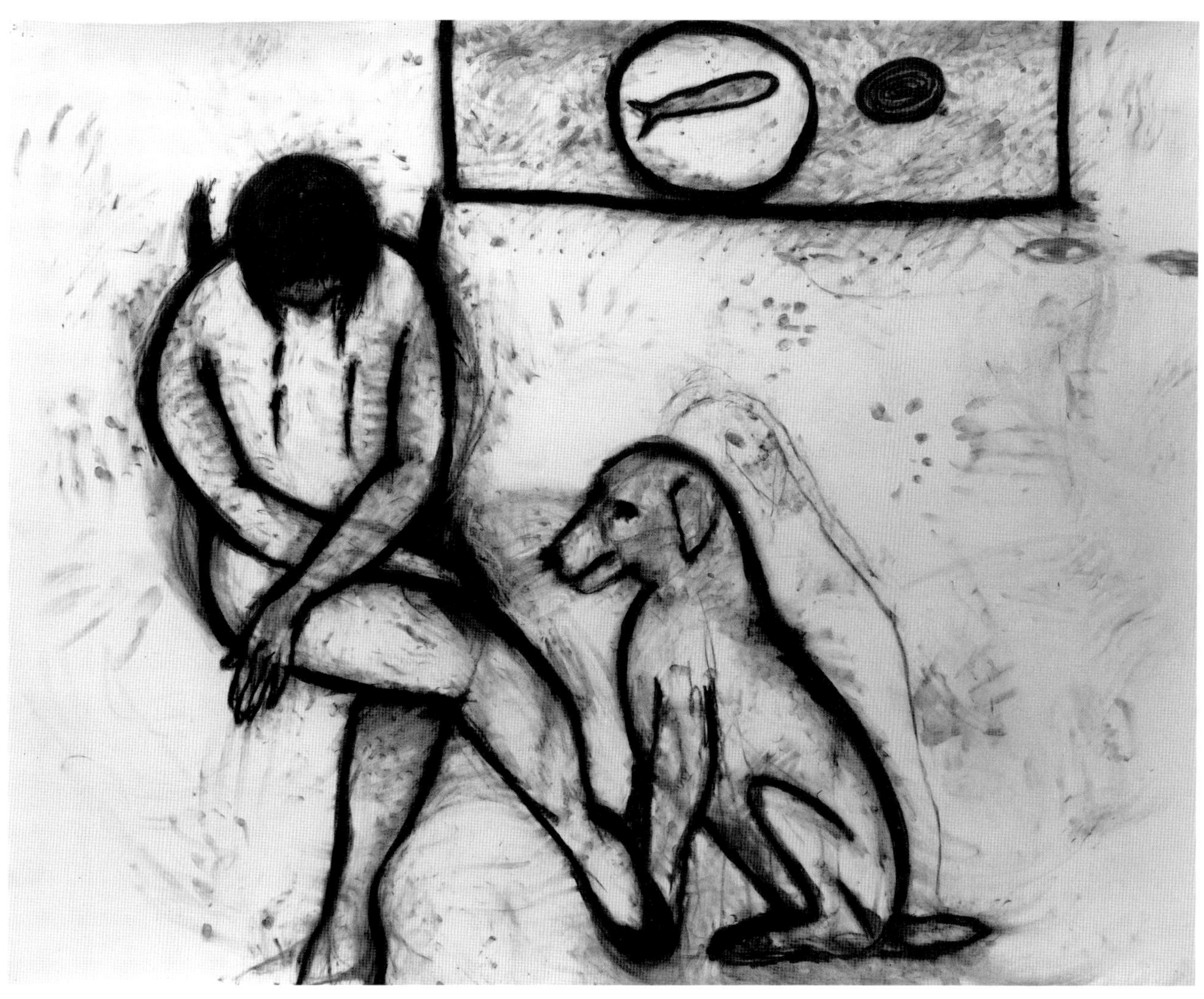

9. **Companion,** 1984

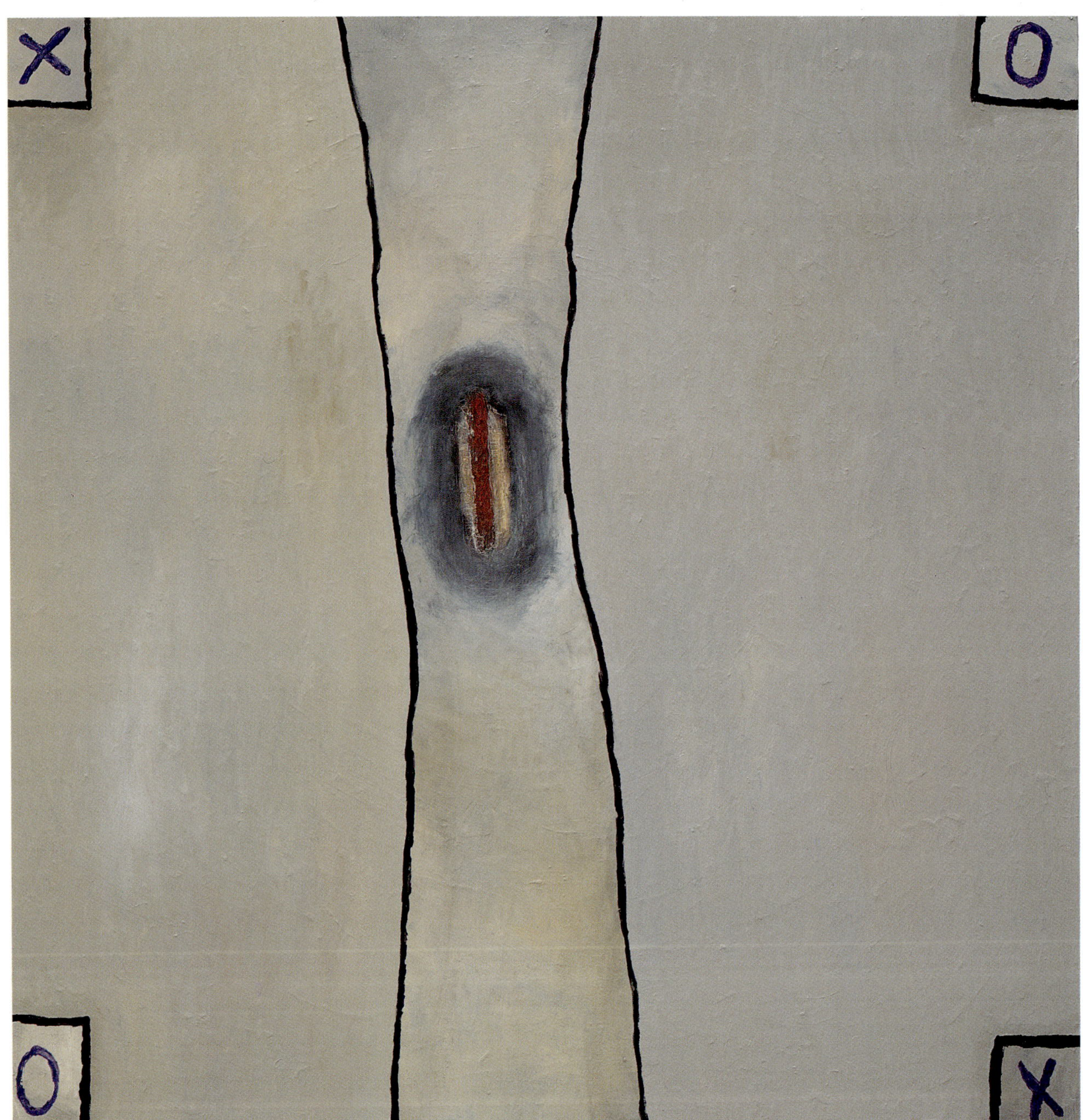

10. **Between,** 1987

Me. Always the water changed, but the river stood still.
Richard Powers

THE MID-1980S BROUGHT CHANGE, both artistically and professionally, for Carnwath. After teaching for a year in Berkeley, she joined the art department at the University of California, Davis, in 1983. At that time the department was distinguished by a faculty associated with Bay Area figurative painting and funk art, among them Robert Arneson, Mike Henderson, Manuel Neri, Roland Petersen, and Wayne Thiebaud. While she continued for a while with her charcoal drawings, Carnwath's painting began to change, from soulful self-searching to taking a wider view of the world. In her own words her canvases became "less needy . . . less infantile."[35] Perhaps Carnwath was taking to heart some of the criticism that had come her way. Reviewing her 1984 exhibition at Hansen Fuller Goldeen, Suzaan Boettger wrote in *Artforum:* "Carnwath's repeated focus on a single female figure, in fantastic environments and surrounded by symbolic elements, exudes a darkly obsessive air which at once suggests an infantile state of self-absorption and the projection of an intelligent artist struggling to clarify her consciousness of being in the world"[36]

"The early work was more 'me-first,'" the artist acknowledged, as reflected in *Head Ache,* a self-portrait of the artist suffering a migraine. "Even at the time, I was calling myself Me-first Carnwath, as a kind of nickname. It's really important to get to the universal. If you don't know what being personal is, you can't get to the 'us.' I don't want the work to be only my experience. I think my experience and somebody else's are similar, and the specificity of why I did something is not something that anyone else needs to know really, because there's a general kind of information that we all get that's underneath language. We understand it because it's visual. It's not just my experience, it's your experience, it's our experience."[37]

The changes that occurred in Carnwath's painting were, of all things, prompted by her interest in her dog's toys—fake carrots, squeaky balls, rubber bones. Breaking with her usual reiterative way of exploring subject matter, Carnwath produced relatively few works in this series. But in canvases such as *Between* (1987; p. 28), her rethinking and retooling of her process is immediately obvious. The overtly figurative elements, the suggestion of personal narrative, and the flat handling of paint are gone. In their place are more simplified, almost minimalist, compositions; the search for her own personal kind of mark making; and the quest to evoke a kind of inner light in her canvases. "I started taking the figures out because I wanted the pictures to be about thinking," Carnwath explained. "No one has to recognize themselves in them, or they recognize the part of themselves that makes them universal."[38]

Importantly Carnwath also refocused her attention on her painting technique. As early as 1979 she was working with oil paint and alkyd, a material used to build up glazes on a canvas; but many of her early works had a certain flat quality about them. With her paintings of dog toys, Carnwath began concentrating on creating a sense of luminosity in her canvases. She found this turn in her work exhilarating. "I feel like my new work, the work on dog toys, has a lot to do with a certain maturity, a certain growing up, a lessening of a psychological dependence," Carnwath said in an interview. "They are compelling basic shapes, almost primitive and real primary."[39] She also responded to the "nastiness and eroticism" of her new subject matter, as embodied in the toy hot dog depicted in *Between.*

Carnwath gradually became interested in the ways in which paintings and their subjects are received. When Wayne Thiebaud painted a row of hot dogs in the early 1960s, no mention was made by critics of the sexual suggestion of the hot dogs nestled in their buns. To her surprise, viewers of Carnwath's *Between* perceived the work as libidinous and interpreted the hot dog as a sexual reference. The Xs and Os in the painting's corners allude to the gamelike, puzzling quality of perception that she was gradually discovering.

This discovery led to a preoccupation with perception and cognition and what Carnwath describes as the "intimate act of looking." Her thinking involves not only the work of contemporary painters such as Thiebaud, but that of artists ranging from Gustave Courbet to Marcel Duchamp—artists who have addressed the seductive act of looking, whether overtly or secretly. Among the historical works Carnwath cites is Courbet's *L'origine du monde* (*The Origin of the World*), an 1866 painting that presents a foreshortened view of a female nude with her legs spread, exposing her clitoris and dark pubic hair. At the time of its painting, genitalia was not an acceptable subject for public display, so the owner of the work, who commissioned the painting from the French master, hid it behind a curtain. When the work changed hands, Courbet produced a canvas depicting a snowy village landscape, which was positioned over the scandalous image, leaving it hidden except to those privy to the subterfuge.[40] In Carnwath's eyes, *L'origine du monde* is one of the first and most important conceptual artworks to have been produced. Brash and confrontational, the painting is also about secrecy and what is hidden.

Duchamp once declared that the practice of painting should be put "at the service of the mind." He believed that "painting should not be only retinal and visual; it should have to do with the gray matter of our understanding."[41] Duchamp also clearly stated his interest in Eros, in what he defined as the universal force of creative energy and potency. "Eroticism is a subject very dear to me . . . In fact, I thought the only excuse for doing anything is to introduce eroticism into life. Eroticism is close to life, closer than philosophy or anything like it; it's an animal thing that has many facets and is pleasing to use, as you would use a tube of paint, to inject into your production, so to speak."[42]

As the historian Arturo Schwarz has observed, Duchamp's view is very close to the archetypal concept of Eros, which is conceived "not merely as the god of sensual love, but as a power which forms the world by inner union of separated elements."[43] Freud expanded on this notion, suggesting that human creativity derives its dynamism from the forces of Eros. Like Duchamp, Carnwath perceives the medium of paint as replicating the behavior of bodily fluids. She sees the thinning and thickening of the medium, the slow buildup of painted layers, the drips and splatters in her canvases as both sensuous and sexual. "Drips [of paint] are like sex to me. They're a signifier of that kind of life force. And the scarred surfaces are a signifier of what the body goes through to exist."[44] Carnwath also admires Duchamp's willingness to reveal something of himself through his work and words. Art making, he said, is making the invisible visible. "People are afraid of art—that it will reveal something," Carnwath has wryly observed.[45]

> Painting is an act of devotion.
> A practiced witnessing of the
> human spirit.
> Squeak Carnwath

PAINTINGS SUCH AS *BOUNDARIES* (1987; p. 31) and *Grace* (1989; p. 34) mark the beginning of Carnwath's mature work. Here one discovers the painterly hallmarks and distinctive content of Carnwath's art that incubated in her work of the previous decade—the importance of symbols and words; the ambiguity of perception; the quality of luminosity that she first discovered in her charcoal drawings; her preoccupation with creating paintings that are records of the human hand, thought, and the passage of time. These paintings also speak, in coded terms, to another challenging time in her life. In 1988 Jay DeFeo, a friend and sister artist, was diagnosed with cancer; not long thereafter, Carnwath's husband, Gary Knecht, became seriously ill.

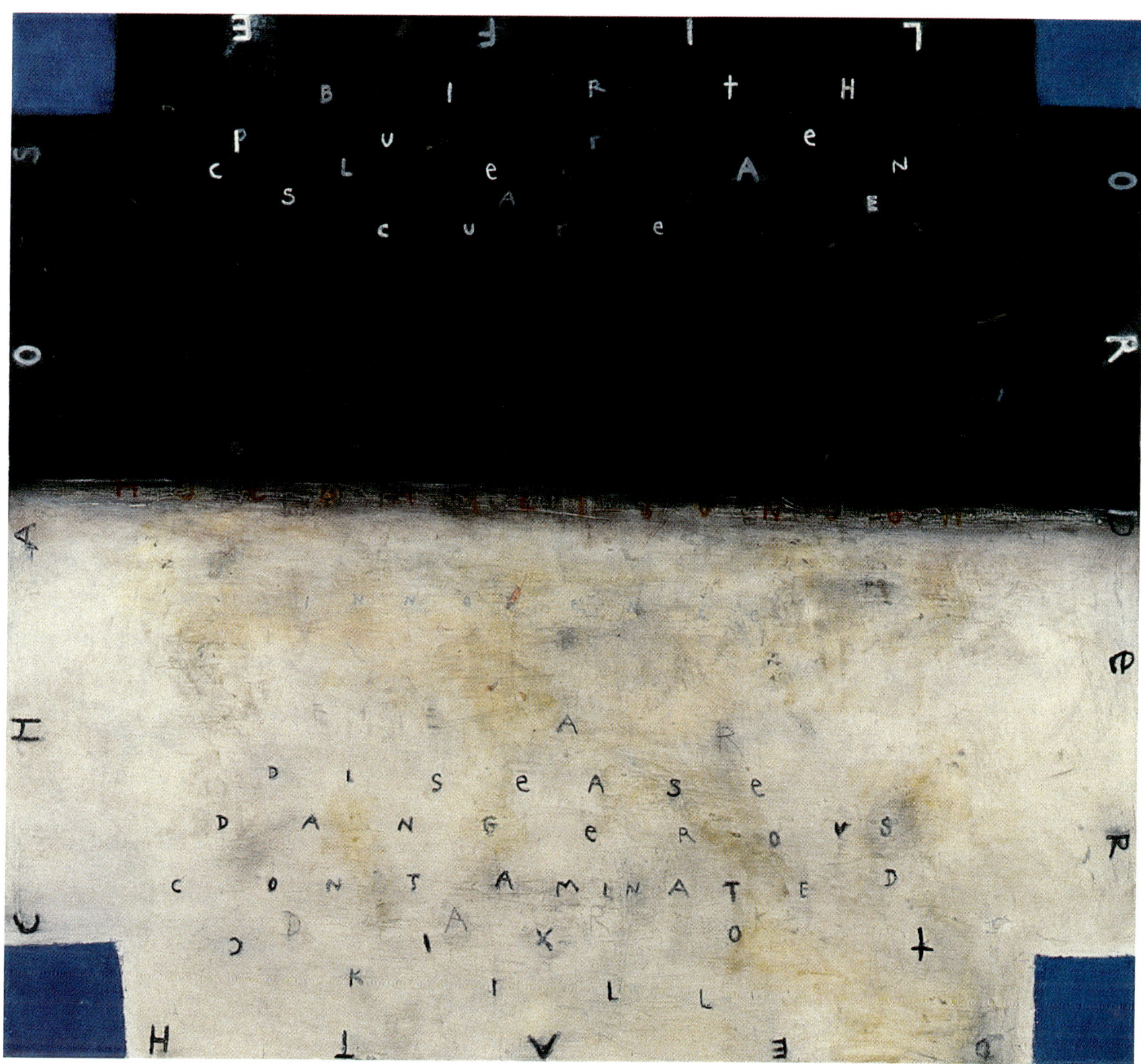

11. **Boundaries,** 1987

Carnwath had a close personal and professional association with DeFeo, although there were eighteen years between them. They enjoyed walking their dogs together, and Carnwath learned from her older friend that a productive female artist can have a satisfying life without children. As Carnwath later asserted in an interview: "[Art] is not a hobby. It is not the second most important thing, it is the first and comes before anything else—before my relationship with my husband, before my job, before everything."[46] When DeFeo died in 1989, Carnwath was one of three friends, including Leah Levy and Ursula Cipa, who sat at the artist's bedside as she took her last breath, then washed and wrapped her body in white.

Boundaries is one of several works completed during and after DeFeo's illness and passing. With its strong horizontal composition and contrast between dark and light, the canvas reflects a distinct relationship to Mark Rothko's work—particularly the paintings he created near the end of his life, when he was beset by health and family problems and drinking heavily. Carnwath seems to be sharing Rothko's desire to express a certain order, a metaphysical truth, through abstract form and color—to paint a panorama of human emotion without being emotional. While there is an inescapable reference to the horizon line of a landscape here, the bifurcation of *Boundaries* is intended more to suggest the internal boundaries that separate order from chaos. Carnwath refers to these horizontally structured paintings as mind-scapes and interior landscapes. Painting them was a way for her to find a sense of subjective order in her mind.

Carnwath fully acknowledges "borrowing" elements from other artists. Just as Rothko's late work bears a certain relationship to paintings by Caspar David Friedrich, Carnwath's methodology is to borrow selectively from other painters, reinterpreting and adapting their ideas to her own work. Thus, one can link Carnwath's thick charcoal lines to the powerful black strokes found in Susan Rothenberg's paintings of horses. The grids in her paintings of the mid-1990s find precedence in the work of Agnes Martin. Her white paintings of 2005–2006 share the same sense of luminosity found in Robert Ryman's minimal canvases. As such, Carnwath participates in the long lineage of artists whose inheritance of knowledge and technique passes from one generation to the next. As she observes, "All paintings share a connection with all other paintings."[47]

Like Rothko, Carnwath conveys meaning through subtle gestures of the paintbrush and the slow, painstaking buildup of pigment so that her paintings appear to have an inner source of light, even in the darkest areas. In what has become an integral part of her formal expression and a signature element of her work, Carnwath also inscribes words in and on her paintings. Words appear sideways and upside down in *Boundaries*, and in positions opposite to what one might assume: "life," "birth," "pure," and "cure" appear in the black half of the painting, "death," "toxic," "disease," and "contaminated" in the luminous white half. The juxtaposition may be startling, but contrary to Western convention, Carnwath sees black as life-giving and white as funereal. Like flies crawling on a white wall or maggots in a dark hole, the contraposition of elements nudges the viewer into a different level of awareness.

The words "order" and "chaos" on either side of the painting refer obliquely to Carnwath's interest in chaos theory. Based in the fields of mathematics and physics, chaos theory is the attempt to understand systems that appear seemingly random, but which actually follow certain rules. For example, sophisticated computers used for forecasting weather cannot do so for more than a few days into the future. This limitation is expressed as the "butterfly effect": the flutter of a butterfly's wings, or the flap of a seagull's, can in theory affect a wind's force just enough to change an immense weather system. Such systems are dynamic, changing over time, but not chaotic in the accepted sense: they can be comprehended as large forces arising from tiny ones. This accords with one of Carnwath's main tenets: one should pay closer attention to the small things.

Grace was completed at a time when Carnwath's husband was ill. The black cross and bloodlike swipe catch the eye immediately; in the center of the painting, the word "waiting" is caught in a whorl—of hope, or despair?—emanating from a hospital bed. Lists of words and numbers appear, in addition to symbols: bed, cross, handprints, outlines of heads. The numbers in the upper right corner will resurface again and again in later works. Perhaps the brief numerical list identifies a negative or positive cell count, or a medical accounting which Carnwath only understood as "good" or "bad," and crossed off accordingly. The words on the left—"mercy," "faith," "pain," "fear," "loneliness," "love," "healing"—could be a litany of supplication for Knecht's well-being.

Words are even more integral to Carnwath's later painting as seen in *Miracle* (1992; p. 35), in which the words "Waiting For A Miracle" boldly fill a black canvas. "I love the way language looks . . . handwriting—evidence of thinking," Carnwath explains. "When I thought of using it, I thought of it as illumination. It is making visible my experience in the world, the fragility of being—on the cusp of being here and not being here."[48]

That words with religious implications, such as "miracle," "faith," and "healing," appear in Carnwath's work should not be too surprising. Although Carnwath is not a "religious" person, she has often referred to her studio as a sanctuary and to her paintings as private prayers. "Painting is an act of devotion," she has written, "a practiced witnessing of the human spirit."[49] As the psychologist Rudolf Arnheim wrote of the powerful combination of language and imagery: "Although image making and writing grew indivisibly out of each other and have never been wholly separate, their recent mutual attraction has come like the healing of a wound that had torn them unhealthily apart."[50]

When *Grace* was discussed in a 1989 *ARTnews* review, the critic Christine Tamblyn saw it as a commentary on the AIDS epidemic. To Tamblyn's eye the numbers in the painting suggested a grim accounting of lives taken by the disease. The words on the left were interpreted as a hopeful counterbalance.[51] No doubt the review pleased Carnwath: as she has often said, she does not want to limit interpretations of her work. While her paintings may allude to narrative, they never tell a story; instead, they furnish just enough visual clues to engage the viewer on some level. The personal meaning Carnwath imparts to a painting is the result of private, meditative time in the studio, but she also seeks to shed light on the universal experiences we all share as human beings. As she observes, "A painter's life is constantly being documented, a body of evidence produced with each stroke, each touch of the brush. A visual record and a beneath language document of existence."[52]

Most artists acknowledge that interpreting and understanding an artwork is not a fixed experience. Love, death, a broken heart are experienced and communicated in infinitely different and intimate ways. As Joseph Campbell mused, "People say that what we're all seeking is a meaning for life . . . I think that what we're seeking is an experience of being alive, so that our life experiences on the purely physical plane will have resonances within our own innermost being and reality, so that we actually feel the rapture of being alive."[53]

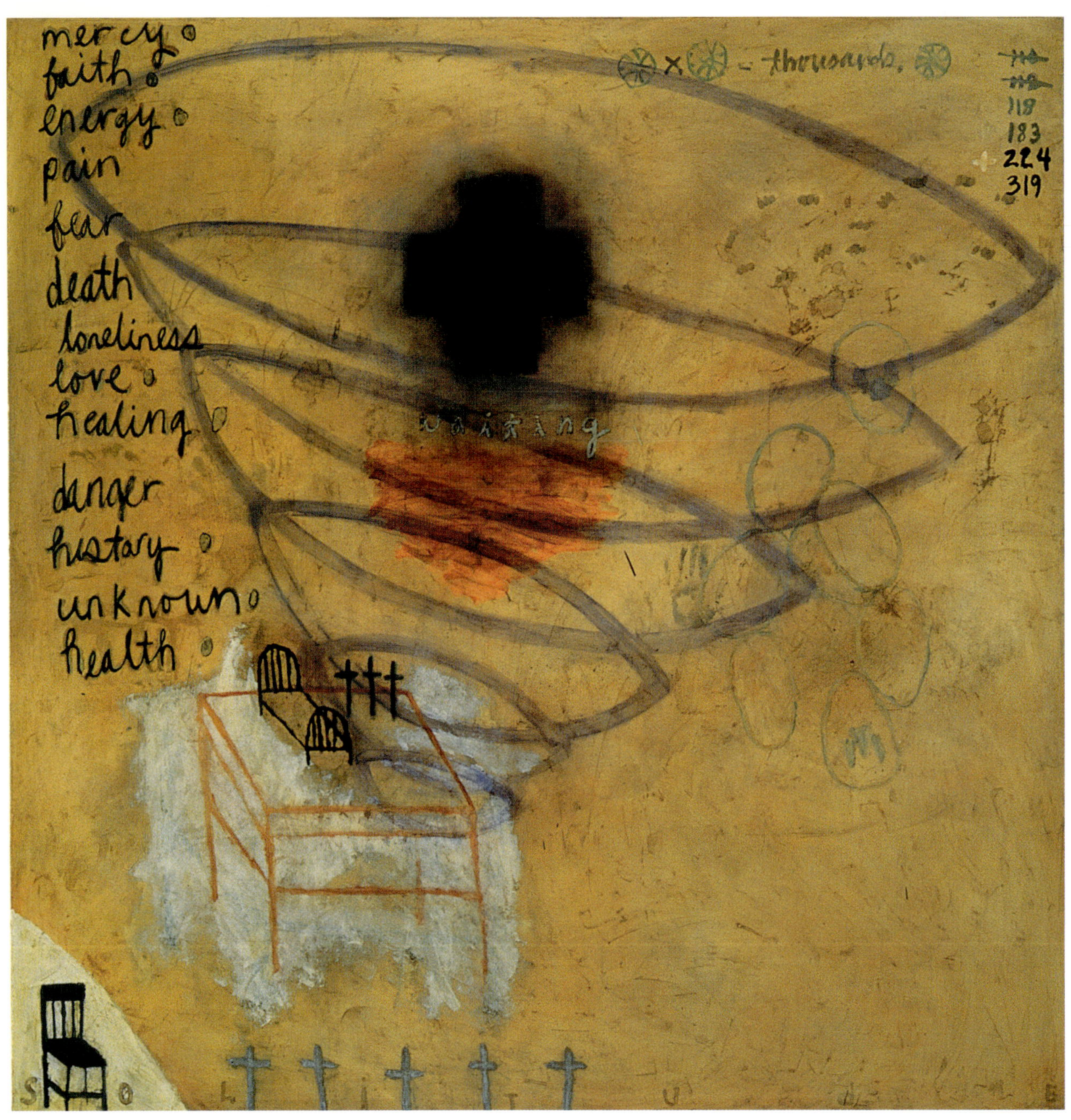

12. **Grace,** 1989

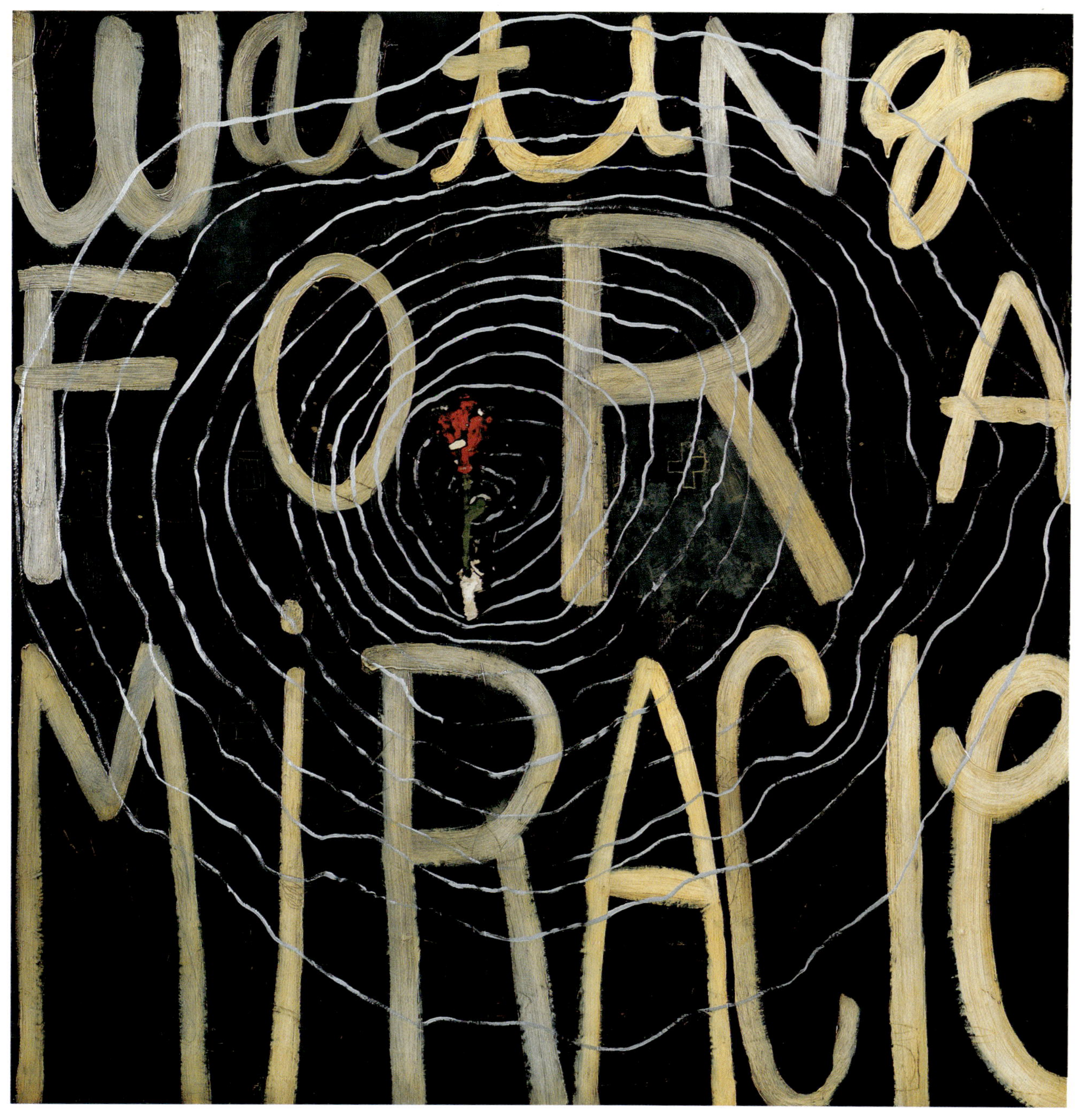

17. **Miracle,** 1992

Disquiet underscores *Grace*, but the canvas also radiates quiet warmth and luminous energy. In some ways it recalls the soft golden hues and rich blacks of Rembrandt's paintings—darkness and light entwined. It has been said that Rembrandt painted as if he was the director of his own theater company, manipulating the light to evocative effect. His later works, especially, suggest private dramas rendered in paint, seamlessly melding the earthly and the spiritual in a kind of utopian light. "Light in a painting for me is not about reflected surfaces. It's about an inner luminosity," Carnwath told an interviewer. "It's recognition of a life force. In the Renaissance light was a stand-in for life, or spirituality, or the presence of a God or a higher self, a soul. I'm interested in having that aspect of light in my paintings."[54]

It may be surprising, perhaps, that Carnwath proposes an overt link between her work and the early-Renaissance master of light and shadow. Yet she admits to catholic tastes in art. She admires Ross Bleckner's ability to create paintings that have spiritual resonance, and she has spoken of her appreciation for artists ranging from Matisse, Duchamp, and Jasper Johns to Cy Twombly, Joan Brown, Jay DeFeo, and Viola Frey. But Carnwath also has deep regard for historical painters such as J. M. W. Turner, Antoine Watteau, and especially Courbet and Rembrandt. She wants her paintings "to *feel* like a Rembrandt painting, but not look like his work."[55]

Another distinctive aspect of Rembrandt's painting that Carnwath emulates is the way he applied his pigment. Early in his career, the Dutch artist carved into his wet paint surfaces with the end of his brush or maulstick. He treated paint as something to be worked *in,* as if it was material to be modeled, applying pigment with his paintbrush, palette knife, or fingers so thickly that it looks as if one could grasp the pearls or gold chains that he rendered. In his hands, paint—the substance itself—became something real, and in the process, he was able to convey the idea that vision is also a kind of touch. Rembrandt celebrated the act and the pleasure of seeing.

Carnwath, too, loves the materiality of paint and how it can act as an uncanny record of time. "In my paintings, the tracing—the pressure of the actual hand—gives them an imprint, a record of time passing, snail trails," she has explained.[56] Brush and trowel in hand, she spends hours slowly fleshing out her paintings. Layer by layer she fills her canvases with the quotidian—grocery lists, doctor's appointments—and the profound: reflections on women's rights, memories of a lost friend. Slowly, slowly, these thoughts embedded in paint take on an existence of their own as the palimpsest of recorded and erased meanings and experiences builds over time. Dense and mottled, haphazardly marked and scratched, Carnwath's paintings feel both aged and immediate, with subtle hints of color, words, and thoughts surging just beneath the final skin of paint.

Carnwath relishes the way the underpainted strata seep through the top layers of pigment, affecting the color, vibration, and feel of the finished work. People may not be able to see the original colors, but they can feel them. She wryly refers to her methodology of paint application as "Carnwath science," but the intent is serious. "I'm trying to be good at painting. I want to make stuff that comes from the hand and I want to get better at that . . . Even though it might seem unfashionable, I'm interested in developing my own sense of material expertise—a sensitivity to the material and how the material can telegraph my feelings."[57] Indeed, she likens the accretions and irregularities of her paintings to human skin with its uneven pigmentation. "I think that painting is a stand-in for the body. It becomes the host. That's part of its conversion. It becomes a host for the spiritual. It's a symbol for the life force, but I think it actually becomes that . . . Good paintings enable us to believe in the palpability of its skin. Of the existence of the body."[58] As Willem de Kooning once observed, flesh was the reason for the invention of oil painting.

When you start owning your own symbology or way of working, you really want to take care of it. It also changes and evolves.
Squeak Carnwath

SYMBOLS, BOTH PERSONAL AND UNIVERSAL, are hallmarks of Carnwath's mature work. In the painting *Four Months* (1994; p. 39), the artist presents a diagram of those that are particularly significant to her and repeatedly quoted throughout her work. The painting's structure is almost that of a scientific schema, reinforcing the idea that Carnwath approaches the creative process as both a "scientist and poet-scribe," as Leah Levy has written.[59] The artist observes, absorbs, and then records in her work the process of examination and the expression of her experiences. What Carnwath seems to affirm through her symbols is that seeing and thought come before words. *Four Months* also speaks to Carnwath's fondness for window grids as compositional frameworks, on canvas and off.

Symbols, by definition, mean something other than themselves; for example a nose may mean "smell," but not "nose." Some that appear in *Four Months* seem straightforward in their meaning: the phone stands for communication, the cake with candles for a birthday; the nose, mouth, eye, and ear refer to the senses. But as Hans Biedermann, a specialist in cultural icons, has written, many traditional symbols are multivalent: "Not every dragon in every culture is evil; the heart does not always stand for love."[60] Biedermann also declares that symbols offer a "dreambook of humanity;" people have long seen in the images that surround them a chance to understand their place in a cosmic plan. Many create their own mythologies and personal symbols, as the artist has done. Carnwath similarly acknowledges their "elasticity" and ambiguity. For example the image at upper left can be read as a gun or as a phallic symbol. The glass is either half full or half empty or may refer to Carnwath's concern for the environment and the unseen chemicals that contaminate the water we drink.

As reflected in *Four Months*, numbers are crucial talismans for Carnwath, and counting has a significance approaching ritual. Sometimes this takes the form of painting the digits one through ten, or counting by each number's first letter: O (one), T (two), T (three). At other times numbers appear to relate to the day of the week: *5* (Friday), *6* (Saturday). Numbers were sacred in some of the most ancient traditions; the Babylonians used whole numbers to name their gods, with fractions for lesser spirits. For Plato, numbers represented the harmony of the universe; for Aristotle, they were the origin and substance of all things. In Taoist paintings, they signify the idea of change.

For Carnwath, counting and painting numbers are a way of animating her awareness of being in the universe, a reminder to pay attention to each breath and passing moment. She counts or writes number sequences to give the days to come the same substance and certainty as the days that have passed. Carnwath grew up in a world of counting games—*One, two, buckle my shoe / Three, four, shut the door*—and the grid of numbers at the bottom of *Four Months* may allude to the hopscotch games Carnwath played as a child. When she walked to school, she did not step on a sidewalk crack lest she "break her mother's back." Such children's superstitions would never have been more than half-believed; but Carnwath was always alert to where her feet were.

Other contemporary artists share Carnwath's interest in counting and numbering. In his ongoing *Today Series*, the Japanese conceptual artist On Kawara daily paints a small canvas that records the date when the painting was executed. If he does not complete the painting by midnight, he destroys it. Numbers play a part in Jonathan Borofsky's work, as well. Borofsky began counting in the 1960s, as a meditative activity, and thereafter often incorporated into his artwork—the painting *10524810* (2001), for example—the number he had counted to on the day a piece was completed.

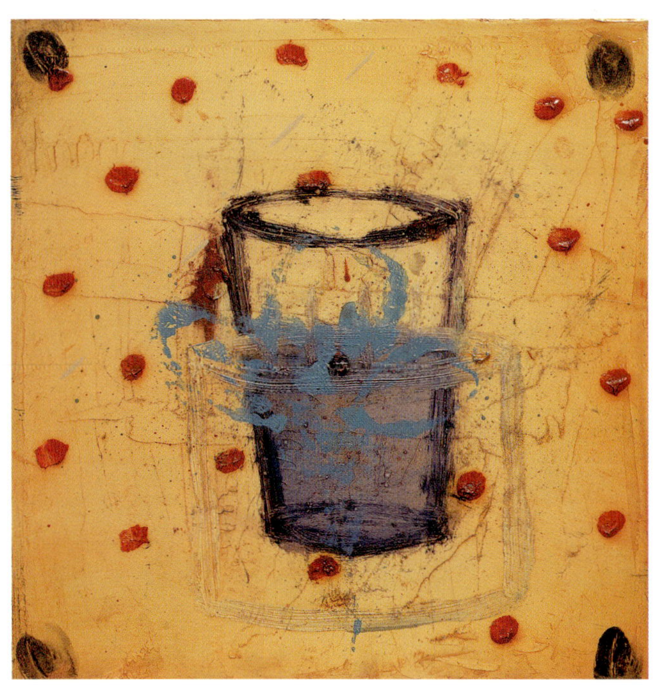

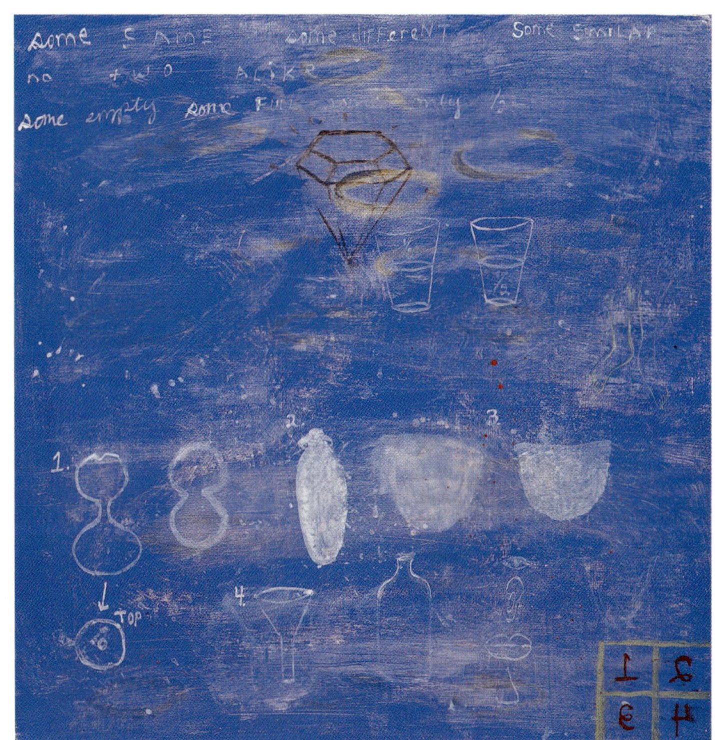

23. **Water Cake Lily,** 1994 (above)

21. **Some Same,** 1994 (below)

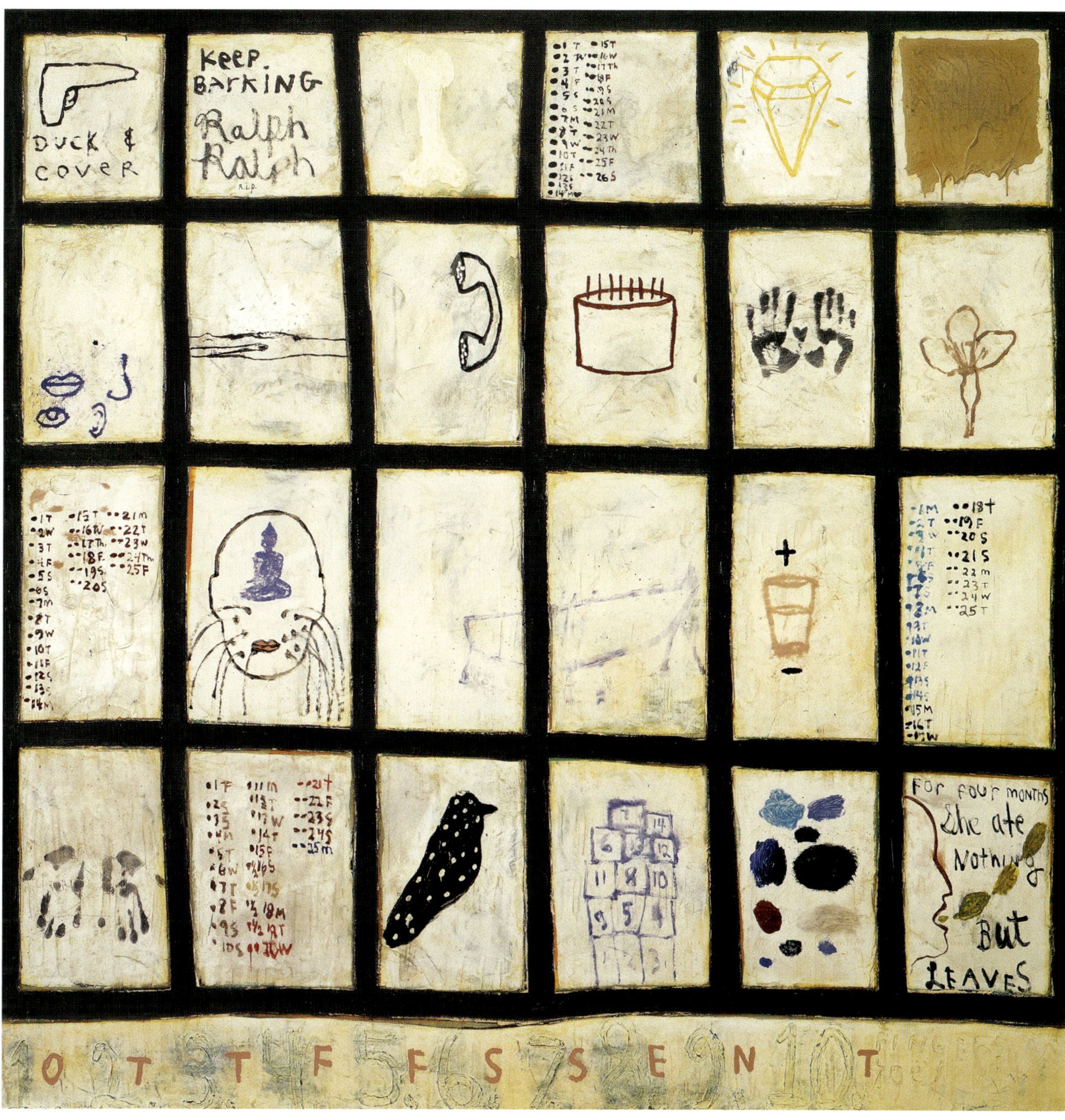

20. **Four Months,** 1994

Handprints appear again and again in Carnwath's canvases, as in *No More, No More*; *Things I've Heard or Seen in Person* (1998; p. 66); *True Life* (1998; p. 67); and *Plaid Lost*. Reaching back to the earliest cave paintings, the handprint is a charged image, variously representing power, strength, providence, and blessing. To Aristotle, the hand was the "tool of tools." In the now outlawed Hindu practice of suttee, a widow would impress her handprint on the temple wall before joining her deceased husband on his funeral pyre; the woman's death was a way to rid society of unproductive women. Jackson Pollock put his handprints on his canvases, then obscured them beneath skeins of paint. When Jasper Johns pressed his oil-covered hands and face to a sheet of paper, critics associated the result with Veronica's veil, the cloth with which, according to medieval legend, Christ dried the blood and sweat from his hands and face during the Passion and which retained his image. Trinkett Clark observed that Carnwath uses her handprints not only as an affirmation of identity, but as a tool to arouse in the viewer the idea that something is confined beneath the handprint's surface, longing to be revealed and released.[61]

The Buddha on the brow of the forlorn head in *Four Months* is known in Mahayana practice as Bhaisajyaguru, the Medicine Buddha. Carnwath created the painting during a time of personal unhappiness and describes that head as an ideogram of the state she was in. The deep blue Medicine Buddha, who reappears in later paintings, such as *The Story Of Painting* (1999; p. 68), *Trying Simply To Be Happy* (2000; p. 74), and *Numbered Moments* (2001; p. 71), remediates spiritual, psychological, and physical ills. But Bhaisajyaguru is not worshiped solely for his healing powers: his is the form of Buddha-nature that one may aspire to realize in oneself.

In the lower right corner of *Four Months,* Carnwath has drawn a face in profile with the words: "For four months she ate nothing but leaves." This is probably a scrap of something she heard on the radio, saw on television, or read in a newspaper or magazine. An ardent reader and one actively absorbed in contemporary culture, Carnwath often transmits in her paintings what she has taken in—absurd, humorous, or touching as it may be. In her painting *An Inability to Remain* (1992; p. 104) she wrote of hearing on the radio that a joyful man stabbed himself one hundred times and then he died. *Towards Earth (1995–96)* (1996; p. 106) bears the words "High in the sky two objects are hurtling from space. A comet and a Chinese satellite. Scientists expect the satellite to land in the ocean. Inside the satellite is a diamond encrusted frame with a picture of Chairman Mao inside it and a 24-carat chunk of gold. Where will the comet land?"

Carnwath's inscriptions, though often coming from real life, might be interpreted as koans, the puzzling, paradoxical questions and conversations through which Buddhist masters train their disciples. A koan may be beguiling or confounding—"Why is a mouse when it spins?"—but its aim is to further the student's enlightenment. As Allen Ginsberg once wrote, the point of these anecdotes is to exhaust words. "Then man sees anew the universe."

The writing that appears in *Four Months* will be elaborated upon in many later works, to the point that one may read a Carnwath painting almost as much as one looks at it. Carnwath has explained that her writing is meant to act as an interruption, as a way to slow the eye; to put the viewer in real time, there to become the owner of the mark and voice of the painting.[62]

But she also sees handwriting as a kind of DNA marker, a fingerprint, the stamp of individual consciousness. "My handwriting is pretty weird . . . it's more expressive," she observes. "I like its edginess. It has its own pathology. It's an aspect of anger or the unconscious."[63] Whether they appear as a shout or whisper—as in *Promise* (1999; p. 118) and *Please* (2000; p. 119)—Carnwath's words in paint often become inextricable from the rest of the work. Indeed, in paintings such as *Miracle*, they *are* the work. The paintings are object lessons in the integration of articulated thought with visual imagery. As Rudolf Arnheim noted, the avalanche of printed words brought on by the technological advances of the eighteenth and nineteenth centuries led to a "cheapening of language as a visual, aural, and syntactic form of expression." Arnheim quoted the poet and critic Franz Mon: "'Never have we possessed so much written material, and never has written language itself given us so little.'"[64]

Many critics and writers have commented on Carnwath's "childlike" way of image making and writing. The adjective makes her bristle. "I think it's sexist. When they write about men in that context, they use words like 'guileless' or 'energetic' or 'willful,' words that have more power to them. Or if they do say 'childlike,' it's in this glowing way—it's not pejorative . . . Using 'childlike' is a way of making a woman's effort seem less of an important enterprise, of not recognizing that they have an intellectual premise."[65]

Robert Goldwater declared, by contrast, that "the most contemptuous criticism of recent paintings comes from those who say: 'Any child of eight could have done that.' It is also the most difficult of all judgments to answer, since it involves the recognition, but not the admiration, of an apparent spontaneity of inspiration and simplicity of technique whose excellence we have come to take for granted."[66]

D. T. Suzuki spoke of "childlikeness" as an admirable quality:

> Man is a thinking reed, but his great works are done when he is not calculating and thinking. "Childlikeness" has to be restored with long years of training in the art of self-forgetfulness. When this is attained, man thinks yet he does not think. He thinks like showers coming down from the sky; he thinks like the waves rolling on the ocean; he thinks like the stars illuminating the nightly heavens; he thinks like the green foliage shooting forth in the relaxing spring breeze. Indeed, he is the showers, the ocean, the stars, the foliage.[67]

> The whole of science is nothing more than a refinement of everyday thinking.
> Albert Einstein

IN AROUND 1993-1994, CARNWATH BEGAN what she calls the "colored" paintings, a series that explores, interprets, and catalogues the symbolism of various hues. Including *Black Is* (1994; p. 42); *What Is Red* (1994; p. 46); *What White Is* (1994; pp. 44-45); *Purple is Purple* (1995; p. 49); *Yellow Stuff* (1995; p. 47), and another four or five paintings, the series originated in her contemplation of identity politics and political correctness.

At the time Carnwath was having a difficult time at UC Davis as the teaching climate had changed. Several members of the art department faculty—people whom she liked and admired—had retired or died; and a form of political correctness dominated the university's culture. Frustrated, she took a two-year leave of absence, traveled, and worked on these paintings.

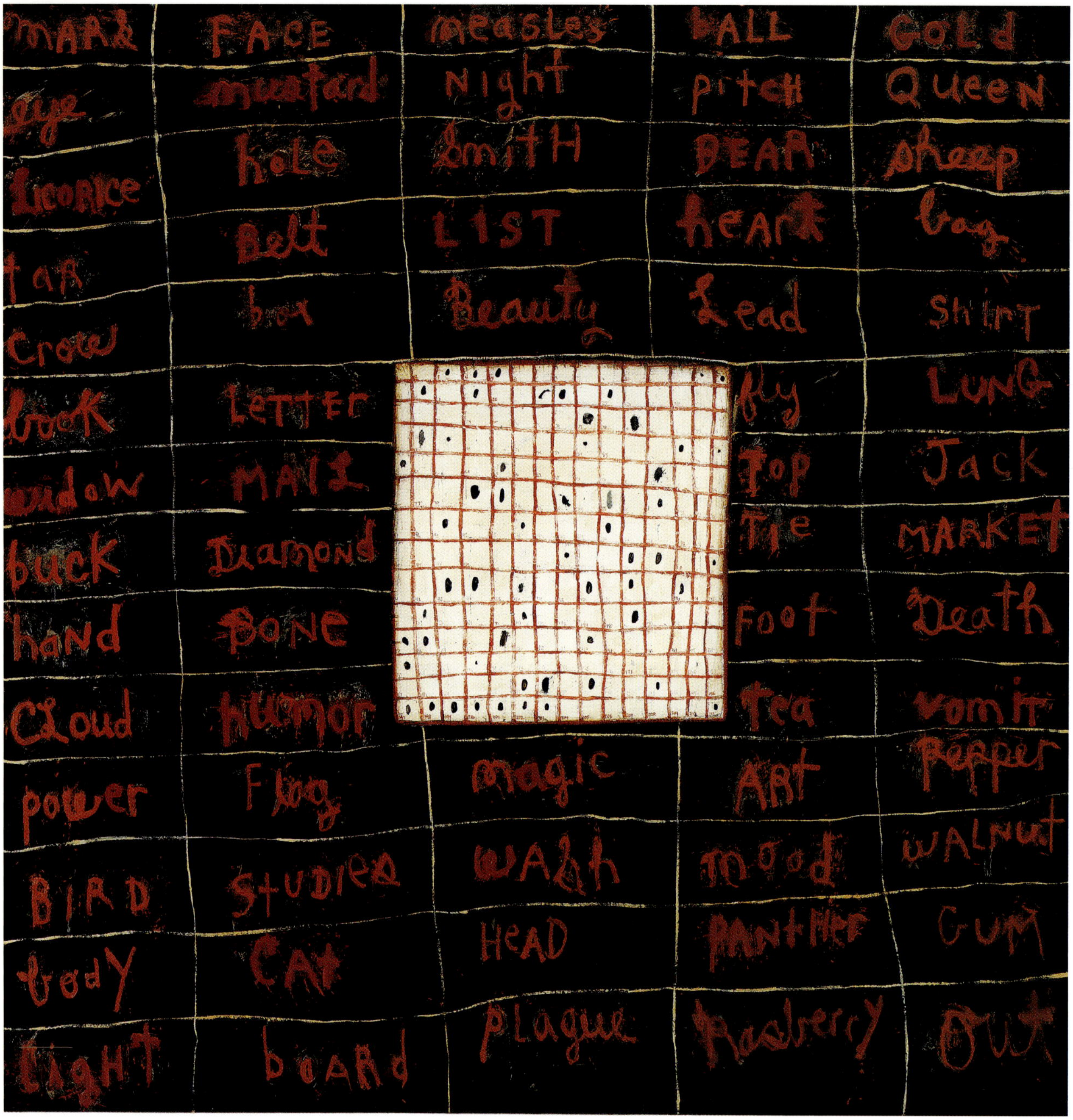

18. **Black Is,** 1994

The largest work of the series, *What White Is* measures almost seven feet by thirteen feet. Carnwath painted 182 different hues of white in the grid on the diptych's left side. On the right she listed sixty-four words associated with white—white cell, white collar, white hot, white cap, white wine, white man, White Sox, white lie, white pepper, pure white, egg white, snow white. The grid-like composition of the painting suggests a scientific sensibility, a schematic organizing device. But the erratically lettered chart and free-associative words subvert scientific rationality and precision. The painting becomes, instead, a metaphor for an open-ended way of defining things, contrasting the dualities of reason and emotion, the cerebral and the sensual, the ordinary and the exotic. In the sciences, white can be defined either as the absence of any pigment or the presence of all the colors of the spectrum. In various cultures white is associated with life and love, death and burial; a white robe can indicate purity, the triumph of spirit over flesh; but white clothing signifies death in Asia, and women of ancient Rome wore white robes to mourn the dead. Investigating the contrary meanings of the color white, Carnwath has produced a visual analogy of humankind's attempt to impose structure and order on unruly meaning.

In *Black Is*, Carnwath lists words associated with black: black licorice, blacksmith, blackbird, black studies, black magic, black hole, black market, black belt, black power, blackjack. Here again she addresses the ambiguity of language and the vagaries of human intellect, the dichotomy between what we see and what we know. In what ways can black power be equated with a black hole, or a blackjack? John Berger observes that "we explain the world with words, but words can never undo the fact that we are surrounded by the world. The relation between what we see and what we know is never settled. Each evening we *see* the sun set. We *know* that the earth is turning away from it. Yet the knowledge, the explanation, never quite fits the sight."[68]

Another list painting, *Purple is Purple*, is full of "Carnwath science": drips of paint suggest blood samples, DNA charts, and chemistry experiments while the word *purple* is linked with people eaters, passion, bruises, hearts. Carnwath is wrestling with one of the questions that have vexed the great minds of the West: what is knowledge? Discussing Bertrand Russell's theory of knowledge, Albert Einstein asked:

> What knowledge is pure thought able to supply independently of sense perception? Is there any such knowledge? If not, what precisely is the relation between our knowledge and the raw material furnished by sense impressions?[69]

In his introduction to *An Inquiry into Meaning and Truth*, Russell himself discussed this dichotomy and offers a window into understanding Carnwath's work.

> We all start from "naïve realism," i.e., the doctrine that things are what they seem. We think that grass is green, that stones are hard, and that snow is cold. But physics assures us that the greenness of grass, the hardness of stones, and the coldness of snow are not the greenness, hardness, and coldness that we know in our own experience, but something very different. The observer, when he seems to himself to be observing a stone, is really, if physics is to be believed, observing the effects of the stone upon himself. Thus science seems to be at war with itself: when it most means to be objective, it finds itself plunged into subjectivity against its will.[70]

The philosophical inquiry Carnwath makes in her "colored" paintings emerges again in works completed a decade later. In *Reflection* (2005; p. 120), a straightforward composition with a blue horizon above a field of white, Carnwath, writing on the canvas, posits the question: "If painting is a language, is this thinking or observation? For instance, is this a picture of the sky? Or a blue-ish patch of paint? And if language represents unique ways of thinking then, painting if it is a kind of language, represents the most unique form of thinking and just to complicate things, painting is the embodiment of time: real and true."

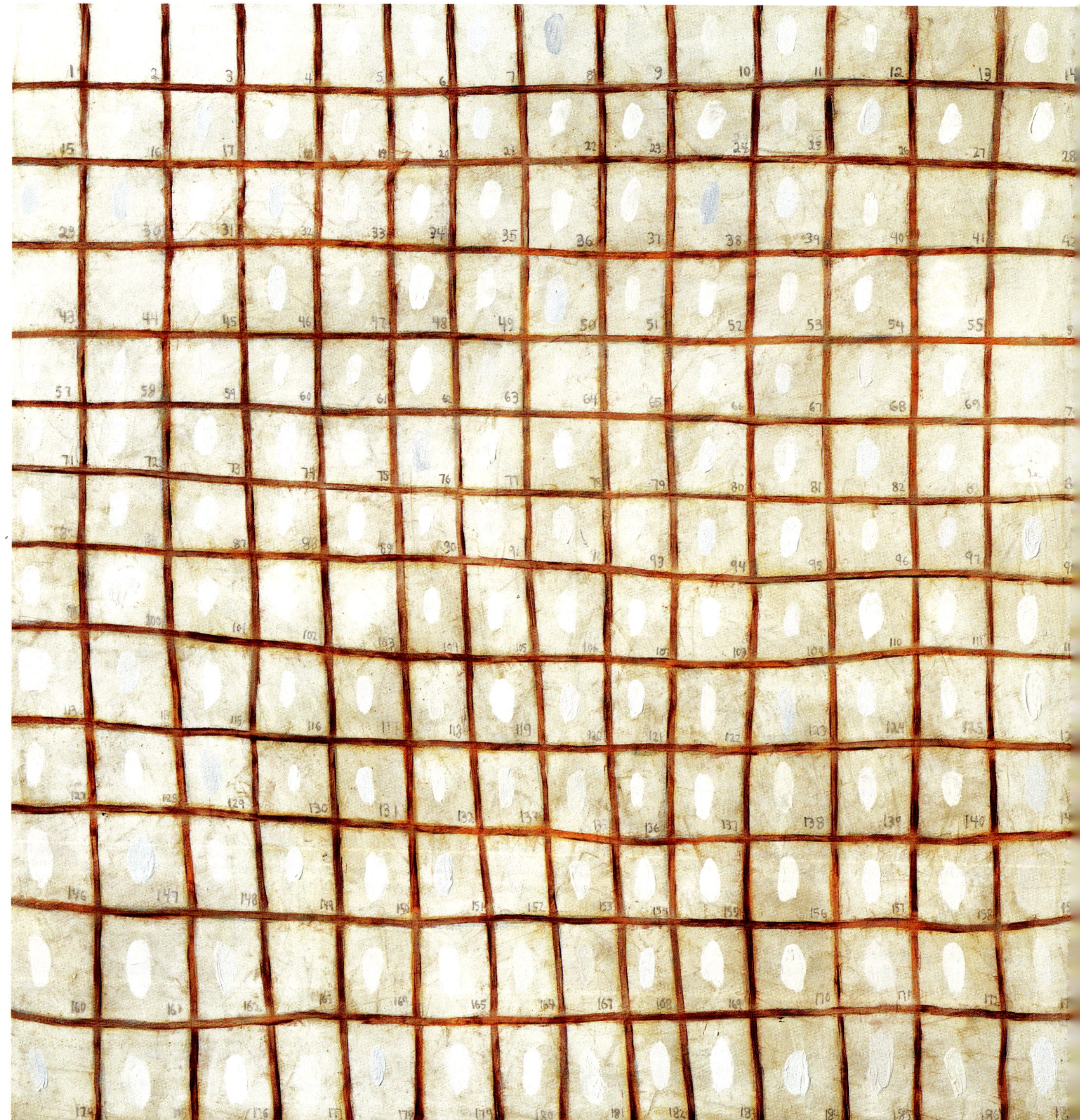

25. **What White Is,** 1994

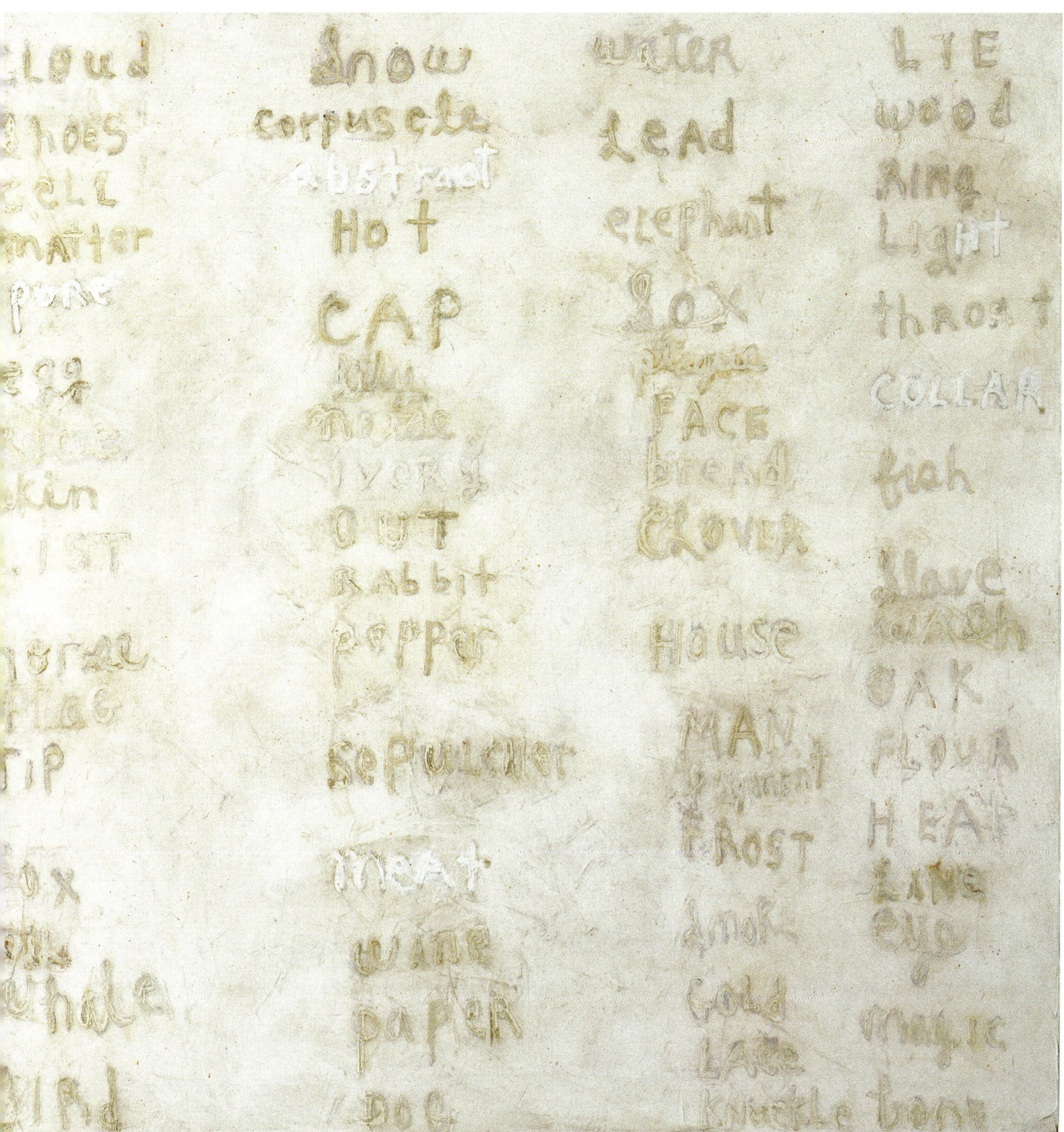
snow
corpuscle
abstract
Hot
CAP
OUT
Rabbit
pepper
sepulcher
meat
paper
DOG
water
Lead
elephant
FACE
bread
CLOVER
House
MAN
FROST
Gold
knuckle
LIE
wood
Ring
Light
throat
COLLAR
fish
OAK
FLOUR
HEAT
magic
bone

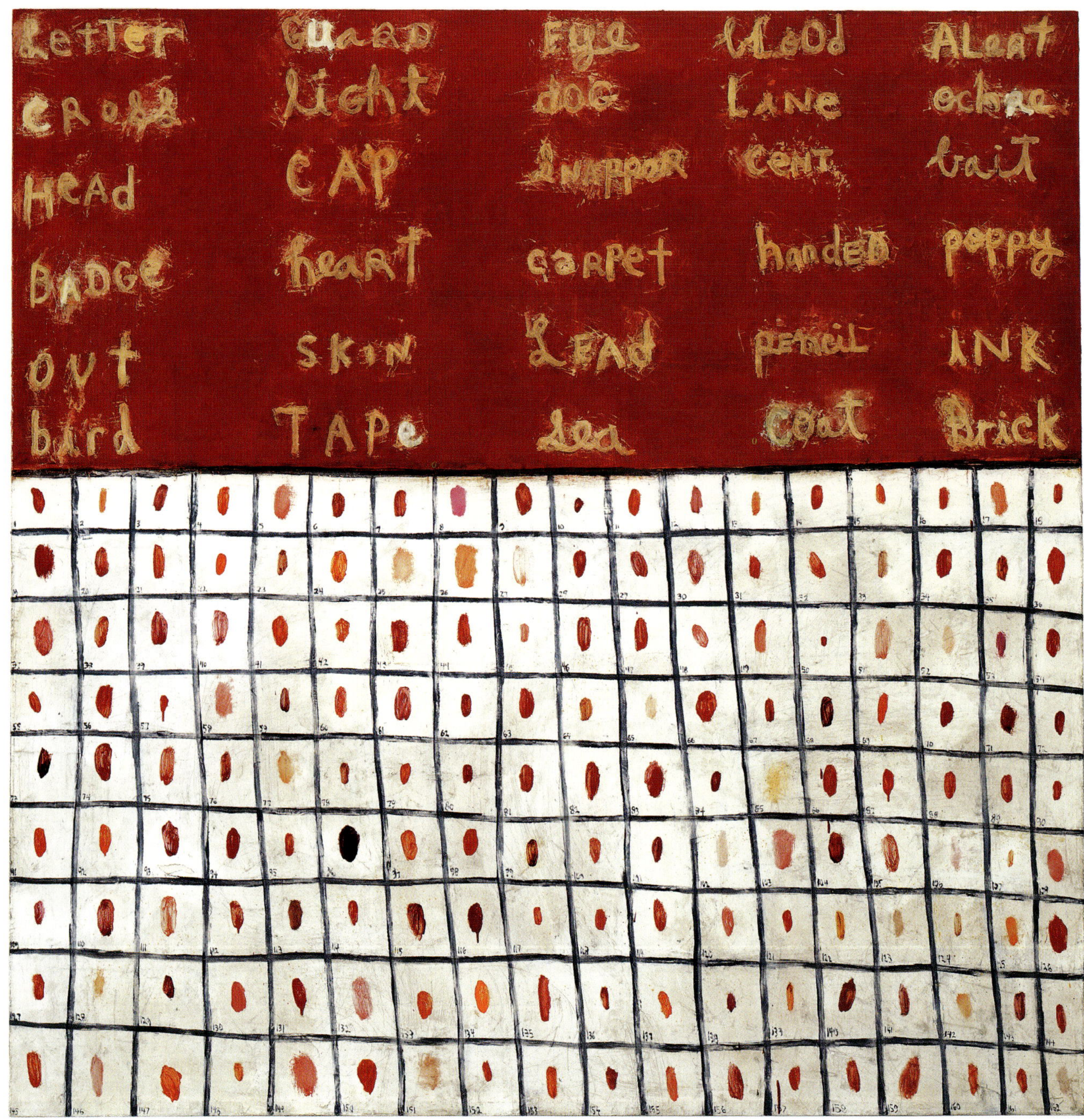

24. **What Is Red,** 1994

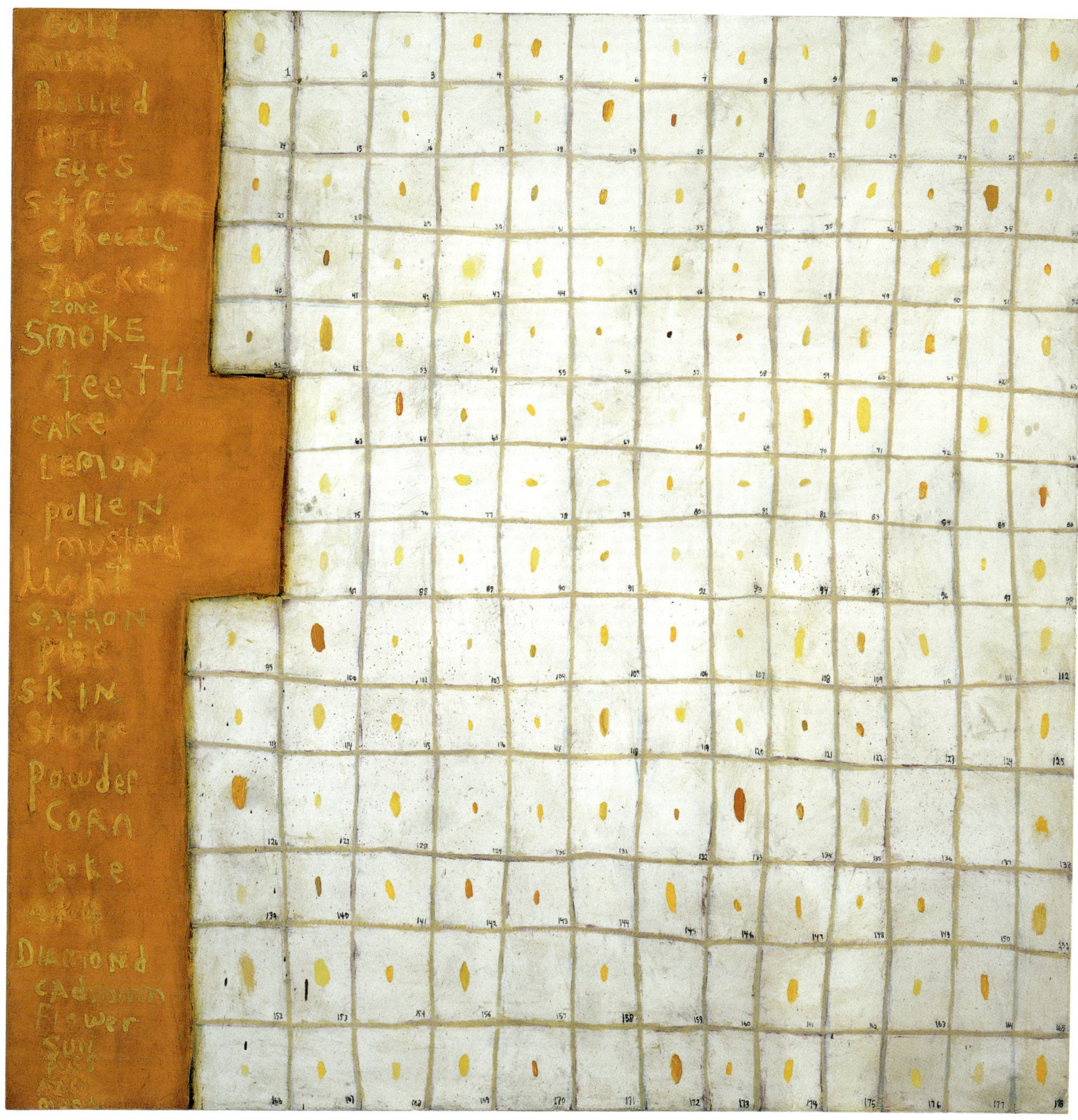

30. **Yellow Stuff**, 1995

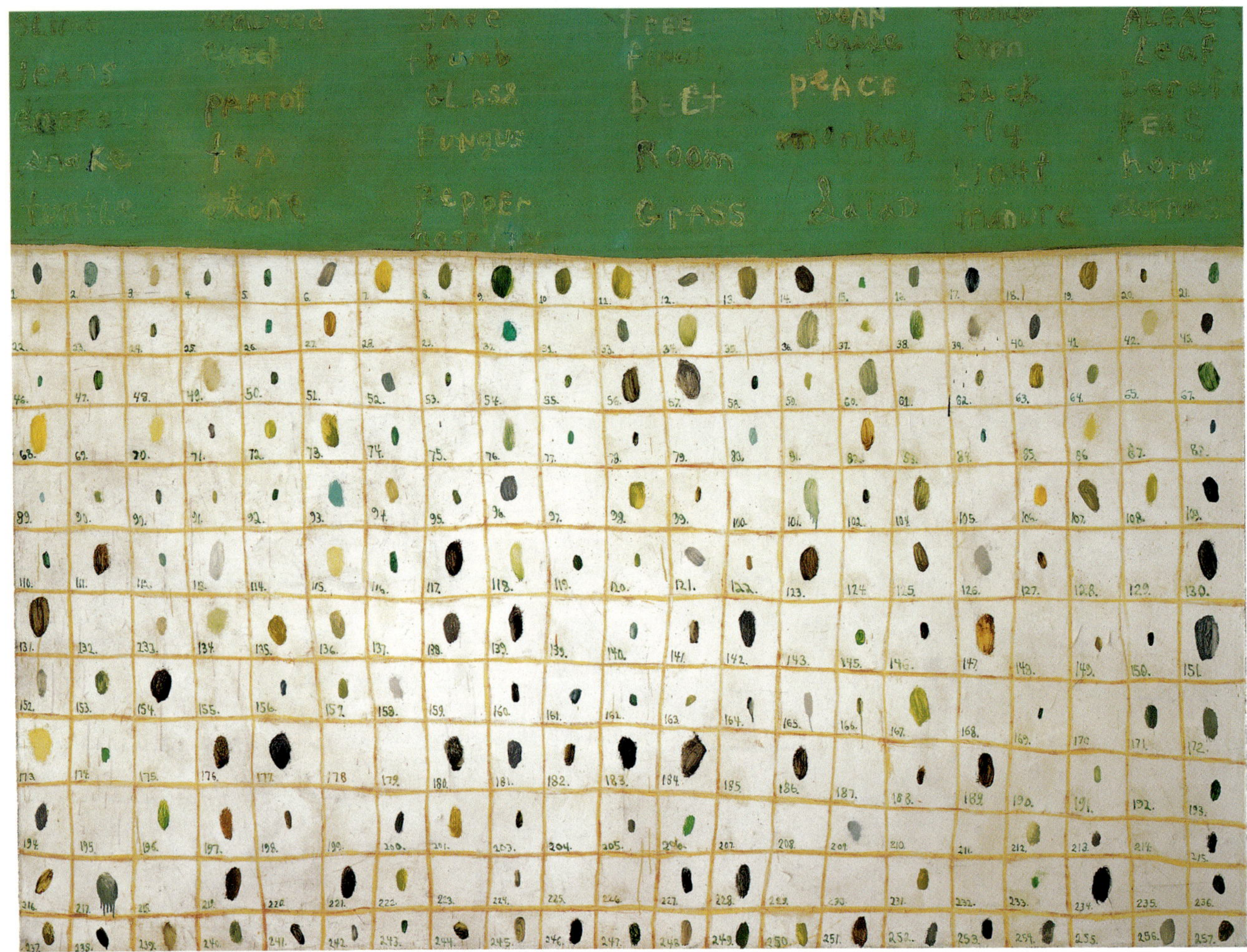

29. **Things Green,** 1995

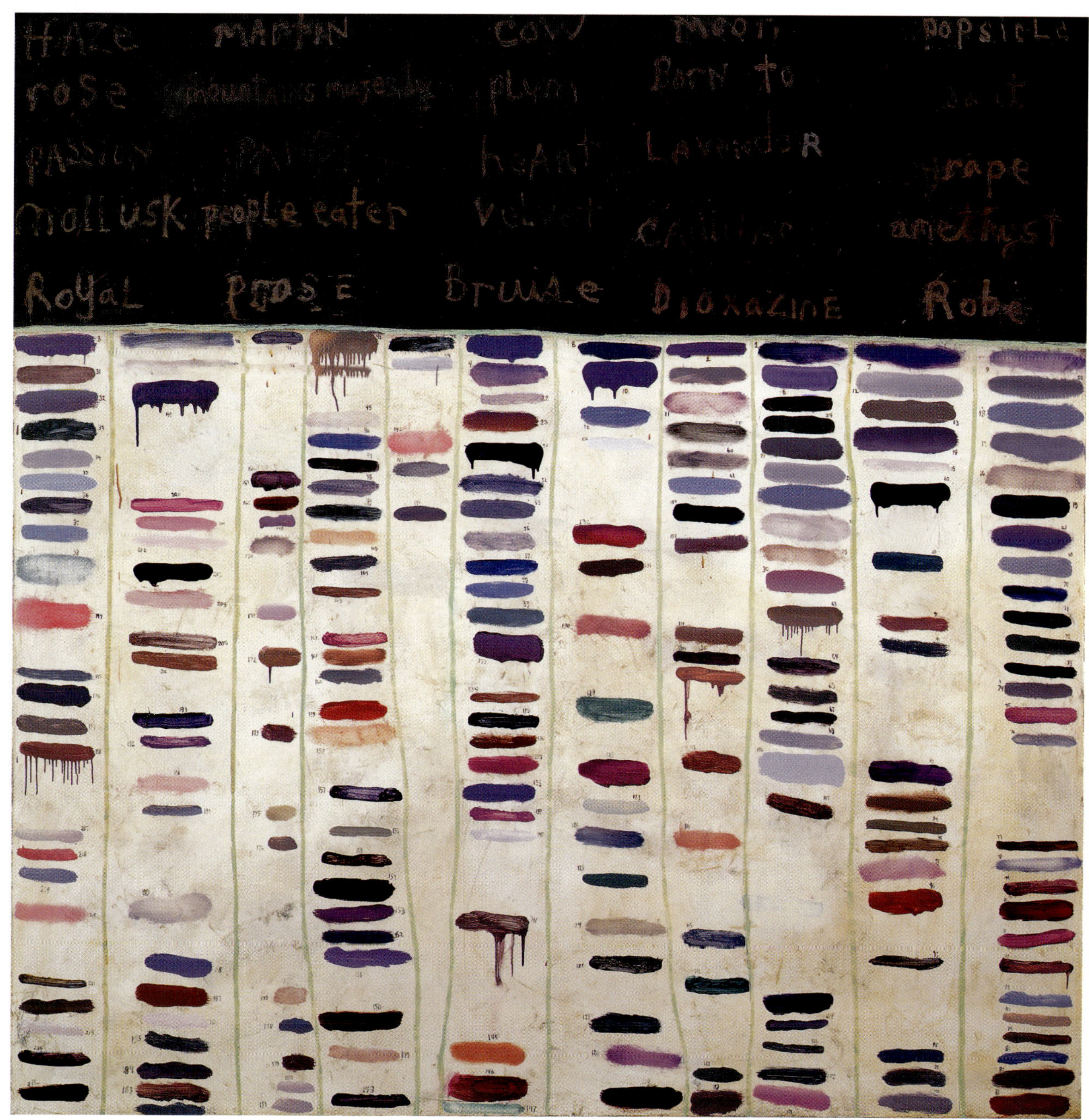

28. **Purple is Purple,** 1995

Carnwath's investigations in *Reflection* and related canvases such as *Manifestation* (2005; p. 121) are not unlike the inquiries many conceptual artists have addressed such as John Baldessari, Ed Ruscha, and Lawrence Weiner. For example, in Baldessari's *Everything is Purged from This Painting* (1967–1968), the following sentence appears in simple black letters on gray canvas: "Everything is purged from this painting but art; no ideas have entered this work." Like Baldessari before her, Carnwath is exploring the very foundation of the concept of art as it has come to be identified. Is art something on a canvas, or is it something in the mind?

The "colored" series of the early 1990s exemplifies Carnwath's practice of repetition and reiteration, just as a scientist reworks and repeats experiments. As she explains, making things is a way to discovery. "If I don't know what I'm doing, I may as well get it right."[71] But unlike a scientist who seeks correct and right answers, Carnwath allows herself open-ended conclusions; art making, after all, is not about following rules and formulas. Thus she allows herself to try things more than once in order to see what will happen: a happy accident or discovery may be hiding around any corner.

Around 1995, Carnwath began painting images of the human brain, including *All That I Know* (1995; p. 52); *Two Minds* (1996; p. 53); and *Red Occupation* (1996; p. 54). Her interest in the subject was stirred during a visit to Lawrence, Kansas, where she had been invited to speak at the Spencer Museum of Art. There she learned that Thomas Stoltz Harvey, a retired doctor who lived in Lawrence, had portions of Albert Einstein's brain in a couple of large mason jars.

Dr. Harvey, the pathologist who performed Einstein's autopsy at Princeton Hospital in 1955, removed, weighed, and absconded with his brain. For years no one knew where it was. In 1978, the brain—sectioned and preserved in alcohol—was discovered in Harvey's possession. When Einstein's brain was analyzed, it was found to be fifteen percent wider than average and had abnormalities consistent with enhanced facility in mathematics and spatial processing. It was also found that his brain lacked a certain groove, suggesting to researchers that his neurons would have been able to fire and work more efficiently with each other.

That Carnwath would choose the human brain as a subject is not that surprising given her scientific curiosity, especially during this period in her life. The substance and story underlying this series of works are intellectually intriguing and tinged with foible, folly, and humor, qualities found throughout her work. But Carnwath made a rather poignant answer when asked why she was so interested in painting images of the brain. By doing so, she explained, she thought she could and would be smarter. As the blue Buddhas she paints are talismans for healing, the act of painting the human brain could be a way to connect with a higher level of knowledge and understanding. Carnwath's personal assessment of Einstein is also revealing. She sees him as the "caretaker" of the knowledge that he possessed, one with the intelligence to understand it and work with it and the generosity to share it with the world. "We don't get to own that stuff." Carnwath observes. "We're only carriers."[72]

Einstein's essay "The World as I See It" foreshadowed Carnwath's observation:

> How strange is the lot of us mortals! Each of us is here for a brief sojourn; for what purpose he knows not, though he sometimes thinks he senses it. But without deeper reflection one knows from daily life that one exists for other people—first of all for those upon whose smiles and well-being our own happiness is wholly dependent, and then for the many, unknown to us, to whose destinies we are bound by the ties of sympathy . . . The ideals which have lighted my way, and time after time have given me new courage to face life cheerfully, have been Kindness, Beauty, and Truth. Without the sense of kinship with men of like mind, without the occupation with the objective world, the eternally unattainable in the field of art and scientific endeavors, life would have seemed to me empty.[73]

In the painting *Red Occupation,* images of the left and right portions of the brain hover in a field of red. The words "current occupation of a body" are scrawled across the top of the canvas. Images on the right of a mouth, tongue, and lips suggest the brain's crucial role in bodily communication.

As researchers confirm, the left and right hemispheres of the brain process information differently. Most people have a dominant side, but learning and thinking are believed to be enhanced when both hemispheres participate in balance. The left brain is said to be the rational side. It processes in a linear, sequential and analytical manner, working from part to whole. The left-brain person is a maker of lists and a drawer of distinctions, adept at deciphering symbols: letters, words, mathematical notations. Such individuals are more controlled in their feelings; they prefer authority structures.

By contrast, the brain's right hemisphere is the intuitive side. Right-brain individuals tend to work more randomly and spontaneously, to see things in a holistic way, and to solve problems by intuition and hunch. They prefer the fluid, the improvised, the open-ended question. They like to be able to see, feel, or manipulate real objects. The right brain draws, the left brain writes.

But questions persist among neurologists, just as they do among artists. How does the brain—"the country of perpetual surprise"[74]—build a mind, and how does it then erect everything else and gain knowledge? Do we have free will? What is the self, and where are the neurological correlates of consciousness? As the protagonist of Richard Powers's *The Echo Maker* observes: "No matter how often I see it, it chills me . . . the naked brain. Scrambling to fit everything together. Unable to recognize that it's suffering any disorder."[75]

In *Two Minds,* Carnwath seems to shift from a relatively detached description of the brain to a more personal assessment of the mind—specifically, of its changing moods as the seasons shift. Here, two female forms represent winter and spring. The winter figure, at left, is a woman who has literally lost her head. The masked woman on the right may represent the soul's rebirth with the arrival of spring: the mask, in many religions and cultures, symbolizes transformation and possession by spirit. Carnwath's wordplay—"(s)he(r)"—subtly reinforces this idea. By definition, "she" is that female who is neither speaker nor hearer. By contrast, "her" relates to her-*self,* as a possessor or the agent or object of an action. This sense of action, of rebirth and renewal, is reinforced by the words at the bottom of the painting: "The grey of winter's darkness. Nearly over. Almost gone. But for the rain. Spring is full of greens, yellows, reds, blues. The primaries. And secondary colors. A full palette. Bright until summer bleaches."

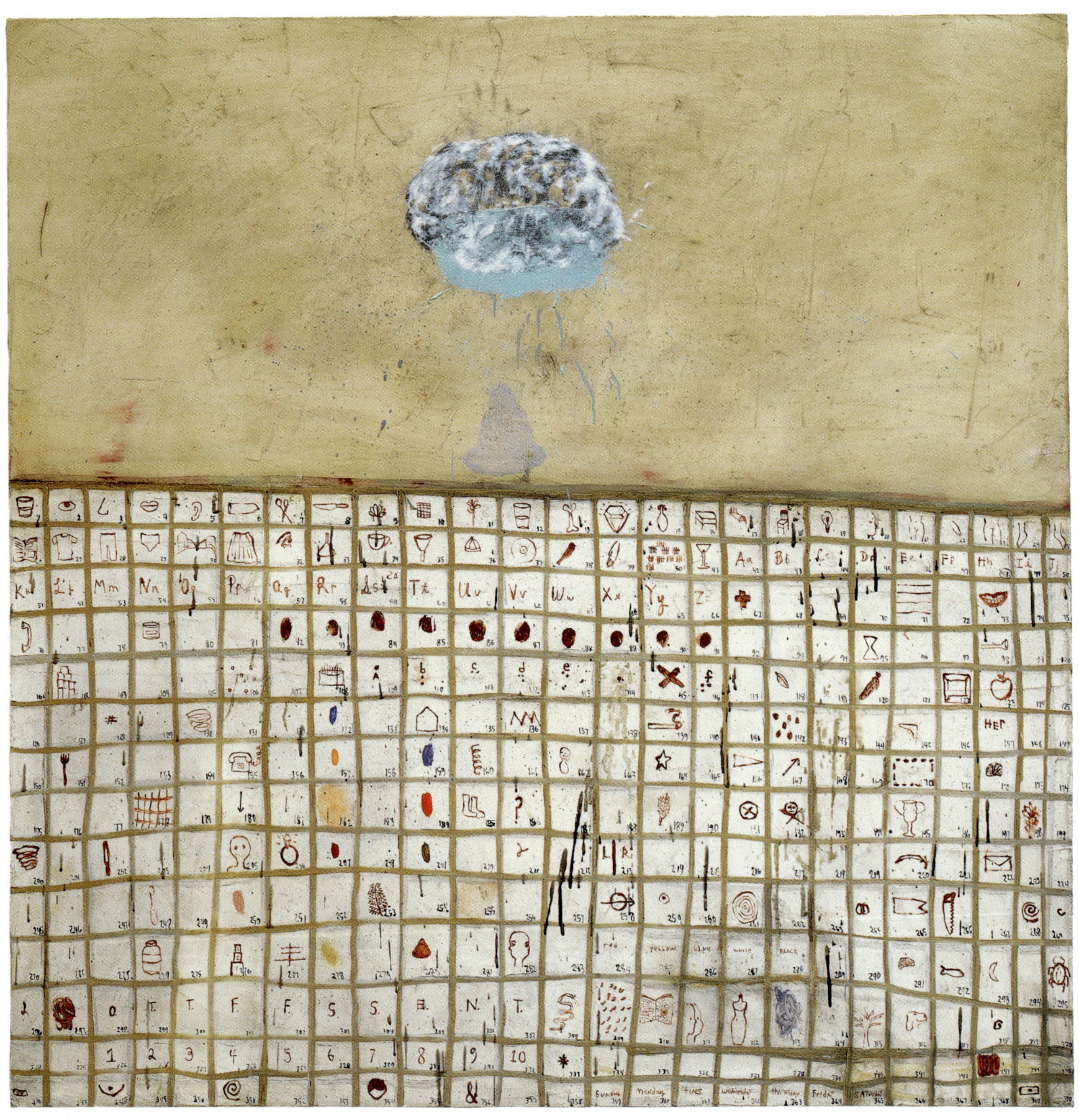

26. **All That I Know,** 1995

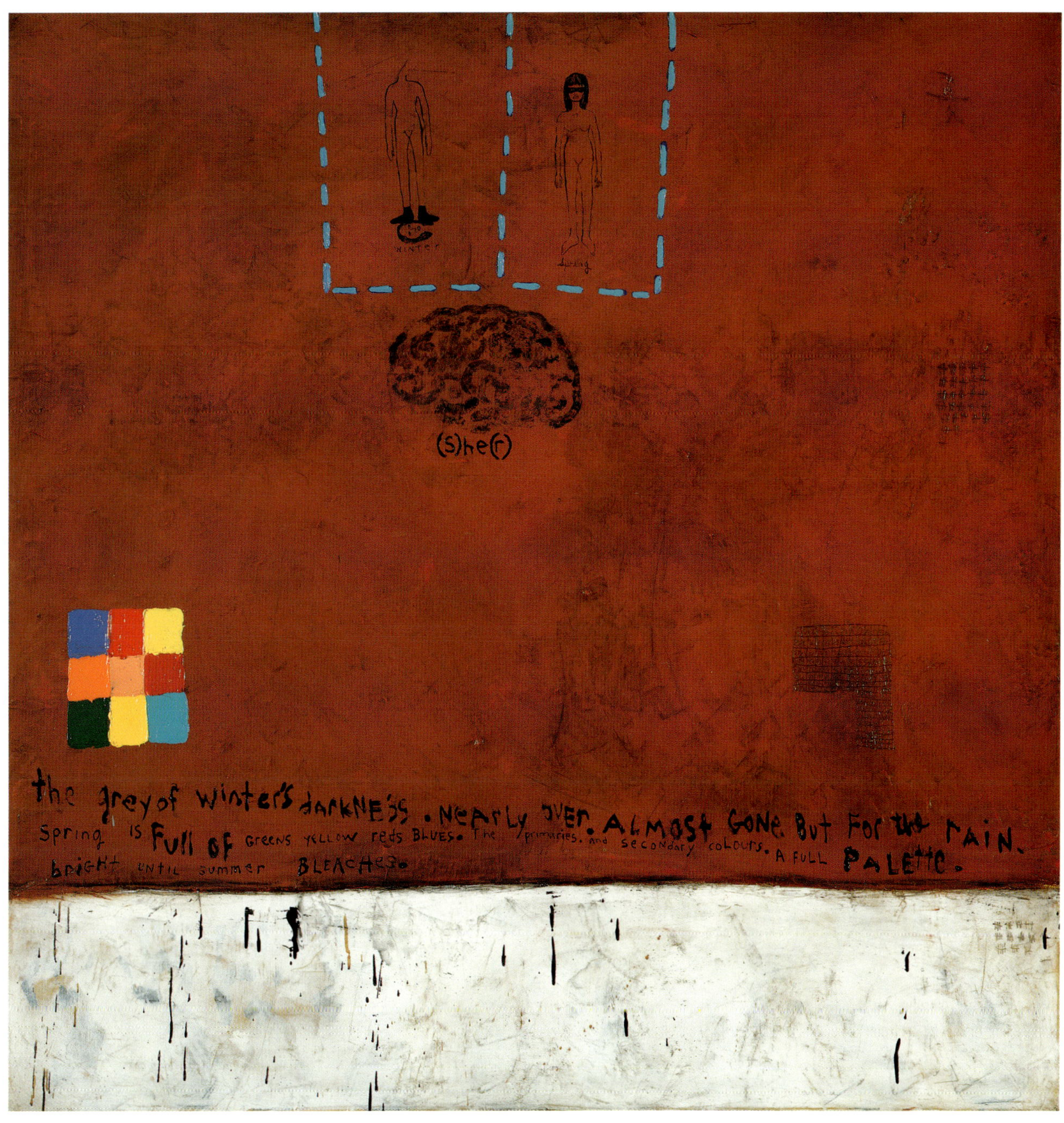

35. **Two Minds,** 1996

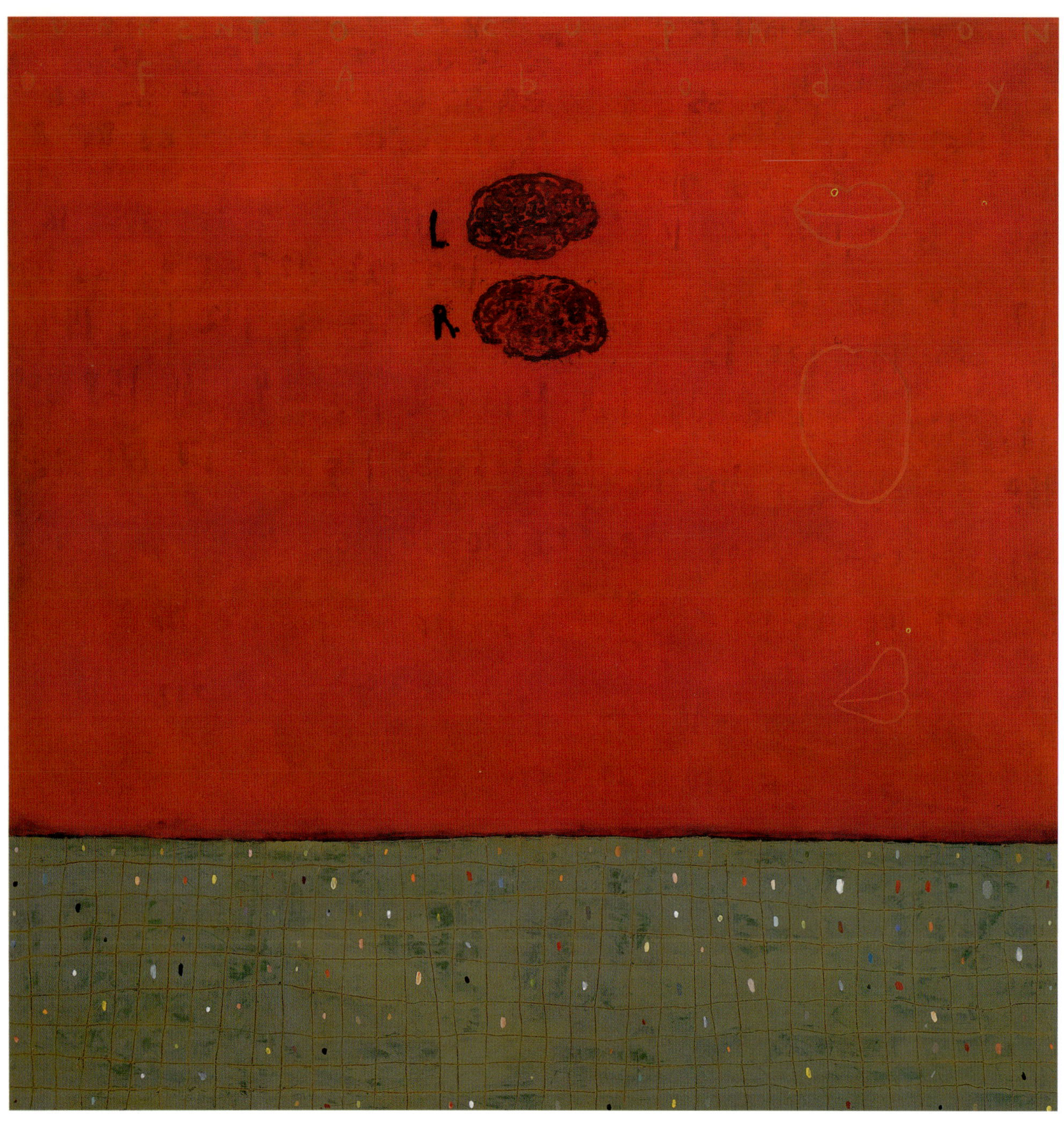

33. **Red Occupation**, 1996

Finally, a small square of colors marks an early appearance of an ideogram Carnwath has invented for herself. In her personal vocabulary of symbols, the three-by-three square of colors represents rationality and order—an extension of the painted grids' function in her "colored" paintings. In the symbolism of numbers, the number three represents creative power and growth; the number nine (three multiplied by three) signifies fulfillment and attainment.

Some of Carnwath's more recent symbols suggest DNA chains, other molecular structures, or constellations. Regardless of the form, these ideograms express the artist's search for order in a world of infinite complexity. The meaning Carnwath assigns to the square, however, does not lie far from longstanding multicultural interpretations associated with the shape. In Hindu culture, for example, the square is the archetype and pattern of order in the universe. Elsewhere, the symbol variously represents honesty and integrity, immutability and integration. The increasing diagrammatic and symbolic content of Carnwath's art speaks to her evolving intellectual curiosity and her appreciation of painting as a critical tool of self-discovery. "Painting is about searching," she has written. "It is about primary research. Each mark reveals something new or something known in a new way."[76]

> If you don't know what the personal is you can't get to the us.
> Squeak Carnwath

IN AUGUST 1996, CARNWATH ACCEPTED a residency at Yaddo, an artists' and writers' colony in upstate New York. Her mother, now living in the nearby community of Amsterdam, encouraged her to do this so they could spend time together. The day before Carnwath flew east, she learned that her mother was hospitalized, with only a short time to live. For the next several weeks Carnwath divided her energy between the hospital and her guest studio. Despite the hardships of the time and her troubled relationship with her mother, Carnwath views the experience as "a final gift" from her.[77]

Two paintings completed around this time express Carnwath's sense of grief, loss, and acceptance. *Green Floor* (1996; p. 58) is a quiet painting with its barely readable words at the bottom of the canvas: "I am willing to entertain the simplicity of my mind." The vague outlines of a column of glasses—half full or half empty—appear as ghostly apparitions, reminders of the glasses of milk her mother drank in the hospital. A "volunteer bug collection" in a whitish rectangle refers to the dead insects Carnwath found on her Yaddo studio floor at the end of each day: a small parallel world of death.

Green Floor is a conversation between Carnwath and the world, addressing both its smallest and its most dramatic moments. The unfolding of such a conversation requires much time alone in the studio. "There I have a feeling of being completely present," Carnwath explains. "It is then that something happens: the alchemical process of painting begins." Often, a mundane object will be the basis for the painting. "I'm looking for the really boring things, the things that people ignore."[78]

The Zen master Soen Nakagawa-Roshi enjoined his students to pay attention to just such boring and ordinary things. "Cooking, eating, sleeping, every deed of everyday life is nothing else than this Great Matter. Realize this! So we extend tender care with a worshiping heart even to such beings as beast and birds—but not only to beasts, not only to birds, but to insects too, okay? Even to grass, to one blade of grass, even to dust, to one speck of dust. Sometimes I bow to the dust."[79]

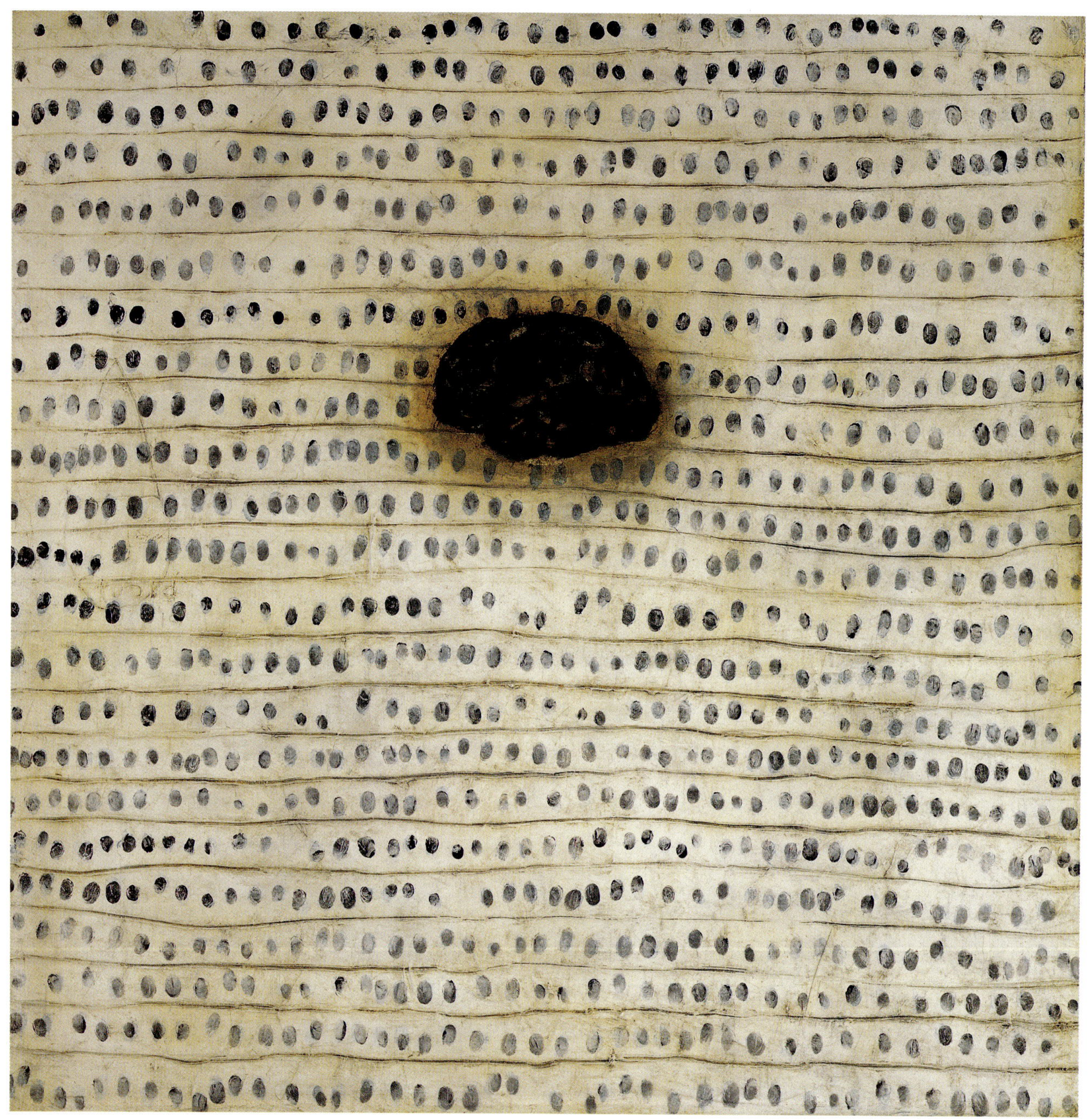

27. **Imprint,** 1995

The painting *No More, No More* (1996; p. 59) stands in sharp contrast to *Green Floor*. A bold black-and-white work that nearly shouts in rage, the painting lists all that Carnwath's mother realized she would no longer have to suffer:

> *No more laundry*
> *No more yelling*
> *No more income taxes*
> *No more crying*
> *No more rust*
> *No more anger*
> *No more burnt toast*
> *No more secrets*
> *No more mopping*

For all its bleak anger, the painting is both elegiac and poignant, a lamentation about life and a sorrowful benediction to Carnwath's mother. "Paintings are not ordinary objects," Carnwath observes. "A painting is not a clock; it cannot tell time but a painting embodies time. It is not a vessel, which can hold water, but painting is a carrier of meaning, of human touch. Each brush stroke or smear of pigment is freighted with philosophical inquiry. Investigations which question reality, occupation of space, physical place, life, and self."[80]

In the years following her mother's death, Carnwath seems to have used painting as a way to purge old sorrows as she sifted through family belongings and untangled childhood memories. Indeed, childhood memories have both dogged and inspired Carnwath throughout her life. "I'm fascinated by my childhood," she once remarked. "I keep thinking I shouldn't be. My parents are dead . . . But it's intriguing—how we were formed, our genetics . . . Some of us keep going over that territory over and over again."[81]

This fascination is reflected in a number of paintings, both large and small, completed around 1997 and 1998. As a child Carnwath always got bad grades; the memory, perhaps conflated with her teaching experiences, is manifest in *Assignment* (1998; p. 111). *Nursery Wall* (1998; p. 60) and *Memory Structure* (1998; p. 61) are touching remembrances, encoded references to her old bedroom wallpaper, plaid school dresses, sibling relationships, and Dick and Jane reading lessons learned in classrooms painted institutional green. In *Memory Structure*, Carnwath has written in small letters: "Change is necessary for growth." Perhaps these inconspicuous words allude to the many times Carnwath's family moved from one city to another and she was told by her parents that the change would be good for her. The vague outline of a rabbit—a "dumb bunny," as Carnwath's father called her in childhood—appears in *Nursery Wall*. The rabbit appears repeatedly in later work, such as *Trying Simply To Be Happy* (2000; p. 74), *Long Happy Life* (2002; p. 78), and *Good Luck* (2003; p. 83). Carnwath has described "him" as pathetic, explaining that she was trying to claim a place for him and to "take care of something that is for me some kind of pain or wound."[82] The recurrence of certain images suggests a healing practice for the artist, an exorcism of sorts. Images are explored until the emotional experience is understood physically and emotionally, and the interior scar gradually heals and disappears.

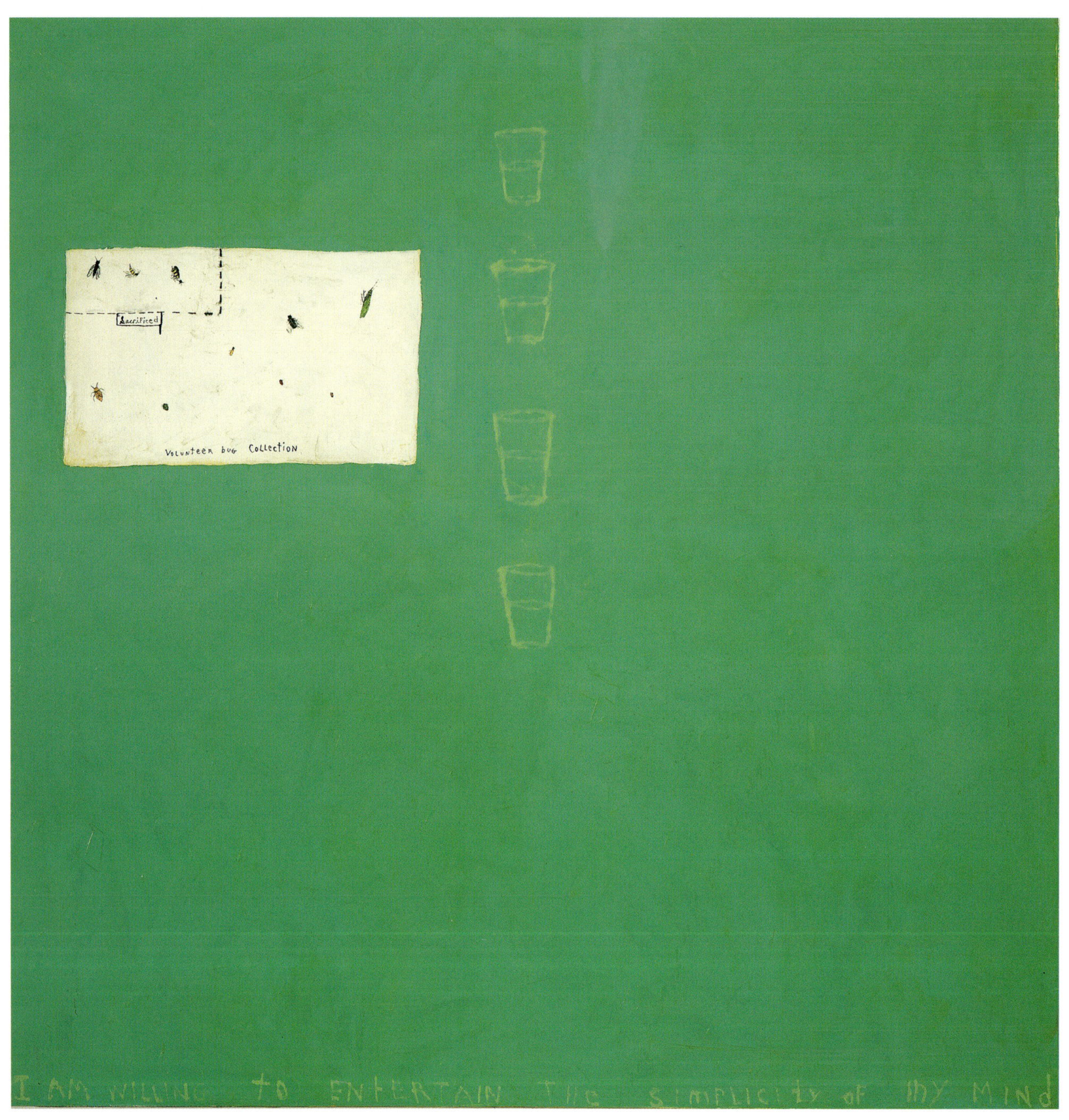

31. **Green Floor,** 1996

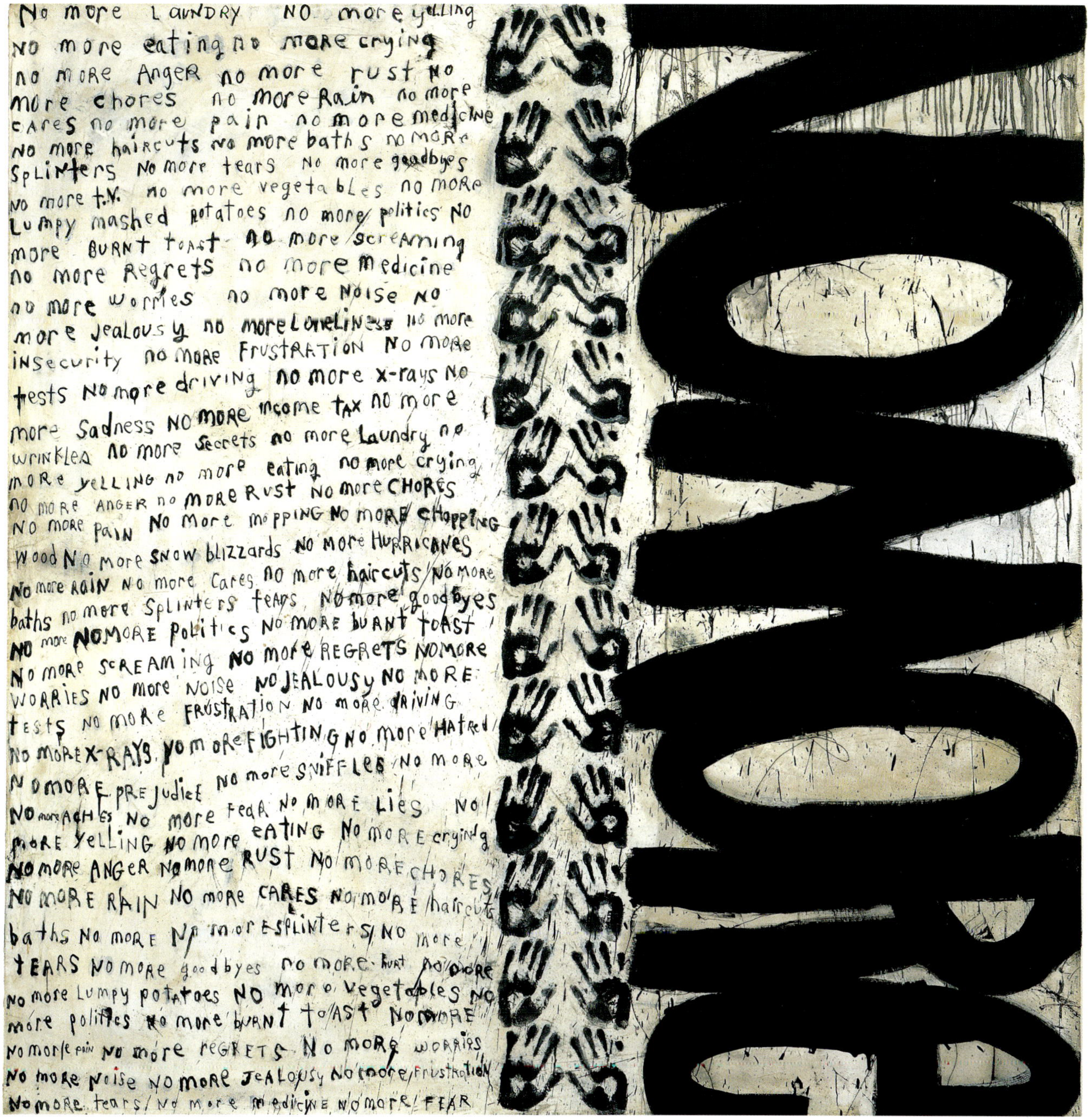

32. No More, No More, 1996

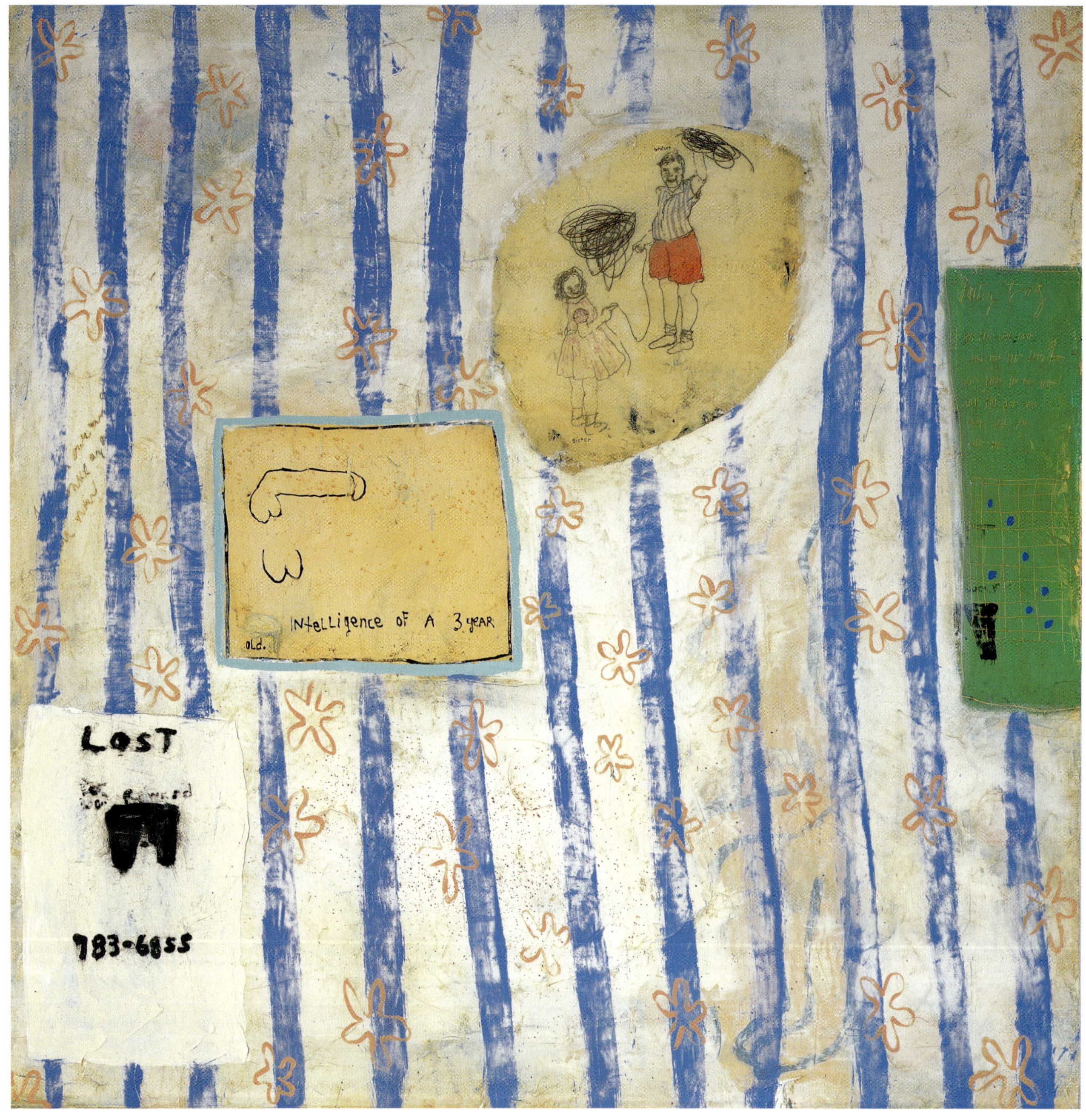

40. **Nursery Wall,** 1998

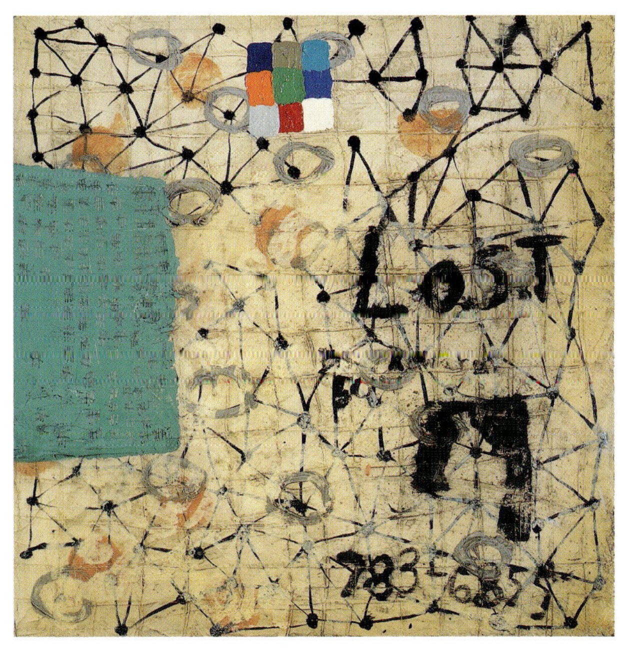

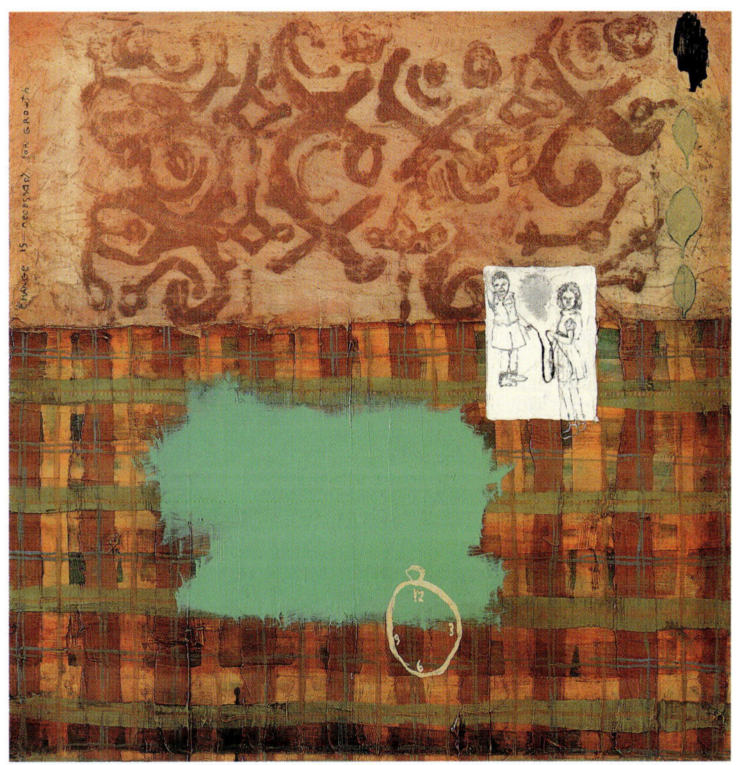

38. **Lost Small,** 1998 (above)

39. **Memory Structure,** 1998 (below)

Carnwath completed the large *Trying To Know Lost* (1997; p. 63) a year after her mother's death. The title itself implies that Carnwath is adrift without her parents. The artist's sense of loss is emphasized by a small flier that advertises a reward for a lost bird. Carnwath received the flier from a friend and in transposing it to canvas she gave it her own contact number. The bold red-and-green pattern, which appears in variation in *Memory Structure* (1998; p. 61) and *Think About It* (1999; p. 69), recalls the upholstery of her family's couch and the designs on the Turkish rug and velvet drapes of her old piano teacher, whom she recalls fondly. Writing of *Think About It*, Maria Porges observed how these sensuous, boldly patterned, and painterly forms, like Matisse's dynamic interpretations of pattern and color, function simultaneously as figure and ground, object and environment.[83] But Carnwath sees the space in her paintings not as deep three-dimensional pictorial space but as the mental space of conscious thought: "Painting or creating is not a replica of life but a tool for insight."[84]

And then there are the black-and-white images and the personal graffiti scrawled on the left side of *Trying To Know Lost*—images of flowers, poised hands, and other random chartings of the artist's emotional subconscious. The words read as calls for help and as acknowledgment of her deep sorrow: "Can't find my toothbrush . . . Can't find my underwear . . . Can't find my sox . . . Alone . . . Head can't hold the small . . . The Big fills Brain . . . Feet stumble lost in place . . . Home not home . . . Hands full can't juggle . . . Eyes sensitive buckets . . . Full to the rim."

A lament for the lost continent of childhood, *Trying To Know Lost* evokes Marcel Proust's *In Search of Lost Time.* Just as Proust's memories—of youth, family gossip, and a world in which he never found a place—start to flow when he tastes a madeleine dipped in linden tea, so one might conjecture the tide of childhood memories that raced in when Carnwath discovered in some closet an old report card or a favorite plaid school dress. Carnwath's paintings from this period represent the adult's attempt to reclaim the child's state of innocence and instinctual faith. "Painting is a kind of call and response," she observes. "During the act of painting one is listening, paying attention to a self, a voice simultaneously recognizable and foreign."[85]

> As the mind explores the symbol, it is led to ideas that lie beyond the grasp of reason.
> Carl Jung

GIVEN CARNWATH'S INTEREST in symbols, it is a temptation to try to assess her paintings in Freudian and Jungian terms. The artist may be both acknowledging and dismissing this thought, or the notional connection, in *Things I've Heard or Seen in Person* (1998; p. 66), with its reference to Freud and a woman's "tit." In the many interviews Carnwath has given over the years, she has never mentioned these eminent theorists of the psyche; in fact she usually declines to discuss or analyze her paintings in detail. "I know less of what I'm working on now than I did years ago," she explained in a 2001 interview. "There would be zones of known territory—like maybe what a color would be—but the parts I liked the best were the parts where I was afraid, or where I didn't know what I was doing. Now that's how it all is . . . It's hard for me even to say exactly what the paintings are about. There are subtexts, which are the real texts, and then there are things like the 'story line,' the thing you thought you saw, but it wasn't the real information."[86]

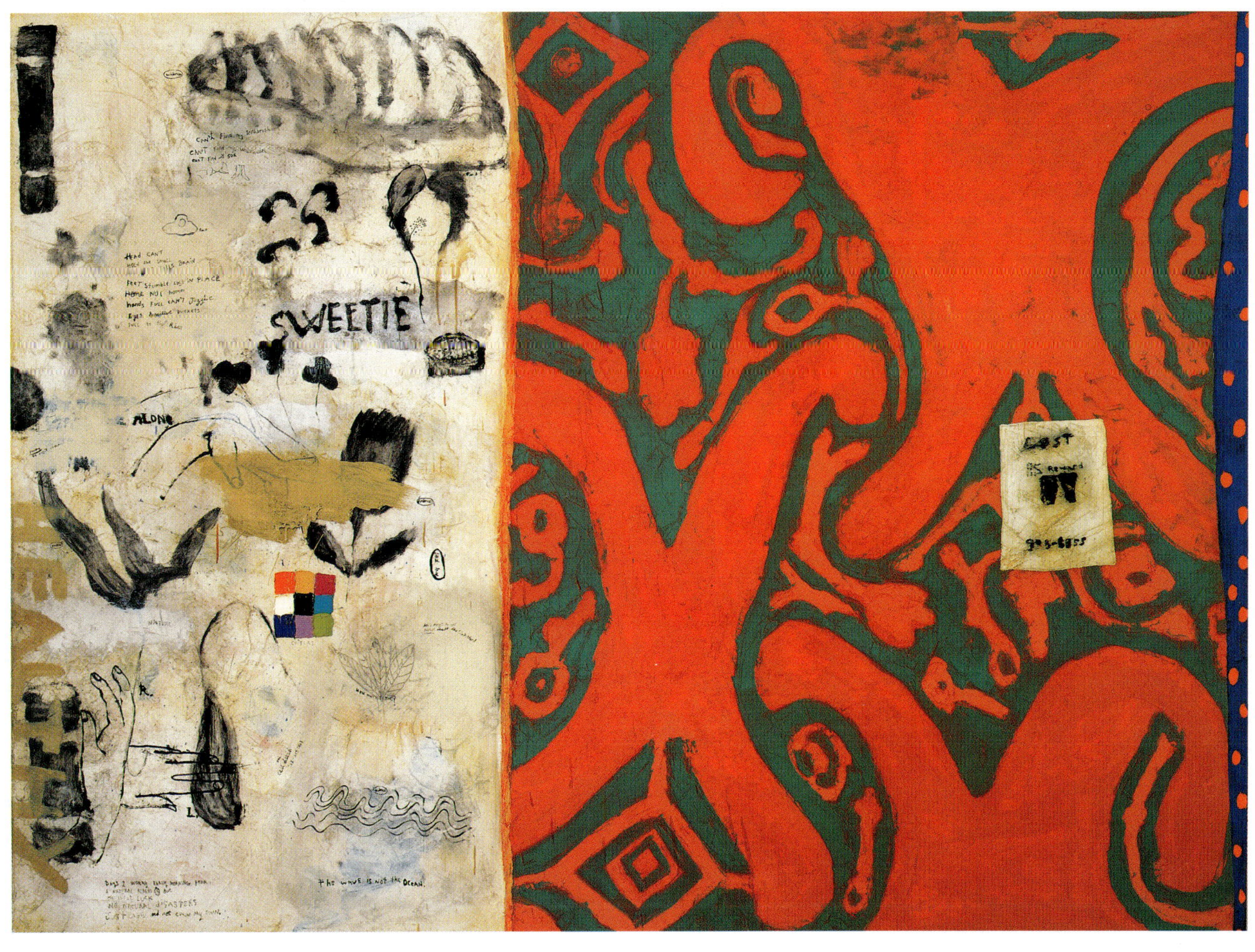

36. **Trying To Know Lost,** 1997

Despite working in this territory of the unknown, Carnwath provides us with just enough tantalizing information to engage the mind and heart. This may reflect what Carl Jung described as the concept of active imagination, a kind of meditation in which the emotions are expressed as images, or entities, or story. Visualization, automatic writing, dance, music, and painting can provide paths to this meditative state. In it, the subconscious conveys—"acts out"—messages to the conscious mind. "My mind becomes totally fluid and receives things in this really great way," Carnwath has said. "And it's from years of painting . . . The more you practice this, the more readily you can get into that zone. And the great thing is there's kind of no boundary, because time doesn't matter—nothing matters but that color, that paint and the pressure, and seeing what it does."[87]

The paintings of the late 1990s and early 2000s find Carnwath and her surrogate, the dumb bunny, taking a more worldly view. In several works—such as *Numbered Moments* (2001; p. 71) and *World Upside Down* (2000; p. 72)—the artist literally paints images of the earth. Intimate and serene though the former painting appears, it powerfully communicates its message of our numbered days on earth. Carnwath sees her paintings as a way to understand "our fragility of being, that we're just specks. And, really, we're just witnesses. It's our job to come to some understanding of that. I want the work to evidence that endeavor."[88]

Often Carnwath's paintings read like large doodle pads in which she records her musings and thoughts about the world at large. She has called herself a kind of radio receiver, with the responsibility to share what she has taken in. Thus, in paintings like *Things I've Heard or Seen in Person*, Carnwath records information about the 1998 anthrax threat and avian flu scare among random paint splotches, swatches, handprints, and a flier announcing a nude drawing class. The flurry of lines in the red dust of pigment suggest a frenzied state of mind—rather like the scribbled cyclones that appear in the thought bubbles of Woodstock, the *Peanuts* cartoon character. In many ways Carnwath, like a good cartoonist, is always on the lookout for the most economical means of expression that will communicate on the broadest possible level.

In various paintings of this period—including *Plaid Lost* (1999; p. 111) and *What We Cannot Control* (2000; p. 72)—Carnwath seems to be struggling with the topsy-turvydom of the universe, as Paul Klee did in his own intimate work. Klee, it has been said, felt an affinity with the insights of "madmen, savages, and children" and the "in-between world" that exists in the interstices of the world our senses perceive. This identification with irrational forces may be what Klee had in mind when he said that "art does not render the visible, but renders visible": art embodies thought. Marcel Duchamp shared the belief, and it is a concept that Carnwath has often articulated and embraced in her work. "I think of myself as high-functioning, but a lot of my work looks like . . . I don't want to say a crazy person did it, but somebody less self-conscious," she acknowledges. "I recognize how close it might be to vernacular, or unschooled, or the art of people who are either institutionalized, or people who sort of live on the fringes and make things."[89] Her menageries of colors, lines, shapes, words, and pictographs are a "subversive way" for people to become engaged, both visually and conceptually, with her work. After viewers are "hooked" into one of her paintings, she hopes, "they will start free-associating to a thing that's familiar and can make sense of the imagery as it relates to their own life."[90]

Painting, then, is a way for Carnwath to share a kind of emotional pantheism, a macrocosm expressed in the microcosm of her work. This sensibility is especially evident in the paintings *Trying Simply To Be Happy* (p. 74) and *In Pursuit of Happiness* (p. 75). The works were completed in 2000, as Wendy Sussman, a close friend and teaching colleague, was fighting cancer and died shortly thereafter. Carnwath explains that the paintings and their titles were meant to be talismanic: if she could imagine happiness, maybe she could be happy in a world where a friend dies too young, the Arctic ice melts too soon, and Earth's ozone layer becomes more ragged by the day. Immanuel Kant put it succinctly: "Happiness is an ideal, not of reason, but of imagination."[91]

In Pursuit of Happiness cites a short story, a fable of sorts, about a midwestern man who has built his own rocket ship and is taking a two-week Russian cosmonaut course as he prepares to go to outer space. The moral of the story is, of course, that happiness takes many forms. But as Eric Weiner observes in *The Geography of Bliss*, happiness is not easily attainable for those that are unhappy. "Today, not only is happiness considered possible for anyone to attain, it is expected. Thus I, and millions of others, suffer from the uniquely modern malady that historian Darrin McMahon calls 'the unhappiness of not being happy.'"[92]

Paradoxically, *In Pursuit of Happiness* is a largely black canvas in which two dumb bunnies face each other in mute dialogue. In Western color symbolism, black often represents evil, the void, the darkness of death. But to Carnwath's eye it is a positive color. She sees in its depths a life force, just as the ancient Egyptians associated black with rebirth and resurrection. Mystics in the Christian tradition regarded darkness as a tool for spiritual enlightenment. Saint John of the Cross found illumination in the dark of his cell; the nun Cecilia del Nacimiento, who was also a poet and painter, once wrote of darkness: "I saw everything with such sharpness that it was as if I had the eyes of a lynx, mysteriously penetrating the very heart of things."[93]

New Carnwath ideograms emerge in this painting. The square of colors, her private symbol for rationality, has expanded to a large, irregular field of colored squares representing, perhaps, her sense of internal order run amok. The Necker cube, an impossible object that spatially reads in two different ways and which is used in the study of perception, multiplies and climbs like an ethereal ladder in the color-spangled darkness of the canvas.

Though Carnwath has not articulated the symbolism of the dots and circles, one might see them as positive signifiers. The circle is a universal symbol for, among other things, wholeness, perfection, enlightenment, timelessness, and celestial unity. Some mystical systems imagine God as a circle whose center is everywhere—an expression of perfection and the absolute. On a less exalted level, the circles might also simply represent the happiness associated with colorful balloons or candy dots; on them Carnwath has spelled out the word "happy." But as Carnwath observes, "Happiness or contentment isn't like a goal. It comes and goes. The only way to have it is actually to have the reverse of it as well"—no light without darkness—"to be able to live with that and also to deal with the fears, with the idea of dying and the idea that nothing lasts forever—unless all of these things are realized then happiness isn't really possible."[94]

These paintings are like private devotionals, personal meditations on life and death. Indeed, *Trying Simply To Be Happy* shares compositional features with Tibetan thangkas. Painted or embroidered panels hung in monasteries or at family altars and used as loci for prayer, thangkas are meant to lead one on the path to enlightenment. Compositionally, they are highly ordered and geometric—especially those associated with healing—with Buddhist symbols and deities occupying a grid of angles, circles, and concentric squares.

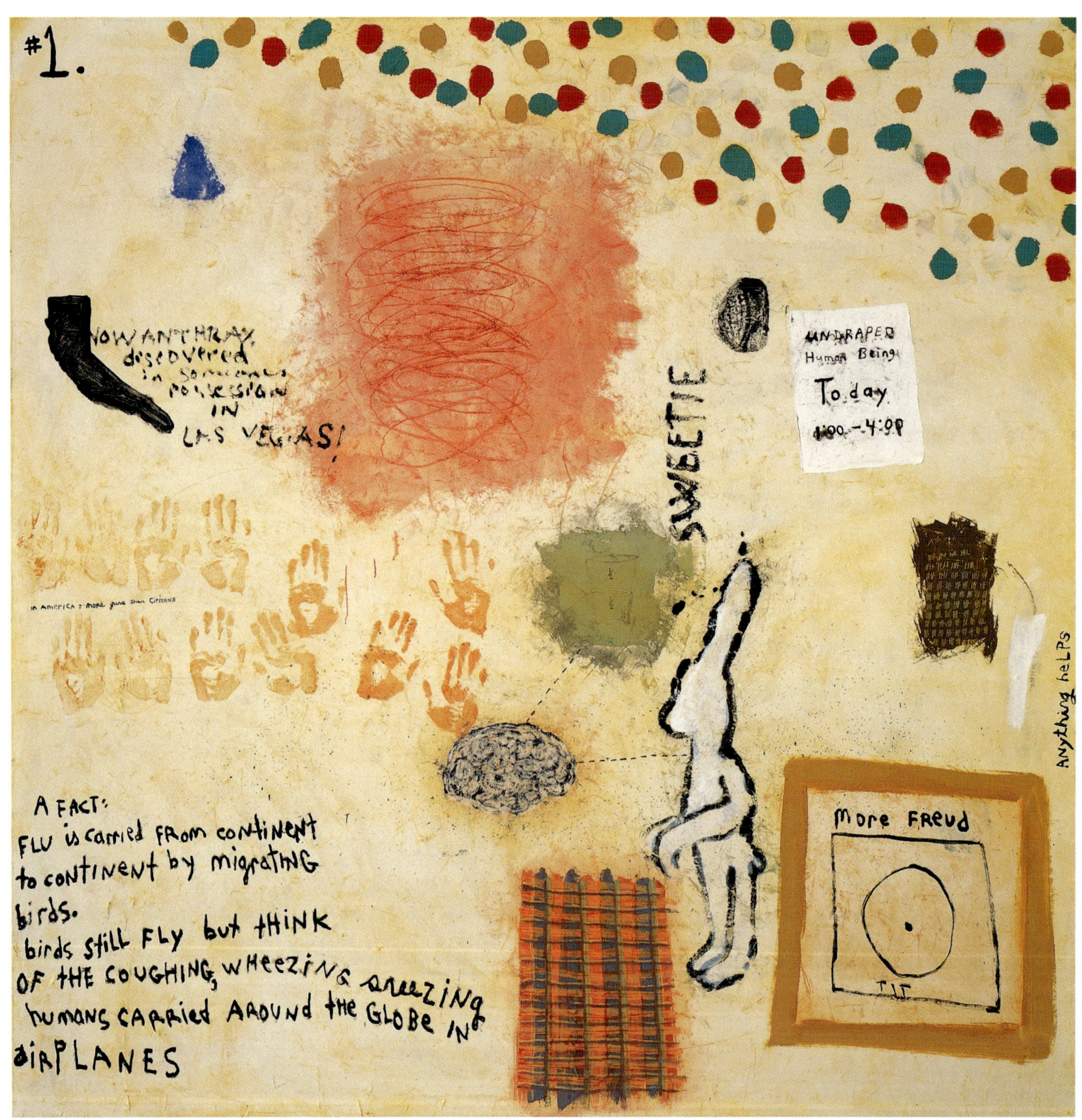

41. Things I've Heard or Seen in Person, 1998

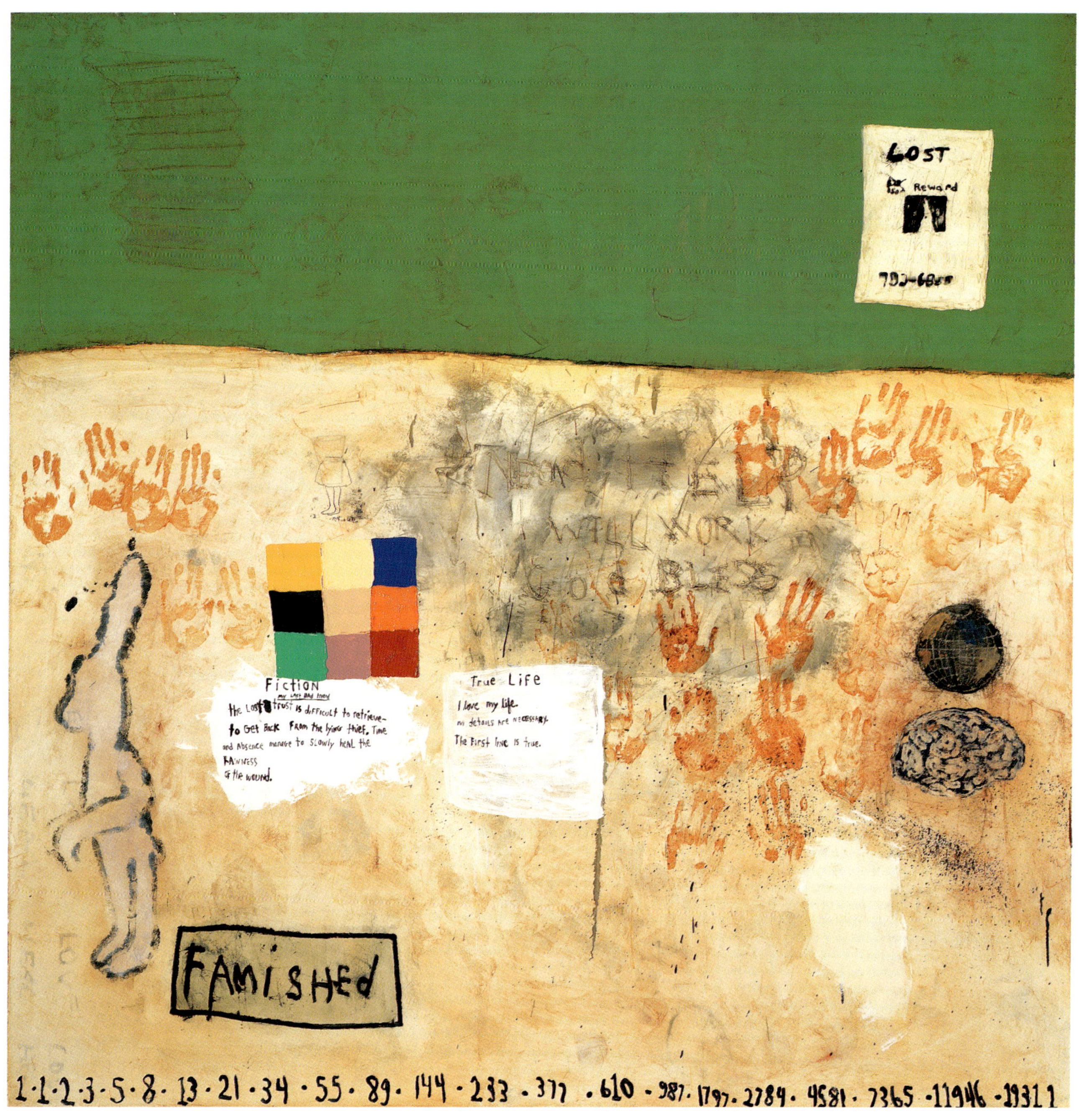

42. **True Life,** 1998

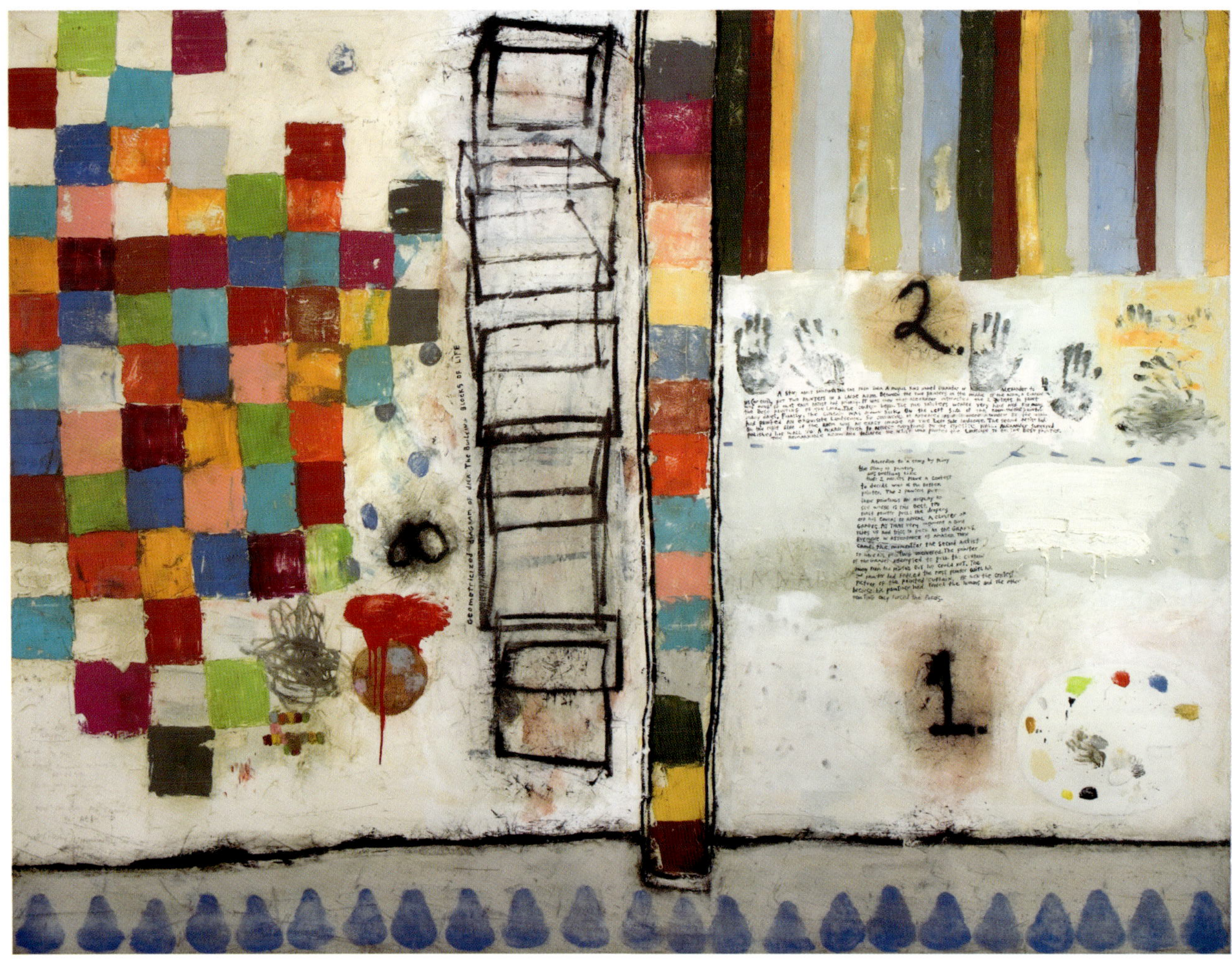

46. **The Story Of Painting**, 1999

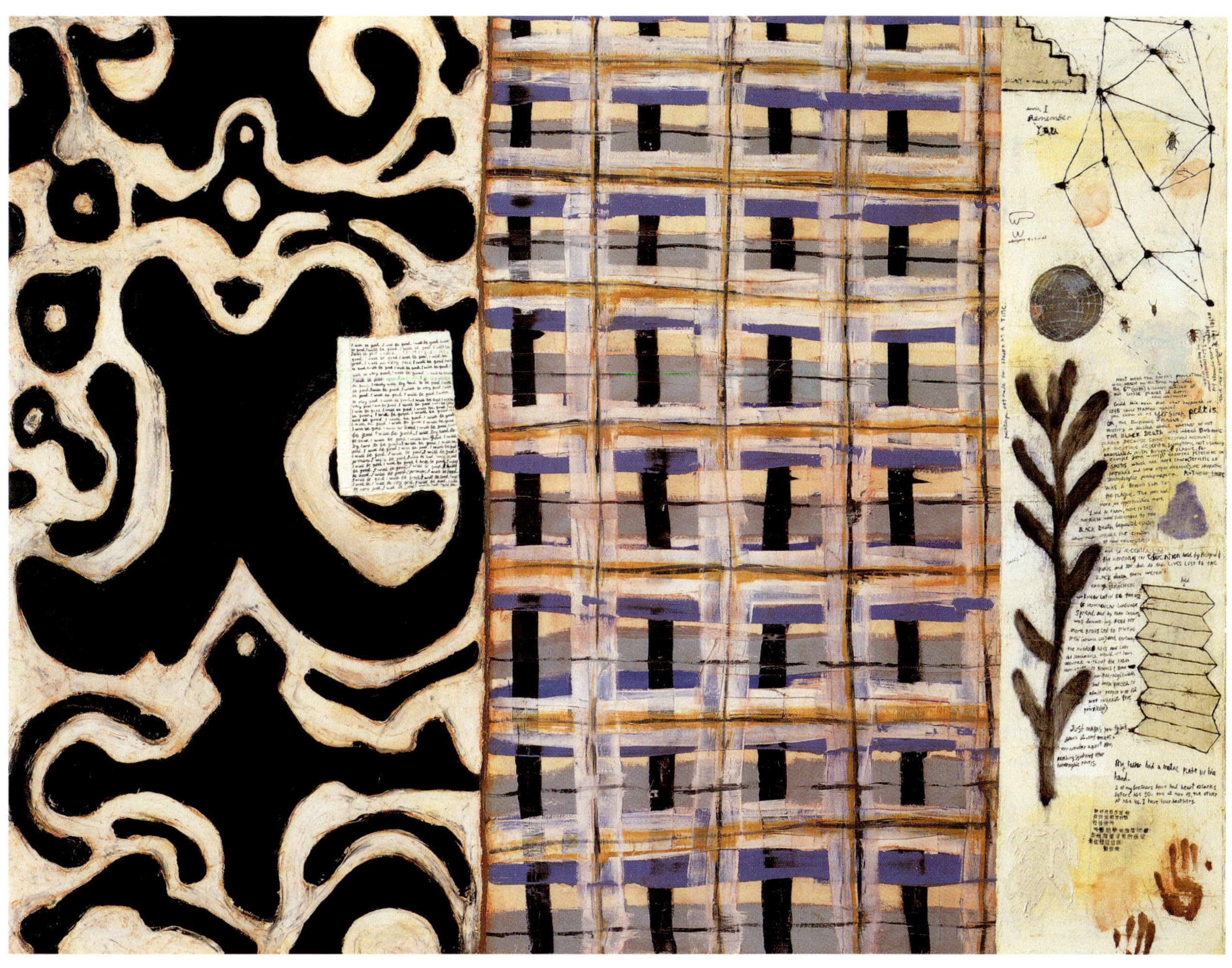

47. **Think About It,** 1999

In *Trying Simply To Be Happy*, rows of blue Medicine Buddhas, simplified to near bell shapes, border a set of nesting squares. A single Bhaisajyaguru is placed off center in the composition, and is somewhat obscured, contrary to the central position the Buddha usually holds in traditional thangkas. Carnwath seems to be suggesting that, like a bell that is sometimes silent, the Buddha in her life, though not always on center, seen, or heard, is always present. Undulating horizontally across the middle of the canvas is what initially appears as a decorative linear design but, on second reading, can also be interpreted as the double helix of DNA, the grand thread of the universe weaving together the living and dead.

> I lost. The unknown refuses
> to collapse.
> Squeak Carnwath

IN 2002, HER FIFTY-FIFTH YEAR, Carnwath created the large diptych *Everything (2)* (pp. 80–81). The title suggests a summation—or struggle—of the artist's creative life. Her rational self, represented by the regularity of the painted stripes and the small square of "order" at the bottom right, claims the diptych's right panel. Markings on three notebook pages signify the elements most fundamental to Carnwath's creative expression: the physical mark of paint, the value of symbols, and the weight of words. Nothing could better express these elements' crucial importance than the written statement: "It's the painting that takes care of me."

The left panel of the diptych shows Carnwath's intuitive side in action. In stark opposition to the painting's orderly right side, it communicates guilt and loss, unambiguously represented in the large words "Please help" and in a scatter of lost-and-found fliers. Words and images appear almost as a form of automatic writing, cries from the depths of Carnwath's conscious and subconscious. Indeed, random lost-and-found fliers, handprints, numerals, hieroglyphs, and narratives appear so regularly in her works since 2000 that they form a mysterious alternative Carnwath language.

A new Carnwath ideogram appears in *Everything (2)*: an irregular circle of dashes encompassing the words "Guilt Free Zone." In a later appearance, the Guilt Free Zone incorporates a roughly rendered Oakland street plan, as in *Last Frontier* (2004; p. 85), identifying where the artist's studio is located—her personal sanctuary, her safe haven. Carnwath has long realized the importance of this safety zone: "When a person gets out of school, she has to create her own safe environment, so she can take risks in her own life."[95] She explains that the Guilt Free Zone was inspired by a friend who was dying from melanoma. Had the friend been quicker to see a doctor, she might have been diagnosed and treated before the cancer became advanced. "I thought she really needed a guilt-free zone," Carnwath recalled.[96] Characteristically leavening introspection with humor, she continued, "My mother was a Catholic who didn't practice, and we didn't know we were being raised Catholic, but got all the guilt."[97]

Feelings of guilt and the uncertainty of a safe haven can have huge consequences. In Carnwath's 1999 painting *Promise* (p. 118), a visually and verbally aggressive work, the large, black words "Shut up, Shut up" can almost be heard as a scream. Carnwath explains that the painting had its genesis when one day her husband asked her too many questions. She told him to "shut up" and leave her studio. "Solitude is necessary," Carnwath declares. "That's why I never wanted kids. Art is a jealous mistress."[98] The significance of *Promise* resides less in the circumstances of its birth, or even in its bold composition, than in the fact that Carnwath expressed so directly in paint a human instinct that we have all shared.

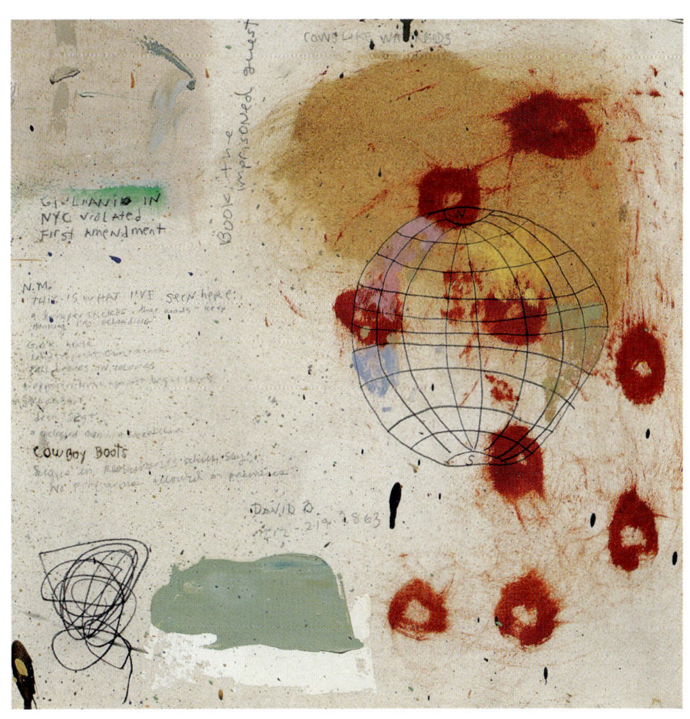

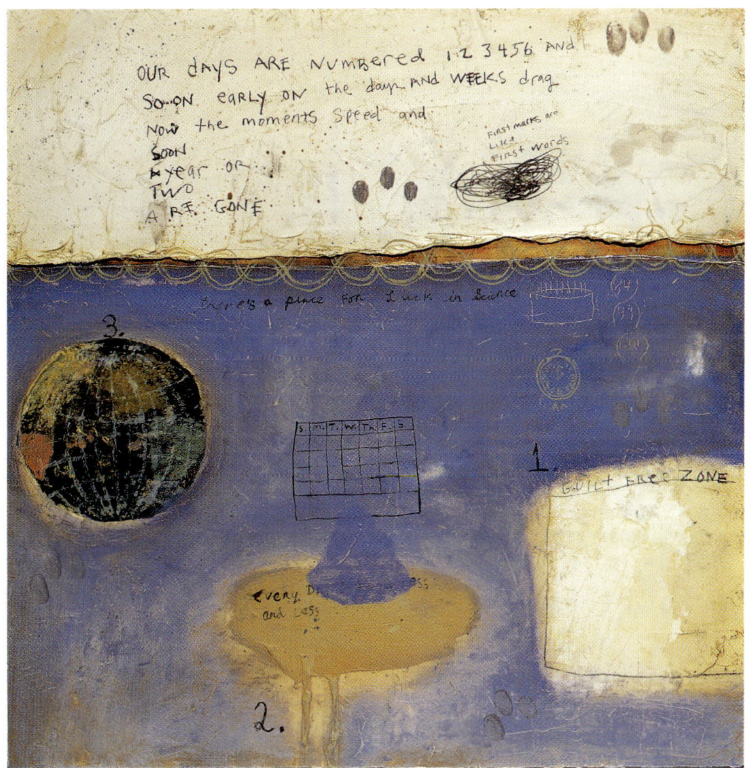

45. **Resident Drawing N.M.,** 1999 (above)

55. **Numbered Moments,** 2001 (below)

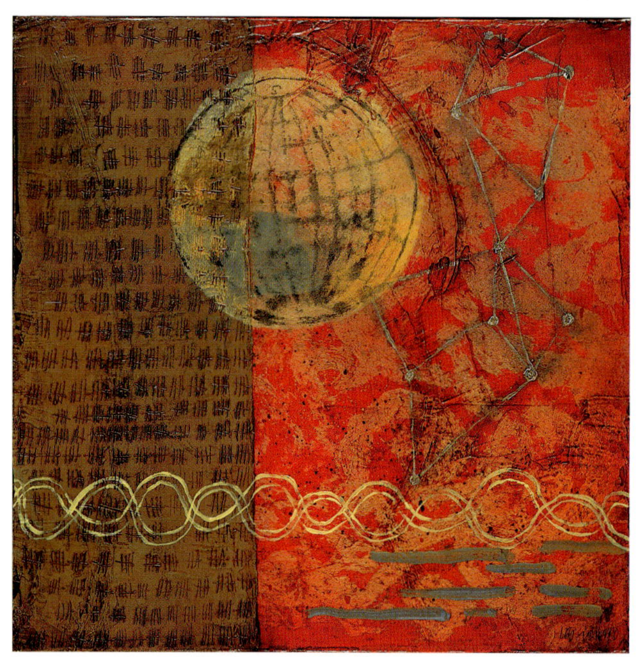

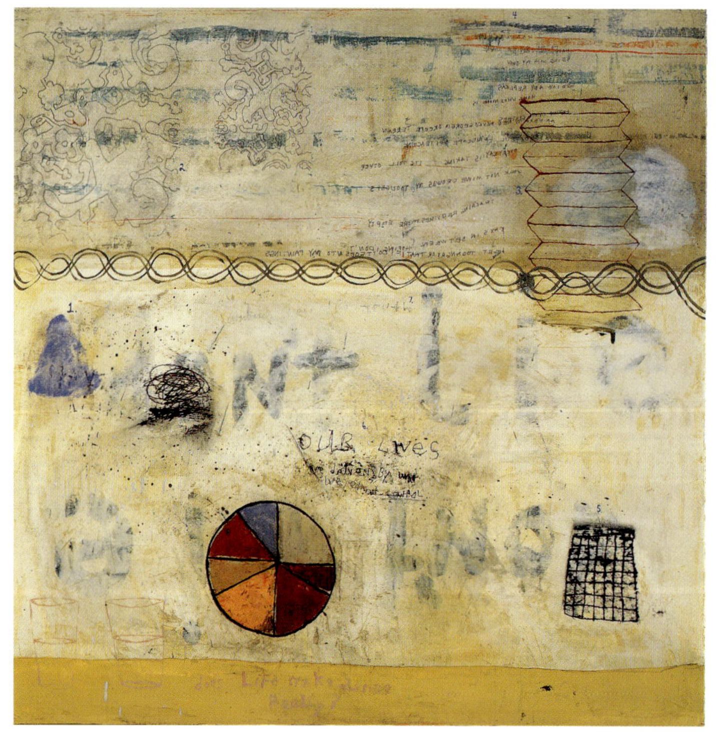

53. **World Upside Down,** 2000 (above)

52. **What We Cannot Control,** 2000 (below)

As a kind of absolution, Carnwath filled the background of *Promise* with handwritten statements: "I will try to be good. I will try to be good. I will be good. I promise I will try to be good. I will be very good." The words initially suggest a mantra, their undulating lines echoing the rise and fall of her voice. But any disgruntled spouse will notice the sly semantic revision. For there is a subtle but distinct difference between "I will be good" and "I will try to be good."

Carnwath continued to expand her personal repertoire of ideograms and symbols. In the 2003 paintings *Good Luck* (p. 83) and *2 Things* (p. 84), for example, these include images of logs, horseshoes, and wishbones. Some of these symbols seem self-evident in their meaning: the horseshoe and wishbone are symbols of good luck. But such interpretations, as usual, are not always so precise. When a horseshoe is turned upward, forming a U, it represents the horns of power and protection. But when it is inverted, it is emptied of power and luck.

The new image of the log alludes to the tree of life. In pagan worship, a tree was a sacred symbol of immortality; in folkloric belief, it signified good luck. Touching a tree was a gesture of respect to the gods when a favor was requested or as a sign of appreciation when a request had been fulfilled. This is where the term "knock on wood" originated. Given Carnwath's political and social leanings, the log may also evoke conservation issues. As John Muir wrote: "God has cared for these trees, saved them from drought, disease, avalanche, and a thousand straining, leveling tempests and floods; but he cannot save them from fools."[99]

Carnwath painted *2 Things* and *Good Luck* in the year when the United States invaded Iraq. A clue is given in the latter painting, which quotes a weary television viewer: "I've turned off the T.V. and taken up painting." But a more personal sorrow may have also compelled her choice of symbols, for at about this time Viola Frey became very ill and Carnwath would soon lose another friend.

In addition to good-luck symbols, these paintings present images evocative of Rorschach tests and classic psychology drawings used in scientific research into perception, such as the Necker cube and Wittgenstein's deliberately ambiguous duck-rabbit sketch. Both the cube and the sketch reveal that perception is a product not just of visual stimulus but also of mental activity. In other words, we see with the mind as well as with the eye. Here again Carnwath explores the ambiguity of perception and consciousness. Are her simple drawings ducks or rabbits? Were there really weapons of mass destruction in Iraq? Do horseshoes and logs really bring good luck? When is the right time for a friend to die?

The identification of these symbols and their meanings might trigger an "iconographic truffle hunt," such as critics and art historians began to undertake when Jasper Johns included, in his paintings of the 1980s, both autobiographical elements and references to other prominent artists. Johns reacted by introducing an image he had used in earlier work and which he deliberately left unexplained. "I got tired of people talking about things that I didn't think they could see in my work," he later remarked. "It interested me that people would discuss something that I didn't believe they could see until after they were told to see it."[100]

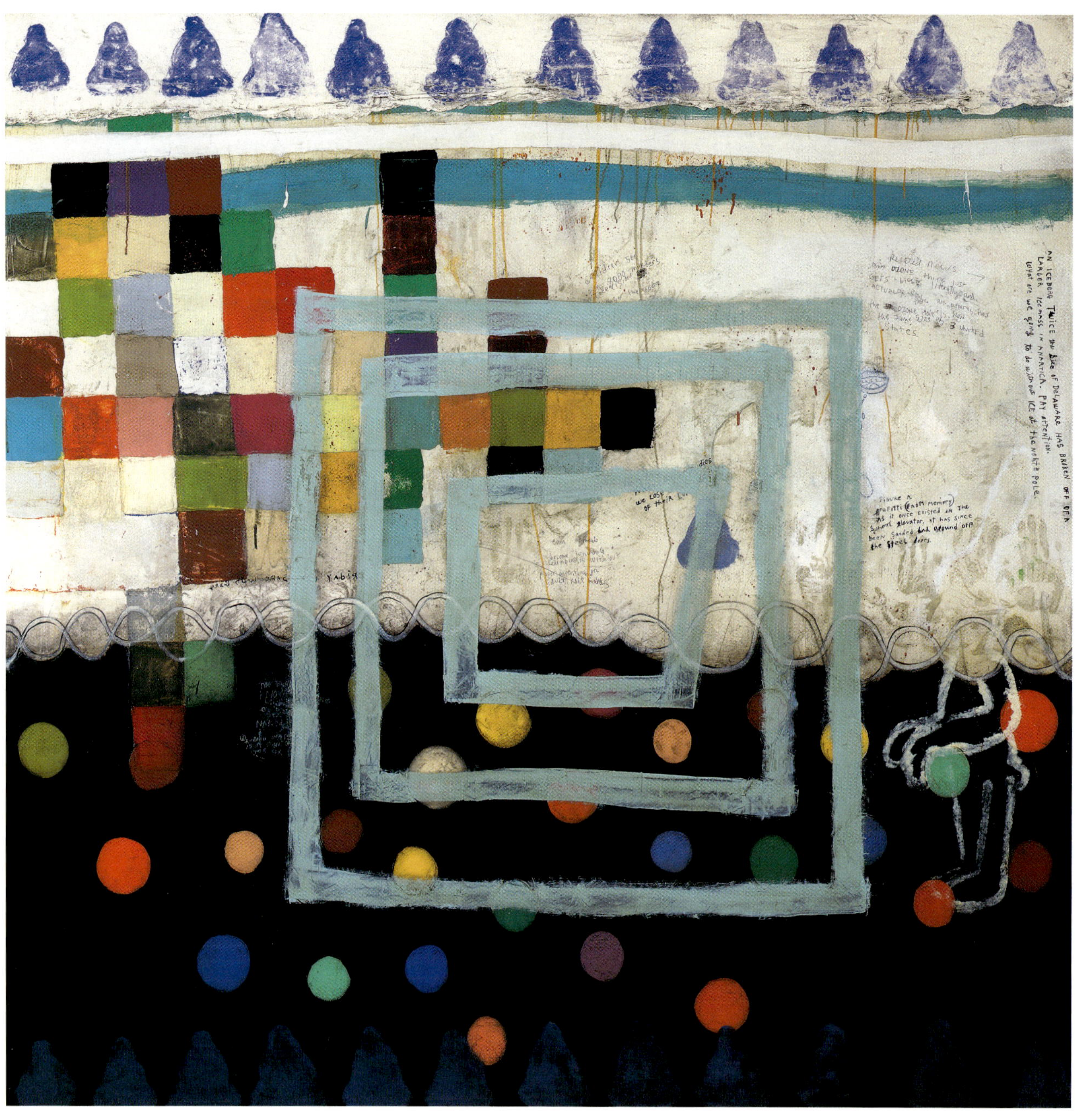

51. **Trying Simply To Be Happy,** 2000

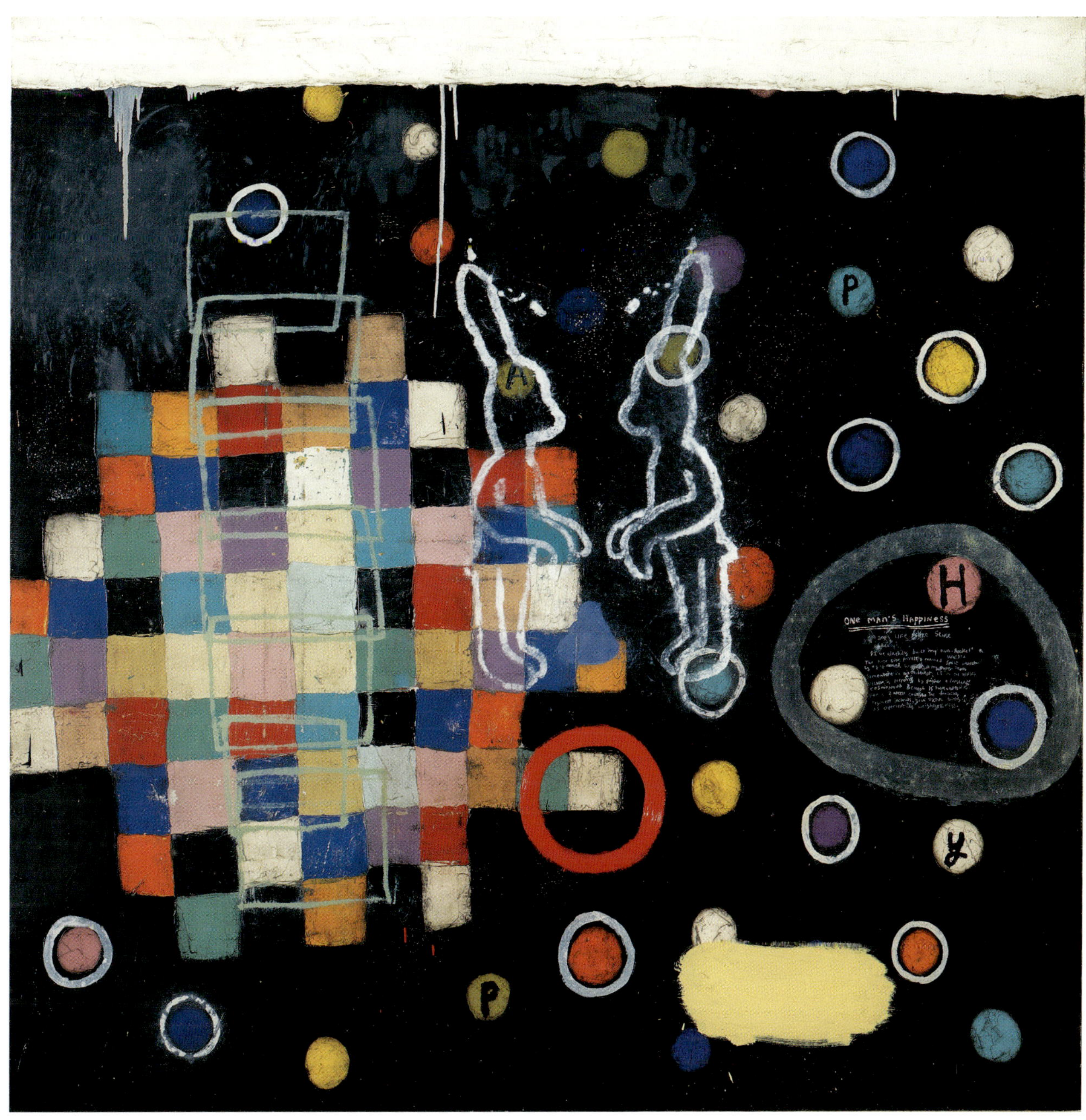

48. In Pursuit of Happiness, 2000

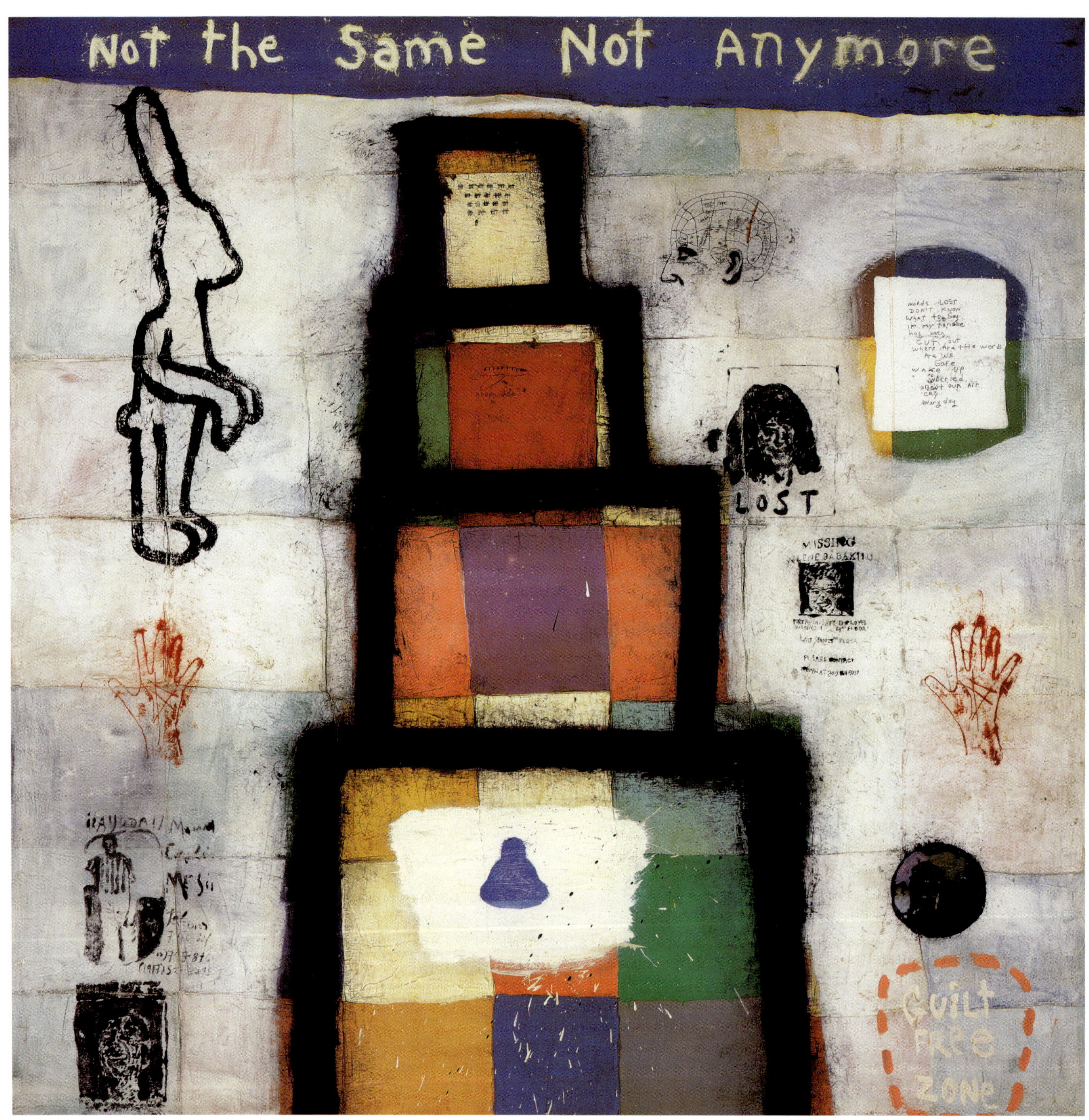

54. **Anymore,** 2001

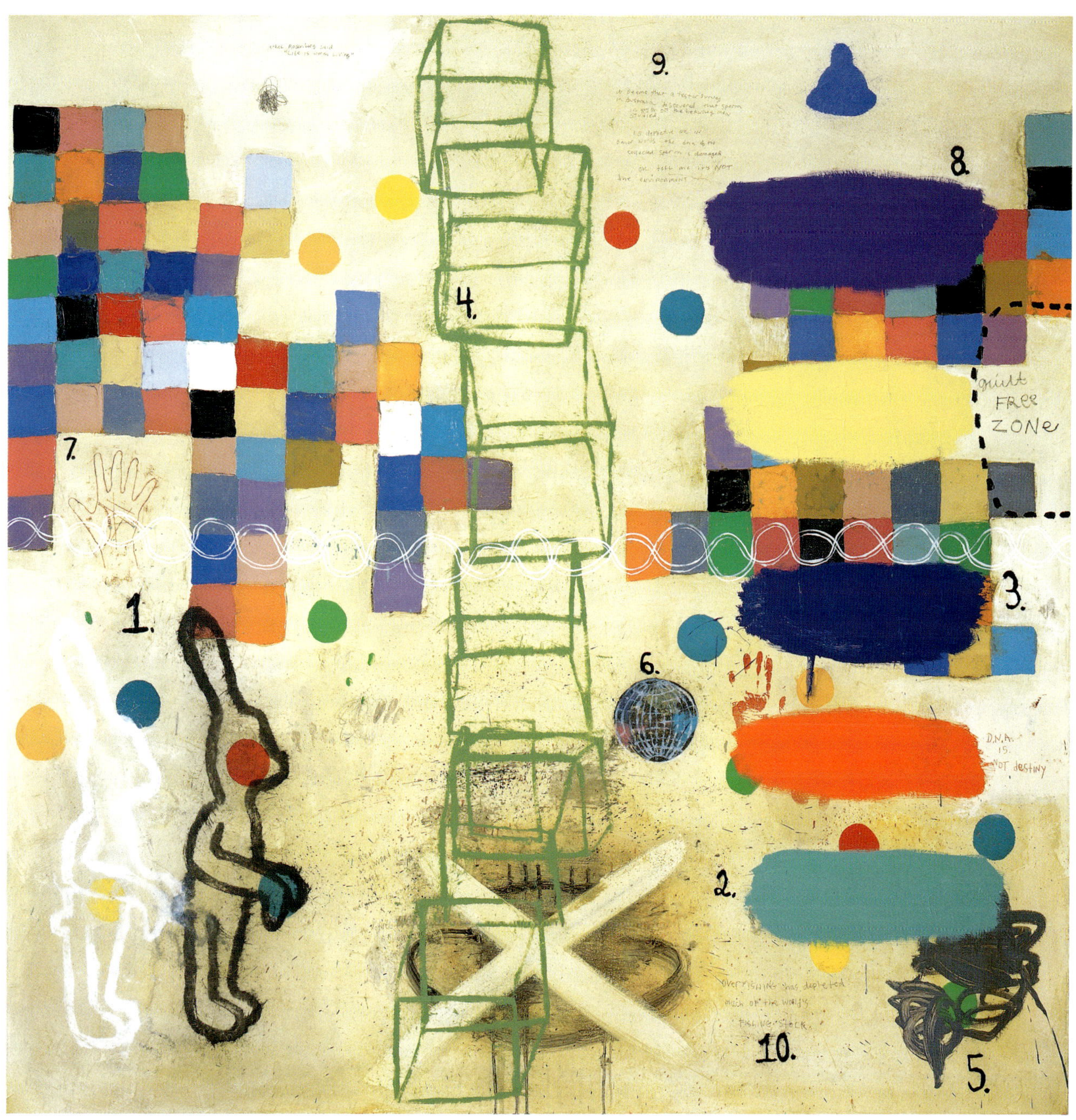

56. **You Call This Happy,** 2001

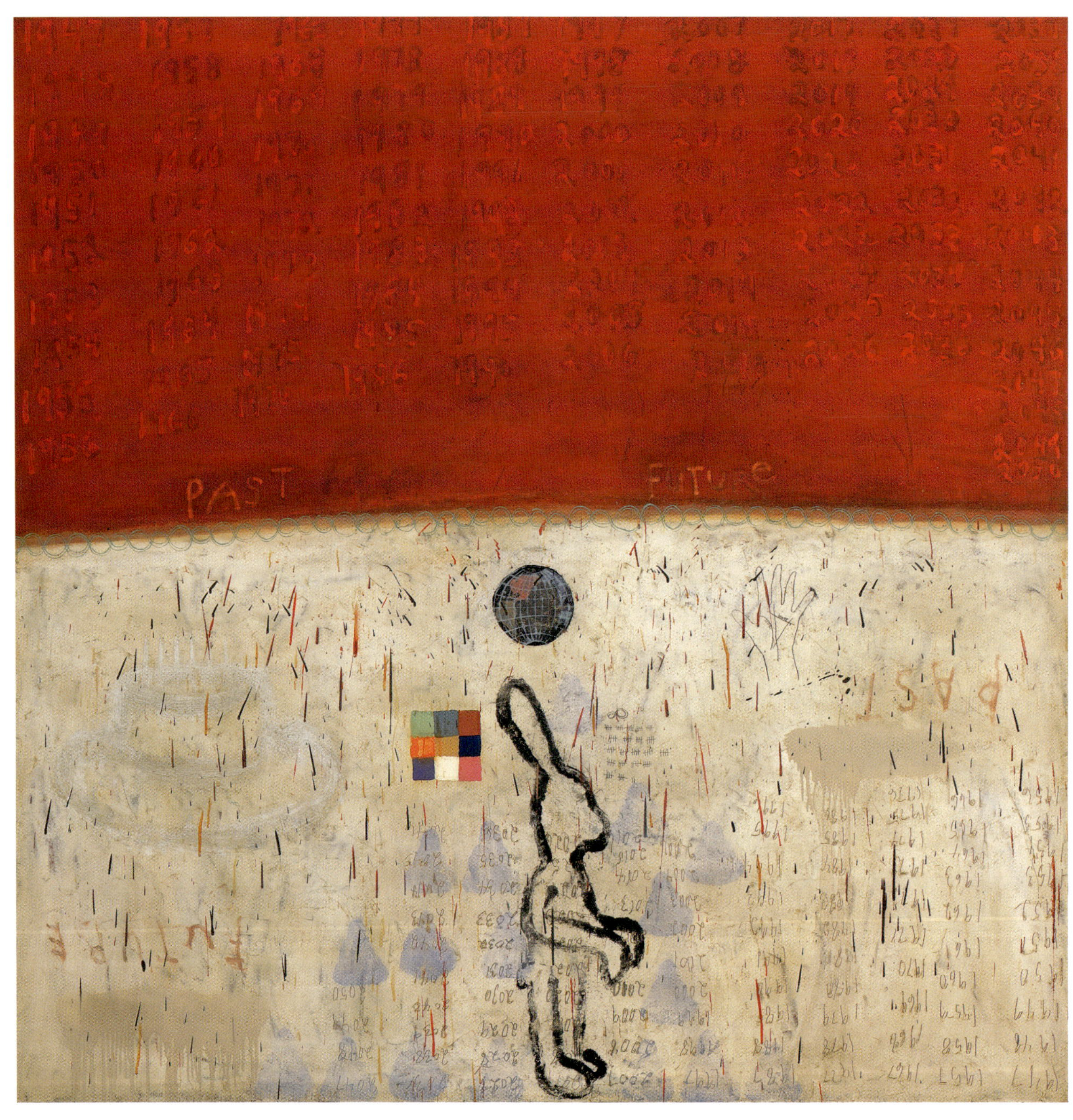

58. **Long Happy Life,** 2002

Although Carnwath has long appreciated the elasticity of symbols and the fact that people read them differently, she has made their decoding much easier in her work since 2004 by providing clues to the meanings she assigns them. Among the new symbols are images of male Etruscan heads, vinyl records, renderings of the ancient Roman Portland vase, and vessels by George Ohr (1857–1918), who called himself the Mad Potter of Biloxi. Without question these images are symbols in homage to the passing of human life—tributes to those Carnwath has known intimately, like Frey, or not at all, such as the recent Iraqi and American dead. The Etruscan heads that line the bottom of her recent paintings, where blue Healing Buddhas once appeared, can be traced to Fayum mummy portraits and depictions of mourners found on tomb walls of Etruscan frescoes. "They're like ancient witnesses to everything that's happened before us," Carnwath explained in a 2007 interview.[101]

Old vinyl long-playing records line the hallway to Carnwath's studio. They found their first pictographic use in *Stolen Borrowed* (2004; p. 128) and *Best Borrowed* (2005; p. 129). In an age when thousands of musical recordings can be heard on a device no larger than a human palm, the long-playing record is a thing of the past. But what a spark of memories an LP can prompt in one who grew up with them—here again are Proust and his madeleine. When examining life and the universe, "man encounters himself" instead of looking for and finding objective qualities, as the physicist Werner Heisenberg observed.[102] But for Carnwath, the symbolism of the black record is very specific. "A record can literally be something like a long-playing record, a record of something that's happened, or it can be about time," as the artist explains. "I only show side one, so for me it's about mortality, or that you only get one chance."[103]

The Portland vase, a Roman glass vessel dating from AD 5–25, is another new image. Viola Frey was very fond of the blue-black vase, with its cameo décor of classical figures, and frequently quoted it in her work. In memory of her friend, Carnwath has incorporated images of the vase in paintings such as *Will or Won't* (2006; p. 91) and *Real and True* (2007; p. 131). From a historical perspective, the vase is interesting not only because of its age but also because it served as a major source of artistic inspiration for Josiah Wedgwood, the eighteenth-century Englishman credited with the industrialized production of pottery. According to the British Museum, where the vase now resides, in around 1786 it came into the possession of the third Duke of Portland; he lent it to Wedgwood, who made it famous through his many copies. Thus, from ancient Rome via Wedgwood and Frey, the vase has become an emotional and creative springboard for Carnwath. "Good ideas r not made they are stolen, or at best borrowed," she writes in *Best Borrowed*.

In many ways, Carnwath's use of images recalls how Jasper Johns has incorporated recognizable everyday motifs in his paintings. He has long been fascinated with the idea of the surrogate, of one thing representing another. Adopting a term from Wittgenstein, Barbara Hess has written that "one might speak of a 'private language,' in [Johns's] paintings, one whose meanings, initially known only to the individual who speaks it, would expand conventional language."[104]

Carnwath also shares with Johns the opinion that viewers should draw their own conclusions. "I think a painting should include more experiences than simply intended statement," Johns asserted in 1965. "I personally would like to keep the painting in a state of 'shunning statement,' so that one is left with the fact that one can experience individually as one pleases."[105] Carnwath elaborates: "What an artist is trying to communicate is often personally driven. They're more interested in understanding their own narrative or their own psychology or the reasons why they're intrigued with a shape than they are with the viewer getting it exactly."[106]

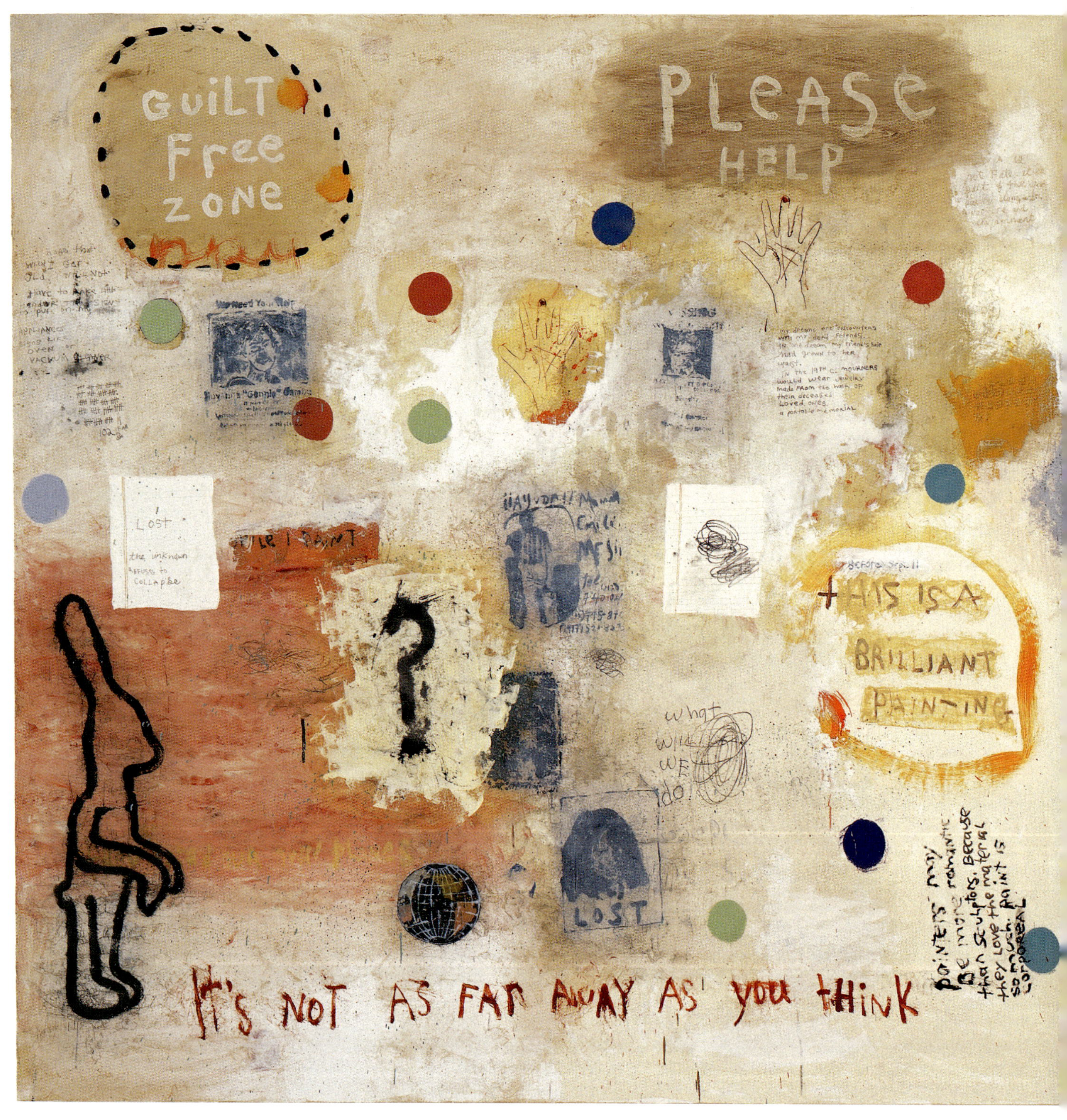

57. **Everything (2),** 2002

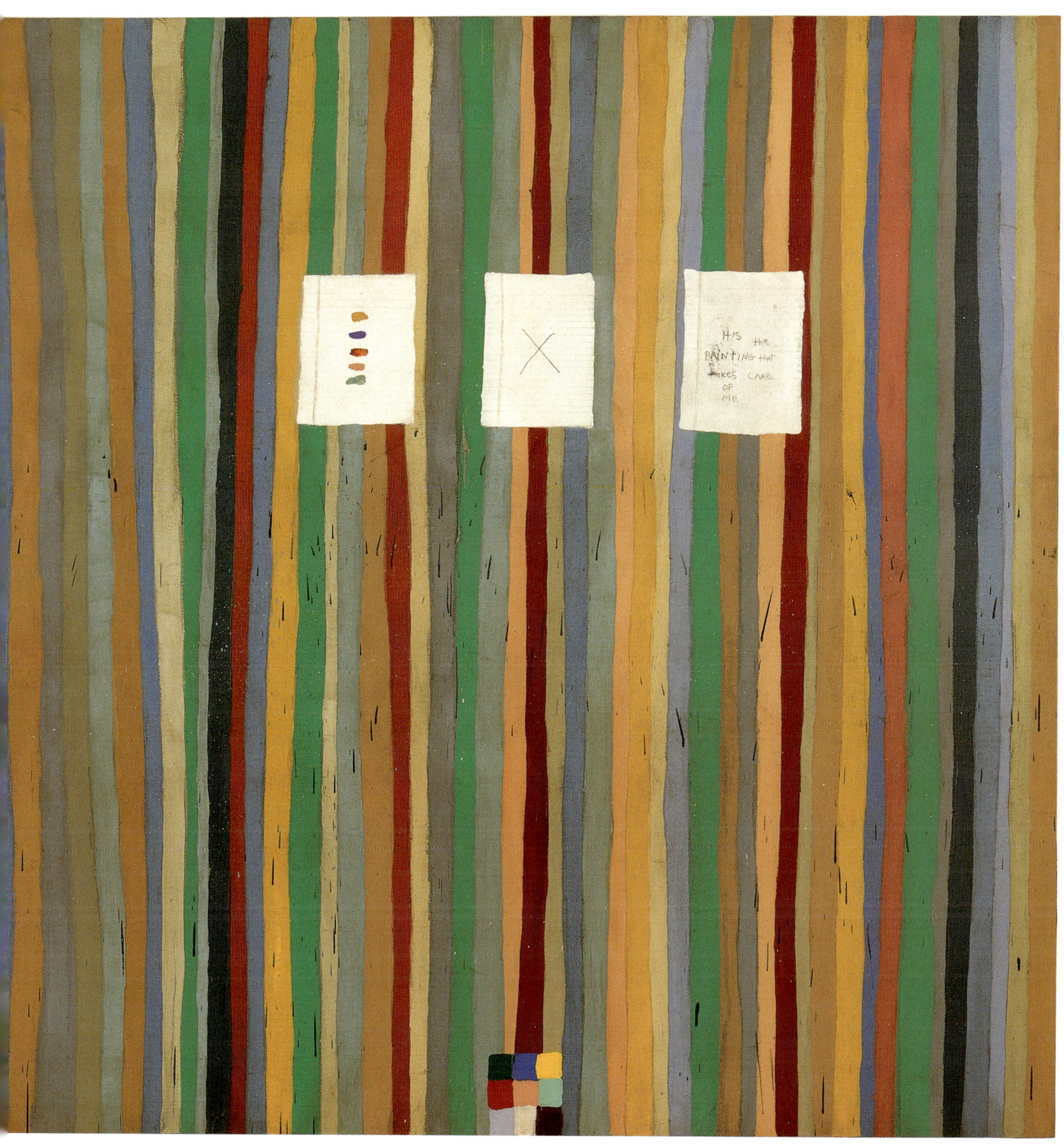
It's the
PAINTING that
takes care
of
me

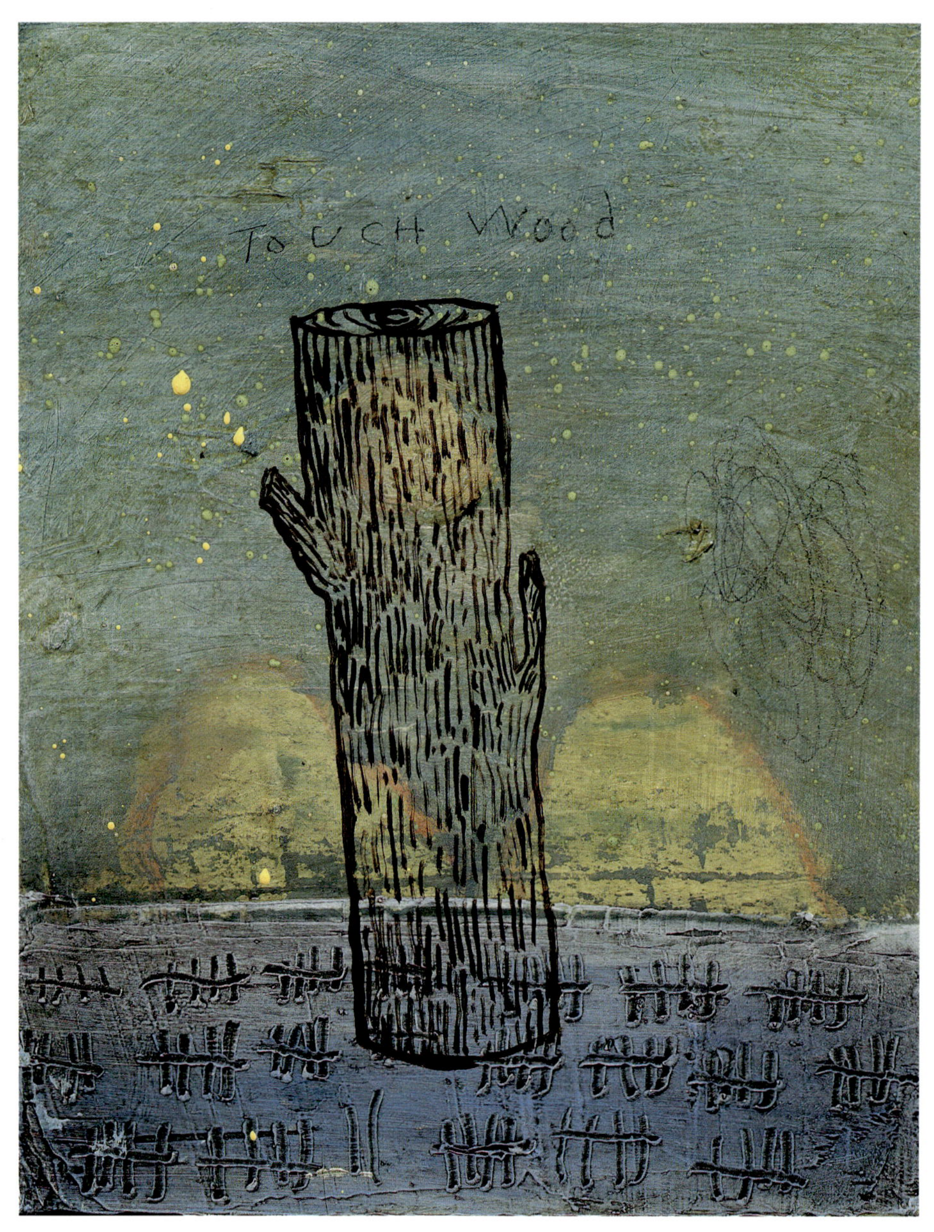

66. **School Demo Tree,** 2004

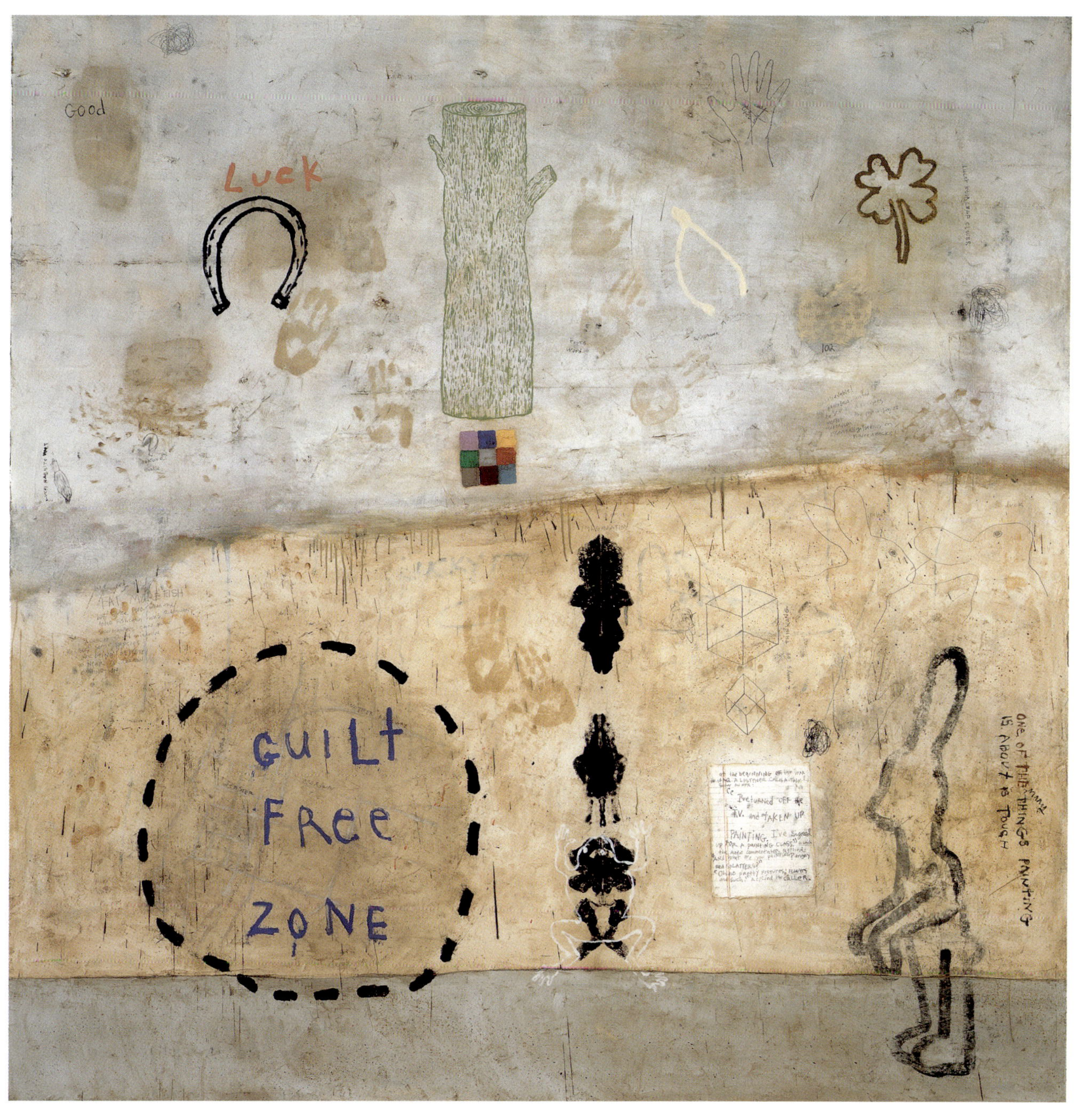

60. **Good Luck,** 2003

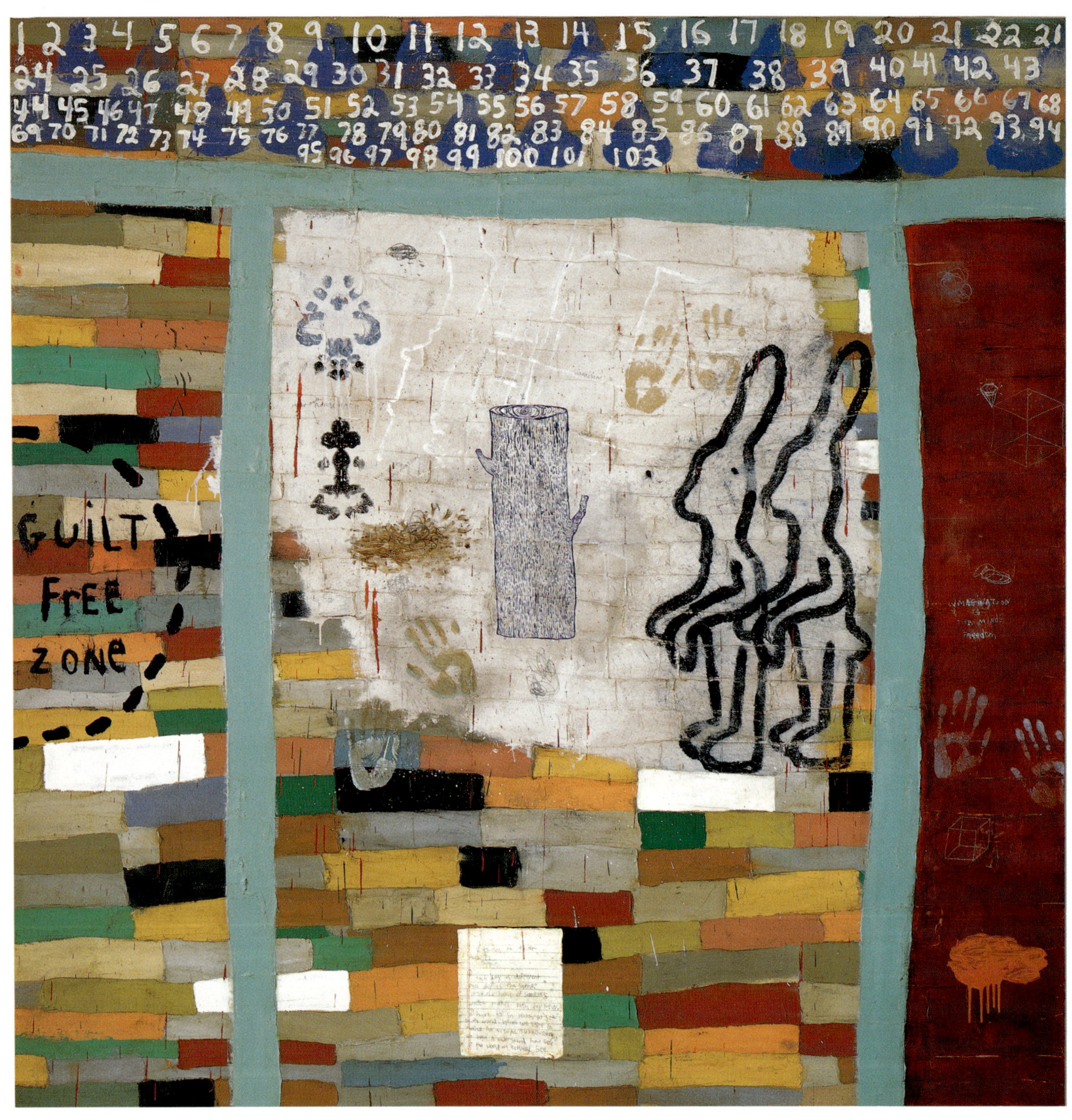

64. **2 Things,** 2003

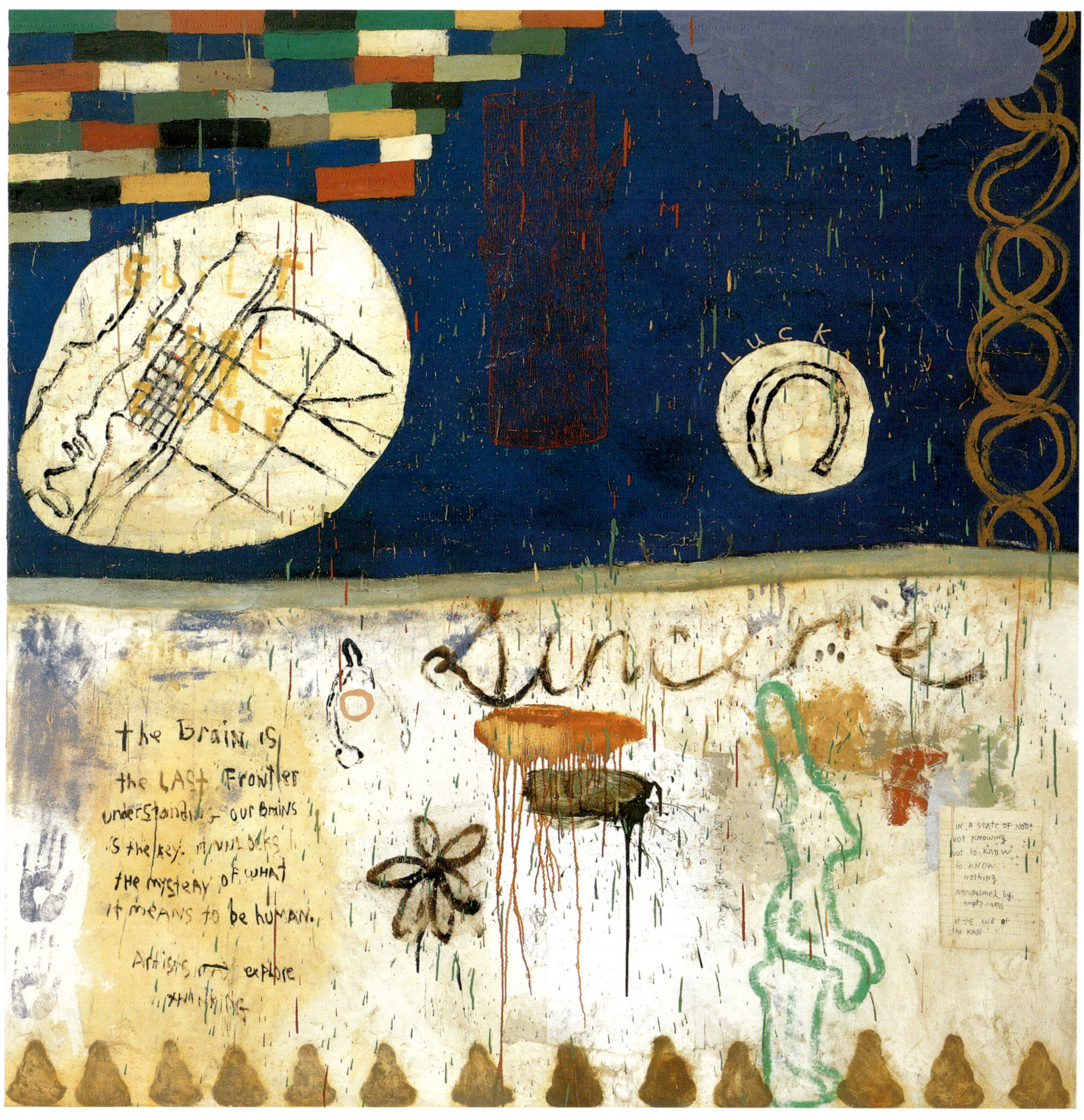

65. **Last Frontier,** 2004

Painting is no ordinary object.
Squeak Carnwath

ARTISTS CREATE FOR MANY REASONS. Who knows where the impulse arises? But as Carnwath has made clear throughout many years of art making, introspection, and conversation, "the matter of being alive is something to be investigated."[107] This seed of belief forms the hidden rhizome from which Carnwath's art has flourished.

That art has grown and matured through confrontation with the demons in Carnwath's life. One of these is mortality—and its flip side, the search for meaning and happiness in life. The experience of death has haunted the artist throughout her life. It is a motif that has snaked in and out of her work from her graduate work on Virginia Woolf to her most recent canvases in memory of Viola Frey. Remembrances of her father, mother, and other family and friends are both obvious and hidden. In her 1999 painting *Think About It* (p. 69), for example, Carnwath scribed in the bottom corner of the large canvas:

> My father had a metal plate in his head. 2 of my brothers have had heart attacks before age 50. One at age 48, the other at 46. I have four brothers.

She completed the painting when she was fifty-two years of age.

One of Freud's most profound insights was that the unconscious does not recognize the concept of age. By that he meant that one may spend a lifetime struggling with issues and emotions acquired in one's formative years, when any conflict or fantasy becomes firmly implanted in the psyche. This point is worth pondering when considering Carnwath's work—how the past shapes a life and finds form as she stands alone her studio, brush in hand. For in many ways the artist is a clandestine autobiographer, layering thoughts and secrets in her canvases as she crawls through thickets of memory, bores through stratified thoughts, probes for a sense of self as she changes and ages. As Carnwath simply states: "Paint is memory. It can hide or reveal."[108]

But Carnwath has too big a heart and intellect to concern herself solely with personal matters. Her painting and mark making also serve as a kind of navigational map for humanity at large as she uncovers and explores our shared world of existence. Wittgenstein called it "the handed-down world," a place and space understood as a given. Carnwath finds that it is this unquestioned, handed-down world that makes questioning possible, especially through art. "Art is the last frontier, the only freedom," she insists.[109] Or, as Jasper Johns once said, "I feel that if all were right in the world that art would not be made."[110]

A highly regarded teacher, Carnwath has always encouraged her students to take risks in their art-making practice, something she herself has done repeatedly over the years. Raised in a family and social environment where contradiction and contrariness, especially from a female, was frowned upon, Carnwath encourages her students to argue and disagree with her. She wants them to have the courage to try anything. "Art is not like other subjects, where you learn a formula or a certain way to do research, and then you apply that methodology to your project. It's primary research. It can't be tested."[111]

Over the years Carnwath's intriguing images and masterly way with paint have seduced many writers and critics who, dazzled, have missed the conceptual and philosophical foundations of her work. Of course, what the artist attempts to achieve in her paintings is no easy task. Working within her private sphere of inquiry, Carnwath explains how she has sought to create paintings that address "a greater memory," to create a human document of consciousness, to reveal herself as a good citizen of the world.

When Jonas Salk, the inventor of the polio vaccine, was asked what the main aim of his life had been, he replied, "To be a good ancestor."[112] Carnwath's goal as an artist is no less noble and humanitarian. Her quest is to create art that can heal the soul, provoke the laugh, pleasure the eye, and stimulate the mind. "Art is evidence," Carnwath states. "Evidence of breathing in and breathing out, proof of human majesty."

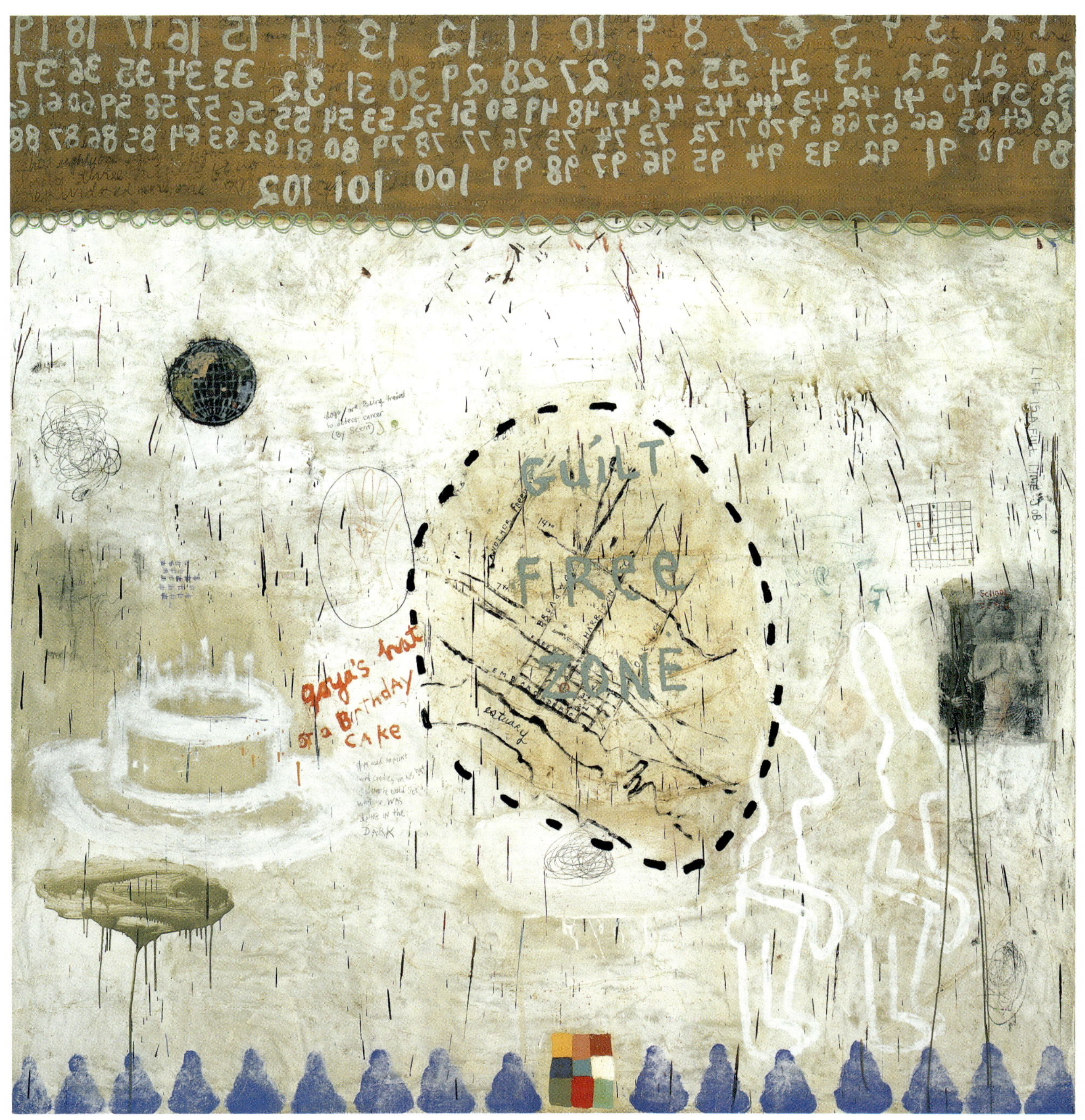

61. **Lucky,** 2003

NOTES

1. Fred Camper, "On Exhibit: Art Chicago 2002's Free Thinkers," *Chicago Reader*, May 10, 2002, p. 34.

2. Leah Ollman, "Wonder of Life Bathes Carnwath's Canvases," *Los Angeles Times* (San Diego edition), May 11, 1990, p. 19B.

3. Anne Gray Walrod interview with the artist, *Connecting Conversations: Interviews with 28 Bay Area Women Artists*, edited by Moira Roth (Oakland, Calif: Eucalyptus Press, Mills College, 1988), p. 23.

4. Audiotaped work, *The I Stories*, 1975, in the artist's collection.

5. Analucia da Silva, "Squeak Carnwath and Viola Frey Have Contributed to Oakland's Art Tradition," *Oakland Tribune*, January 1, 2000, p. 11.

6. Richard Whittaker interview with the artist, *Another Conversation with Squeak Carnwath: Works + Conversations*, March 2, 2001; http://www.conversations.org/story.php?sid=20.

7. John Yau interview with the artist, "In Conversation: Squeak Carnwath with John Yau," *The Brooklyn Rail*, November 2006, p. 49.

8. Wendy Edelstein, "Bunnies, Boring Objects, and the Guilt-free Zone," *Berkeleyan* (University of California), November 1, 2007, p. 8.

9. Walrod, *Connecting Conversations*, p. 23.

10. See Amelia Jones, editor, *Sexual Politics: Judy Chicago's Dinner Party in Feminist Art History* (Los Angeles: Armand Hammer Museum of Art and Cultural Center in association with University of California Press, 1996), p. 237.

11. Walrod, *Connecting Conversations*, p. 24.

12. Paul Karlstrom interview with Viola Frey, February 27, May 15, and June 19, 1995, Archives of American Art, Smithsonian Institution, Washington, DC; http://aaa.si.edu/collections/oralhistories/transcripts/frey95.htm, p. 24.

13. Carnwath made these observations in an undated note in the archives of the Richmond Art Center, Richmond, California.

14. Quoted in *Creating an Arts Career* (Oakland, Calif.: California College of Arts and Crafts, 1984), p. 5.

15. Author's interview with the artist, April 30, 2008.

16. Virginia Woolf, http://en.wikipedia.org/wiki/Virginia_Woolf (accessed May 2, 2008).

17. Author's interview with the artist, April 30, 2008.

18. Quoted in Suzanne Foley, *Space/Time/Sound: Conceptual Art in the San Francisco Bay Area: The 1970s* (San Francisco: San Francisco Museum of Modern Art, 1981), p. 88.

19. Author's interview with the artist, April 30, 2008.

20. Frances Shedd Fisher interview with the artist, *Nielsen Gallery News* (Boston), July 19, 2006, n.p.

21. The other two artists were Suzanne Hanson and Seth Seiderman.

22. Charles Shere, "A Handsome Showing in Various Media at S.F. Galleries," *Oakland Tribune*, September 30, 1980, p. C-9.

23. Steven Winn, "California Reviews: Ramps and Ghosts," *ARTnews*, January 1981, p. 77.

24. J. C. Cooper, *An Illustrated Encyclopaedia of Traditional Symbols* (London: Thames and Hudson, 1978), p. 7.

25. Ibid., p. 186.

26. "Squeak Carnwath in Conversation with Richard Whittaker," *Squeak Carnwath: Life Line* (San Francisco: John Berggruen Gallery, 2001), p. 6.

27. Quoted in Daisetz T. Suzuki, *Sengai: The Zen of Ink and Paper* (Boston and London: Shambhala, 1999), p. 5.

28. Author's interview with the artist, April 30, 2008.

29. Thomas Albright, "Imagism and a New Look," *San Francisco Chronicle*, March 8, 1982, p. 40.

30. Susan Rothenberg,"When Asked If I'm an Expressionist: An Artist's Symposium," in Kristine Stiles and Peter Selz, *Theories and Documents of Contemporary Art* (Berkeley, Los Angeles, and London: University of California Press, 1996), p. 264.

31. Typewritten statement taken from the artist's notebook, 1985–1986, in the archives of the Richmond Art Center, Richmond, California.

32. See Gay Shelton's essay "Making a Human Record," *Seeing in the Dark* (Santa Rosa, Calif.: California Museum of Art, 1998), n.p.

33. Walrod, *Connecting Conversations*, p. 27.

34. Ibid., p. 28.

35. Ibid., p. 25.

36. Suzaan Boettger, "Squeak Carnwath," *Artforum*, Summer 1984, p. 98.

37. Mark Van Proyen and Phyllis Shafer interview with the artist, "Squeak Carnwath: Excerpts from an Interview with Mark Van Proyen & Phyllis Shafer," *Éxpo-See* (San Francisco), January/February 1984, n.p.

38. Quoted in John McCloud, "Not Boxed In," *SF: The Magazine of Design and Style* (May 1991), p. 114.

39. Walrod, *Connecting Conversations*, p. 25.

40. *Gustave Courbet* (New York: Metropolitan Museum of Art and Hatje Cantz, 2008), pp. 380–381.

41. Quoted in Arturo Schwarz, *The Complete Works of Marcel Duchamp* (New York: Delano Greenidge Editions, 2000), p. 73.

42. Ibid., p. 83.

43. Ibid., pp. 83–84.

44. Whittaker, *Life Line*, p. 6.

45. Author's interview with the artist, April 30, 2008.

46. Quoted in Sally Engelfried, "Squeak Roars," *510 Magazine: East Bay Arts and Culture* (Oakland, Calif.), December 1994, p. 35.

47. Squeak Carnwath, "A Simple List," *Parameters: Squeak Carnwath* (Norfolk, Va.: Chrysler Museum, 1994). Compiled by the artist in 1993, this list identifies thirteen points that are critical to her creative philosophy. It has reappeared in various publications over the years.

48. Quoted in "Squeak Carnwath at Shea & Beker," *Cover*, April 1990, p. 17.

49. Carnwath, "A Simple List."

50. Rudolf Arnheim, "Language, Image, and Concrete Poetry," *New Essays on the Psychology of Art* (Berkeley and Los Angeles: University of California Press, 1986), p. 90.

51. Christine Tamblyn, "Reviews: Squeak Carnwath," *ARTnews*, December 1989, p. 174.

52. Squeak Carnwath, "Painting Is No Ordinary Object," *Adelie Landis Bischoff* (New York: Salander-O'Reilly, 2006), p. 17.

53. Joseph Campbell with Bill Moyers, *The Power of Myth* (New York: Anchor Books, 1988), p. 1.

54. Richard Whittaker, "Squeak Carnwath," *The Conversations: Interviews with Sixteen Contemporary Artists* (Delray Beach, Fla.: Whale and Star, 2007), p. 45.

55. Author's interview with the artist, April 30, 2008.

56. Quoted in *Cover*, April 1990, p. 17.

57. Whittaker, *Life Line*, p. 5.

58. Whittaker, *The Conversations*, p. 45.

59. Leah Levy, "Squeak Carnwath: Transformations," *Squeak Carnwath: Lists, Observations & Counting* (San Francisco: Chronicle Books, 1996), p. 5.

60. Hans Biedermann, *Dictionary of Symbolism: Cultural Icons and the Meanings Behind Them* (New York: Meridian, 1994), p. viii.

61. Trinkett Clark, essay for the 1994 exhibition "Parameters: Squeak Carnwath," Chrysler Museum, Norfolk, Virginia.

62. Author's interview with the artist, March 12, 2008.

63. Quoted in Diane Peterson, "Artist's Early Drawings Offer Insight," *On Q: The Press Democrat* (Santa Rosa, Calif.), July 26, 1998, p. 8.

64. Arnheim, *New Essays on the Psychology of Art*, p. 91.

65. Sally Engelfried, "Squeak Roars," p. 35.

66. Robert Goldwater, *Primitivism in Modern Art* (Cambridge, Mass., and London: Belknap Press of Harvard University Press, 1986 enlarged edition), p. 1.

67. Quoted in Sean Murphy, *One Bird, One Stone*, p. 46.

68. John Berger, *Ways of Seeing* (London: British Broadcasting Corp. and Penguin Books, 1983), p. 7.

69. Quoted in Paul Arthur Schilpp, editor, *The Philosophy of Bertrand Russell*, vol. 5 (Evanston, Ill.: Northwestern University, 1944), p. 277.

70. Quoted in Carl Seelig, editor, *Ideas and Opinions by Albert Einstein* (Avenel, N.J.: Wings Books, 1954), p. 20.

71. Quoted in *Squeak Carnwath: Eden in the Studio* (Turlock, Calif.: University Art Gallery, California State University, 1995), n.p.

72. Transcript of interview for Artist Project, Graduate School of Business Administration, Harvard University, Boston, July 10, 1977, n.p., in the artist's collection.

73. Seelig, *Ideas and Opinions by Albert Einstein*, pp. 8–9.

74. Richard Powers, *The Echo Maker* (New York: Picador, 2006), p. 135.

75. Ibid., p. 123.

76. Carnwath, "Painting Is No Ordinary Object," p. 17.

77. The details of Carnwath's time with her mother and at Yaddo were first recorded in Jamie Brunson's essay "Squeak Carnwath: Willing to Entertain the Simplicity," *Squeak Carnwath: Relative* (San Francisco: John Berggruen Gallery, 1996), p. 3.

78. Quoted in Mark Levy, "Squeak Carnwath: Reclaiming Lost Territory," *Artspace*, January/February 1990, p. 35.

79. Murphy, *One Bird, One Stone*, pp. 83–84.

80. Carnwath, "Painting Is No Ordinary Object," p. 17.

81. Peterson, "Artist's Early Drawings Offer Insight," p. 8.

82. Yau, "In Conversation: Squeak Carnwath with John Yau," p. 18.

83. Maria Porges, "Squeak Carnwath," *Squeak Carnwath* (New York: David Beitzel Gallery, 1998), p. 2.

84. Author's interview with the artist, March 12, 2008.

85. Carnwath, "Painting Is No Ordinary Object," p. 17.

86. Whittaker, *Life Line*, p. 6.

87. Fisher interview, n.p.

88. Whittaker, *The Conversations*, p. 41.

89. Artist Project, Harvard University, n.p.

90. Edelstein, "Bunnies, Boring Objects, and the Guilt-free Zone," p. 8.

91. Eric Weiner, *The Geography of Bliss* (New York: Twelve, 2008), p. 154.

92. Ibid., pp. 2–3.

93. Barbara Catoir, *Conversations with Antoni Tàpies* (Munich: Prestel-Verlag, 1991), pp. 41–42.

94. Whittaker, *Life Line*, p. 8.

95. Whittaker, *The Conversations*, p. 38.

96. Camper, "On Exhibition: Art Chicago 2002's Free Thinkers," p. 34.

97. Ibid.

98. Zahid Sardar, "Squeak Carnwath," *Western Interiors*, July/August 2005, p. 38.

99. John Muir, *Our Forest Parks* (Cambridge, Mass.: Houghton Mifflin, 1901).

100. Quoted in Barbara Hess, *Jasper Johns: The Business of the Eye* (Cologne: Taschen, 2007), p. 76.

101. Edelstein, "Bunnies, Boring Objects, and the Guilt-free Zone," p. 8.

102. Carl G. Jung, *Man and His Symbols* (New York: Doubleday, 1964), p. 307.

103. Edelstein, "Bunnies, Boring Objects, and the Guilt-free Zone," p. 8.

104. Hess, *Jasper Johns*, p. 40.

105. Ibid., p. 52.

106. Edelstein, "Bunnies, Boring Objects, and the Guilt-free Zone," p. 8.

107. Whittaker, *The Conversations*, p. 40.

108. Carnwath, "Painting Is No Ordinary Object," p. 17.

109. Edelstein, "Bunnies, Boring Objects, and the Guilt-free Zone," p. 8.

110. Jill Johnston, *Jasper Johns: Privileged Information* (New York: Thames and Hudson, 1996), p. 16.

111. Edelstein, "Bunnies, Boring Objects, and the Guilt-free Zone," p. 8.

112. Weiner, *The Geography of Bliss*, p. 110.

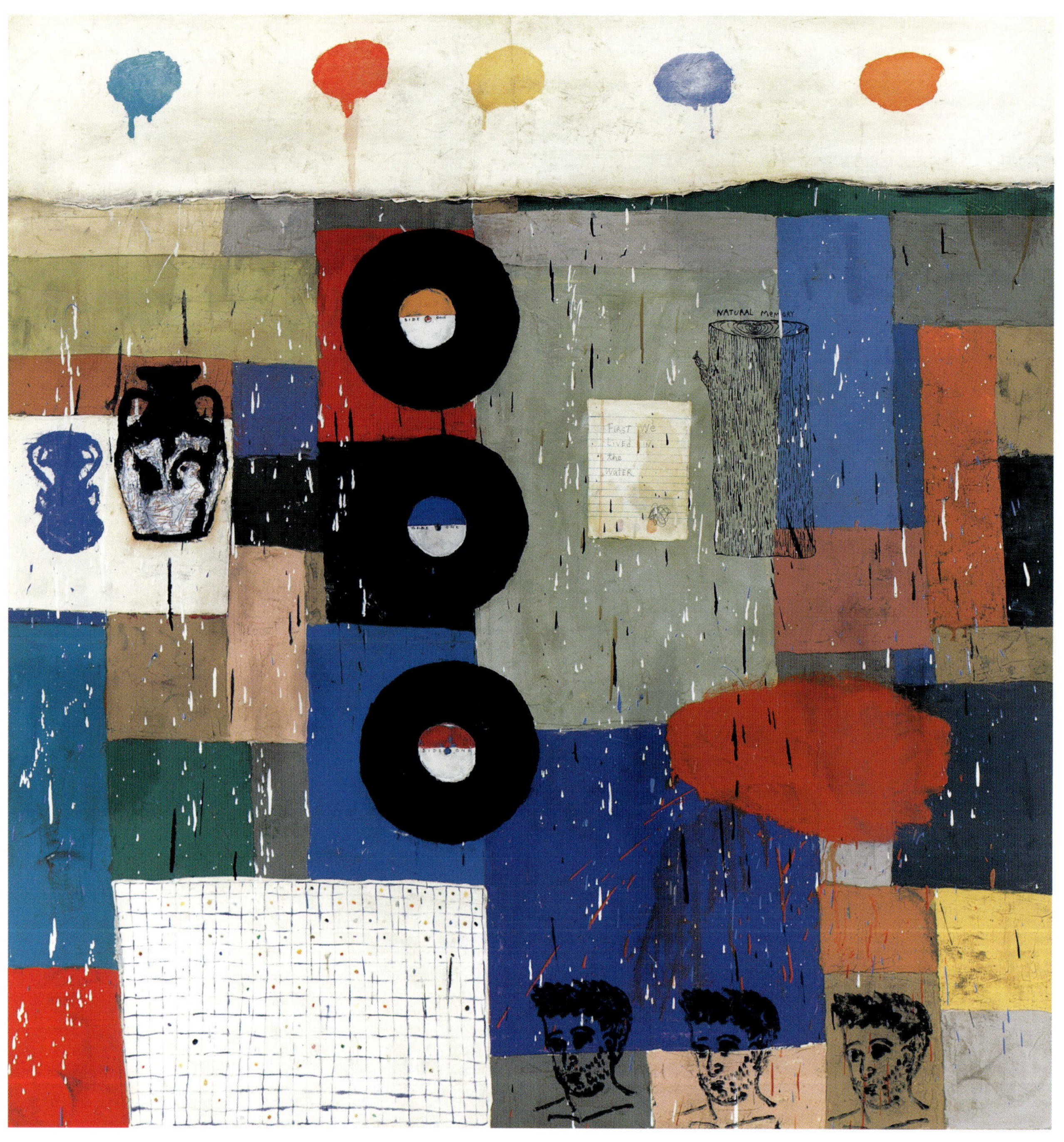

75. **First Water,** 2006

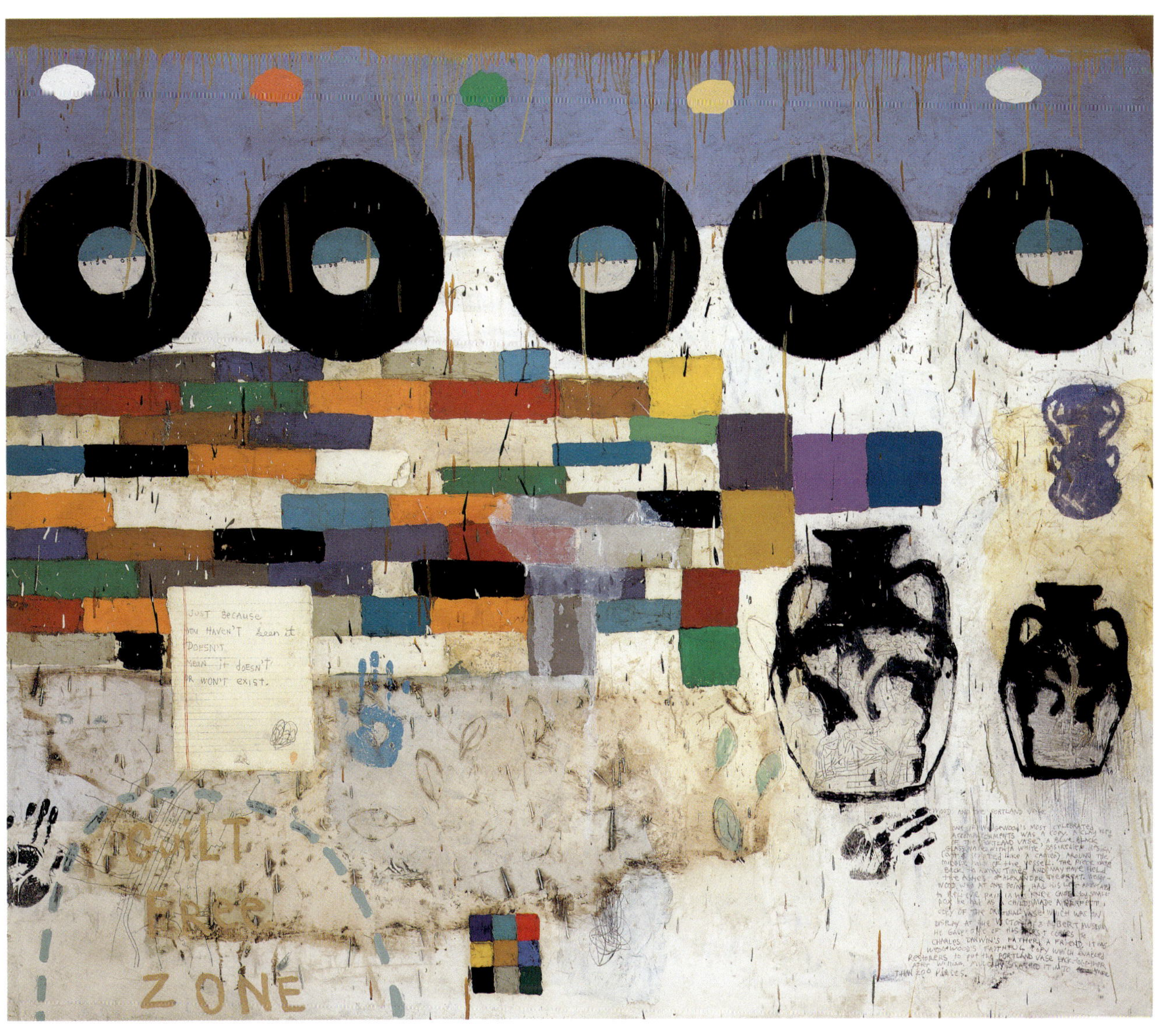

78. **Will or Won't,** 2006

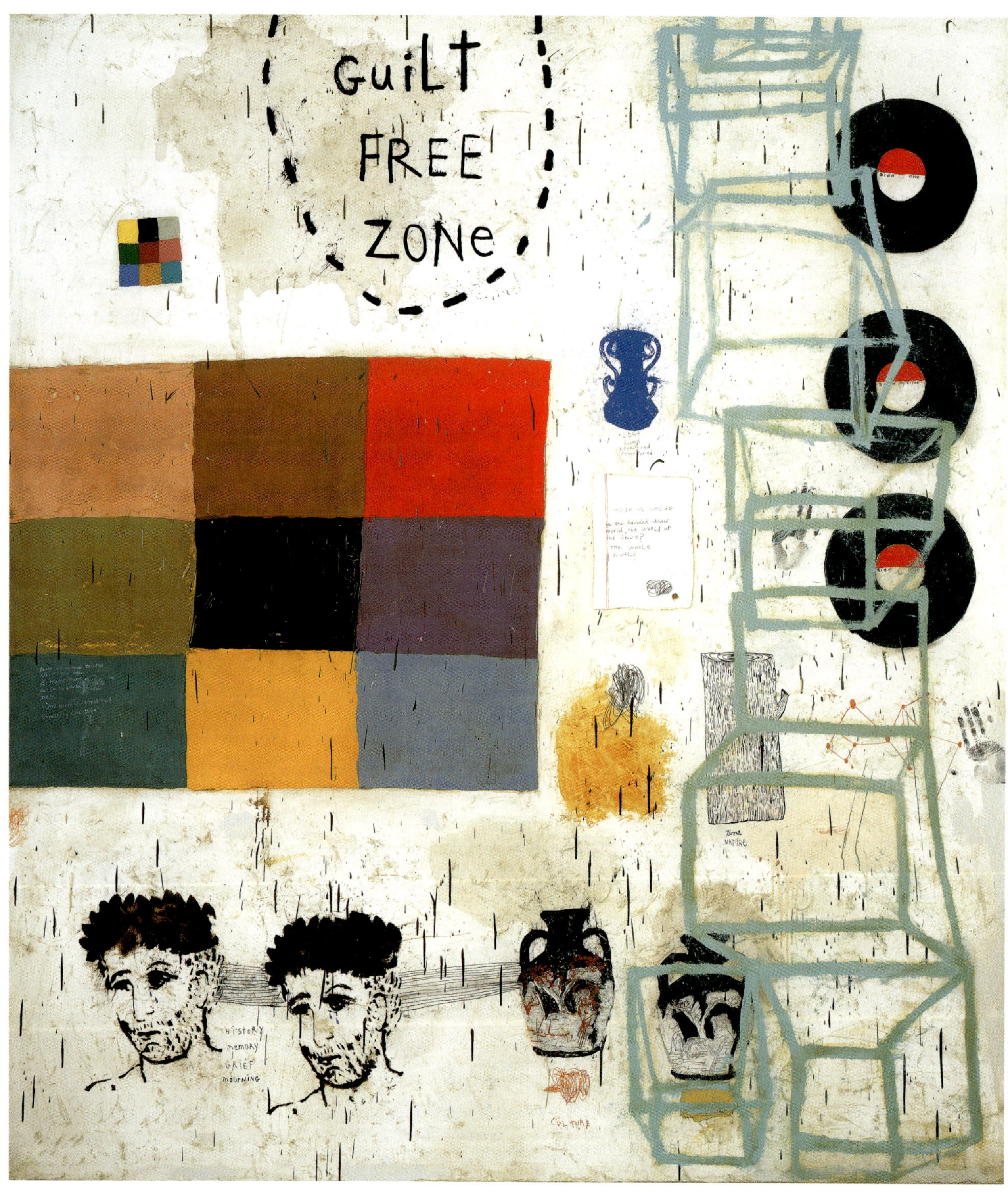

77. **The Whole Truth,** 2006

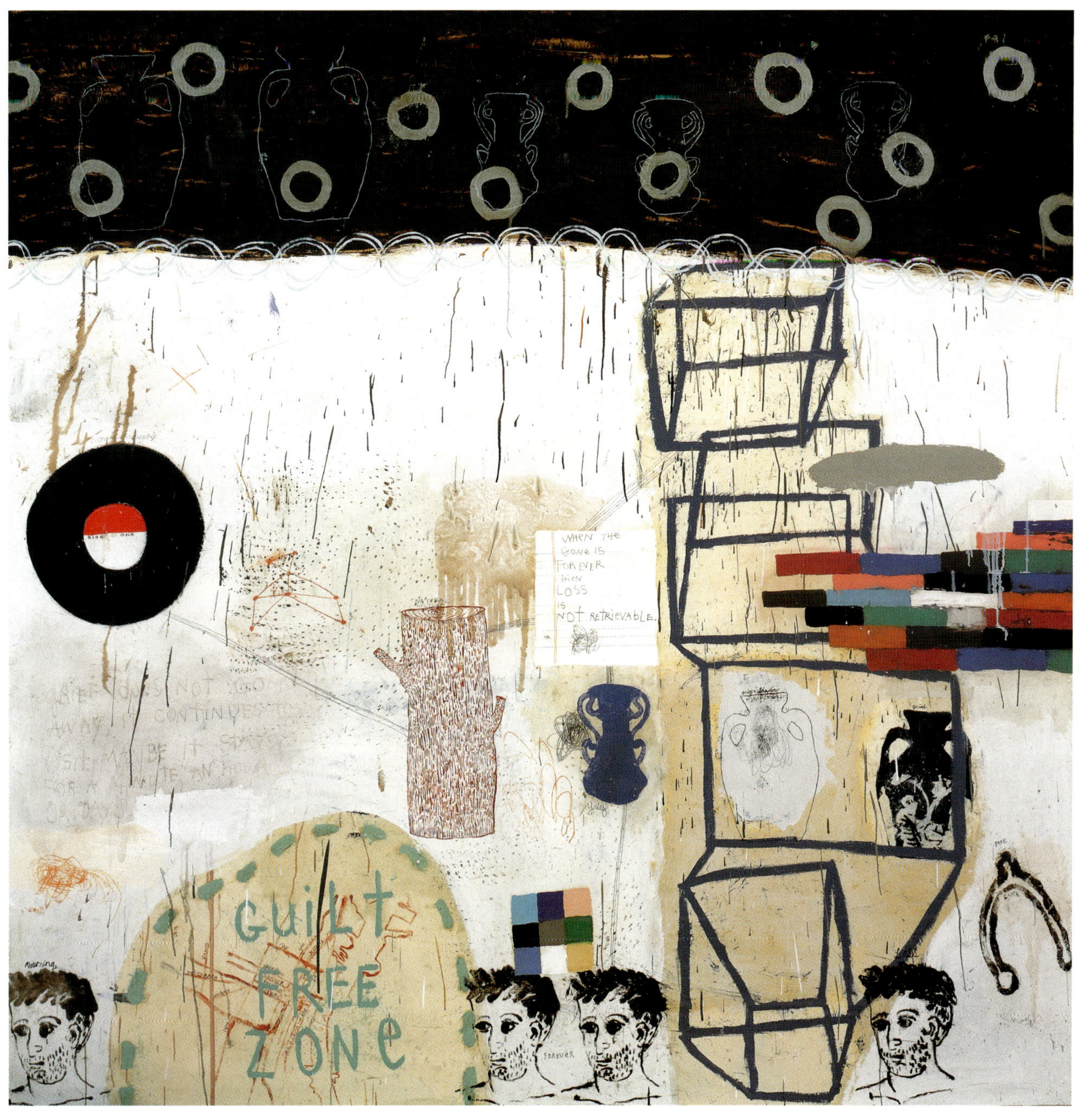

76. **Gone Is Forever**, 2006

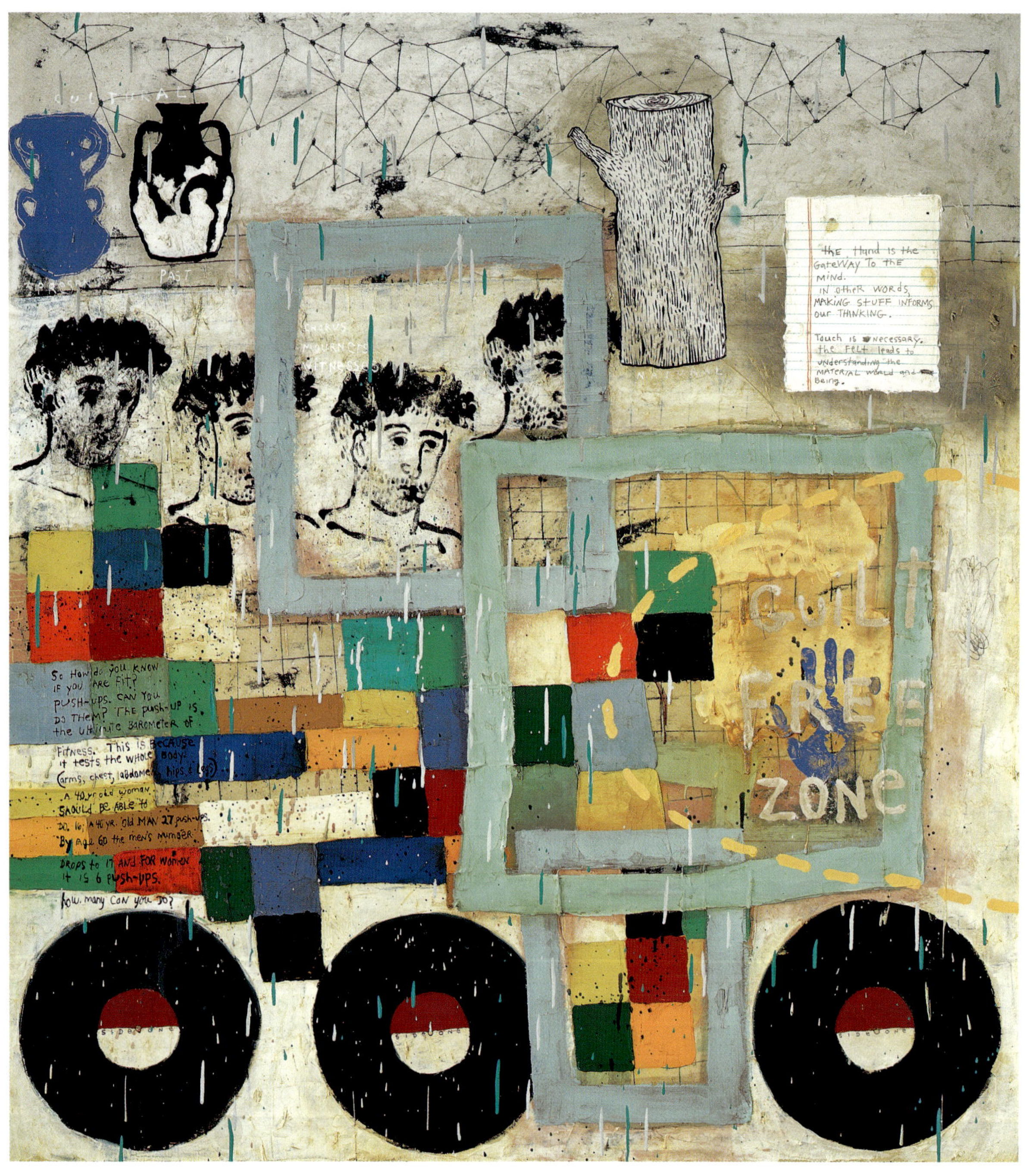

81. **Gateway,** 2008

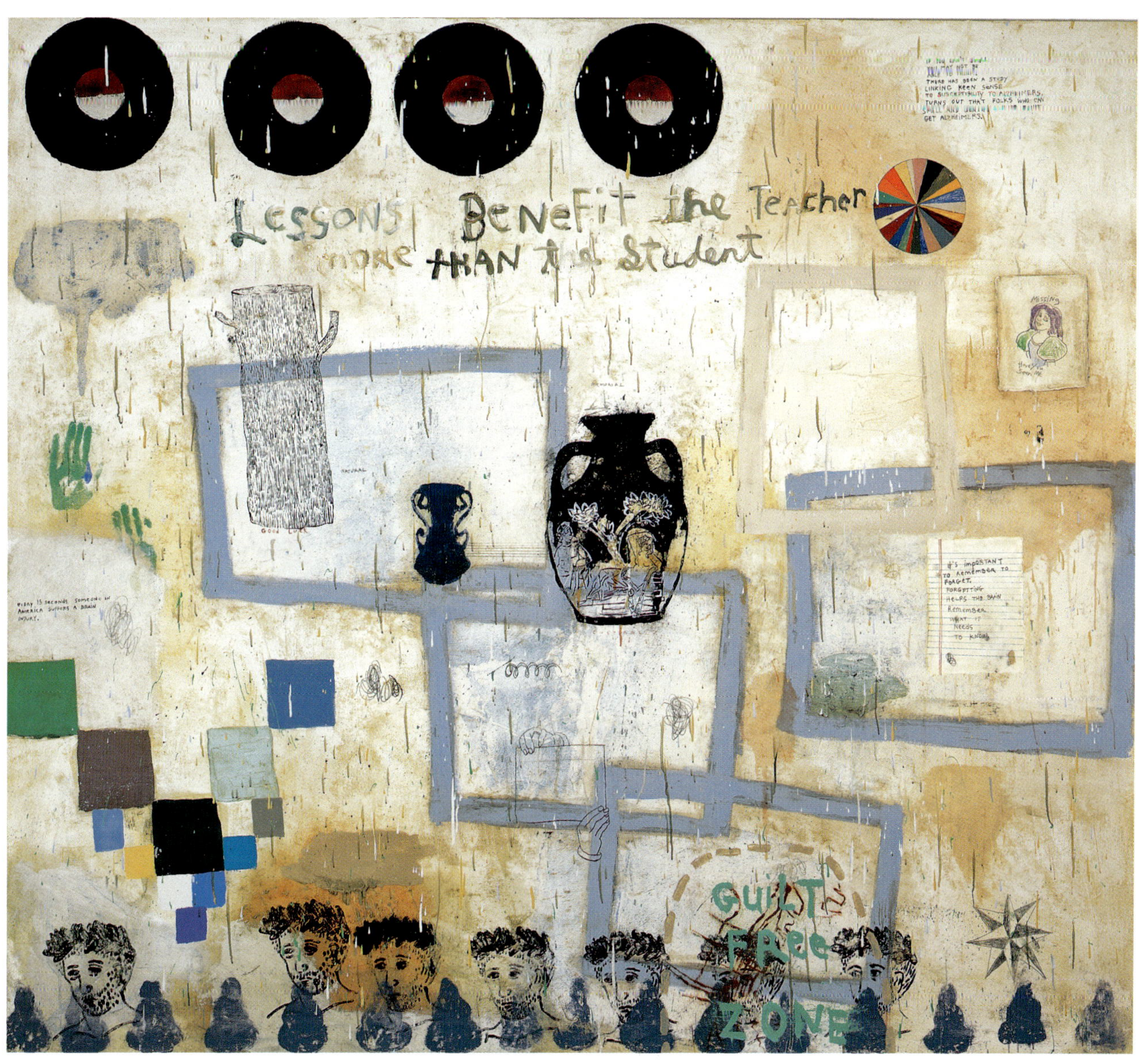

79. **Lessons Benefit,** 2007

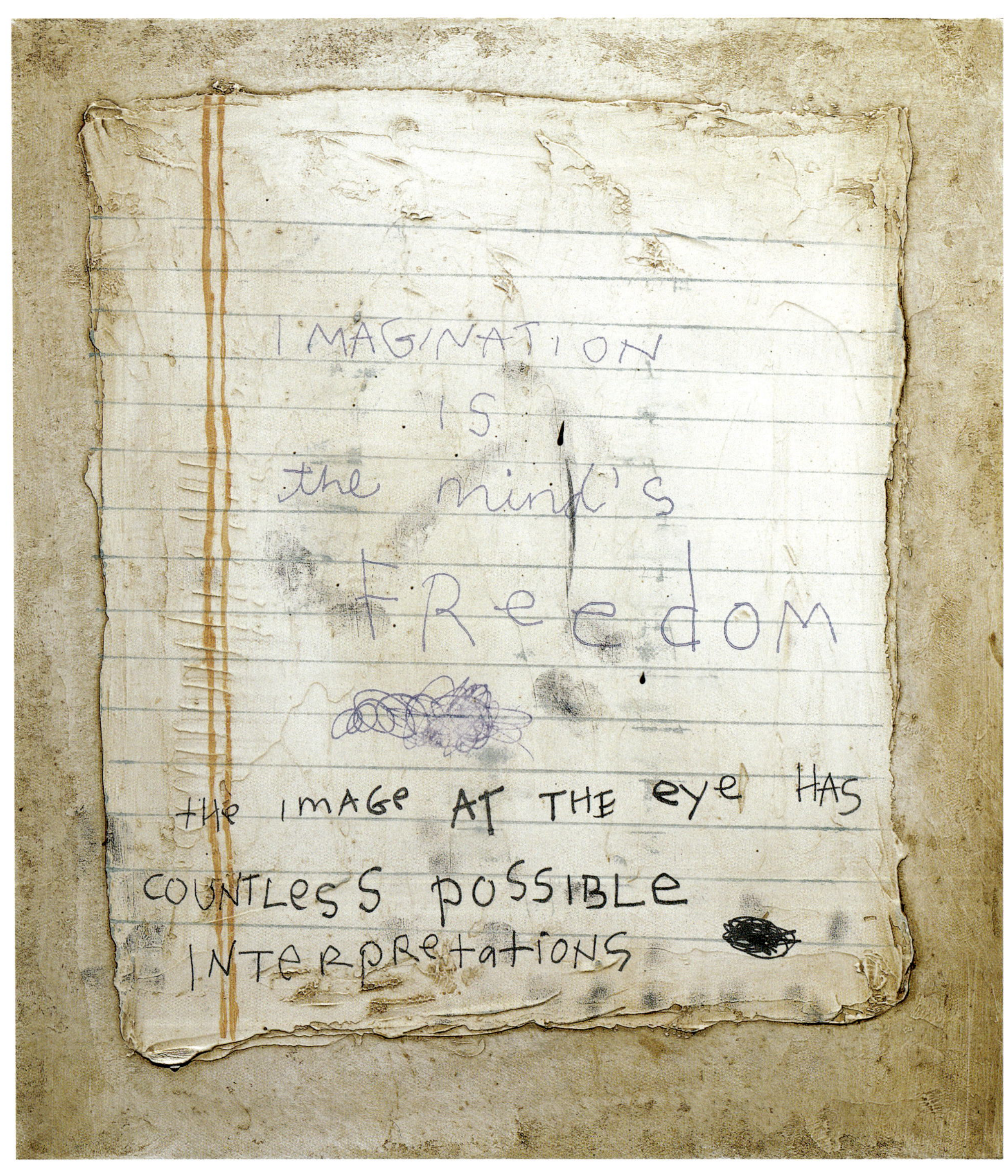

62. **Mind's Freedom,** 2003

painting as language

JOHN YAU

The image at the eye has countless possible interpretations.
Squeak Carnwath

EVERYTHING AN ARTIST MAKES reflects an ethical position. This is one of the dirty little secrets that is rarely mentioned in critical discourse, which tends to focus on terms ("modern" and "postmodern") that have more to do with fashion than with ethics. Recognizing the particular ethical position that an artist takes in his or her work, however, is crucial not only to our understanding of a profound argument about the relationship between transgression and tradition that has been going on ever since Edouard Manet exhibited *Le déjeuner sur l'herbe (The Luncheon on the Grass,* 1863) in the Salon des Refusés in 1863. It also affects our view of contemporary art and the role it can play in our daily lives; whether we approach it as something more than a form of entertainment, a distraction from the quotidian. Because of the importance that Squeak Carnwath places on choice and responsibility, her work embodies an ethical position that clarifies many facets of the argument.

Carnwath's first ethical decision, which also amounts to an artistic challenge, has to do with materials. "It can't be anything but paint," she once told me in an interview.[1] "It has to be on a flat surface, and be all paint. It can't be pencil, crayon, or Magic Marker." This means that she doesn't use collage, even when the focus of her attention is a piece of lined notebook paper or the image of an old vinyl LP that is repeated across the entire width of a painting. For recurring motifs, Carnwath may use a stencil or put on gloves, cover them with paint, and press her hands against the canvas—but she never resorts to mechanical means to transfer images. Everything must become paint in order to exist in her painting; but she allows neither the materials nor the image (or written words) to dominate. Rather, they must become a unified thing, at once visual and substantial.

Carnwath works alone in her studio and employs no assistants. Her paintings range in scale from ones you could hold like a book (ten by ten inches) to others that feel slightly larger than human in their dimensions (eighty-two by eighty-two inches). Their square format places them outside the traditions of landscape (horizontal) or portrait (vertical) painting. In rare instances, she will join two or more paintings together, but the compositions will not be continuous across the seam between the canvases. The square (or abstract) format announces that her paintings are self-sufficient artifices, not mirrors or windows; they stand apart from reality even as the artist responds to, and questions, her understanding of it.

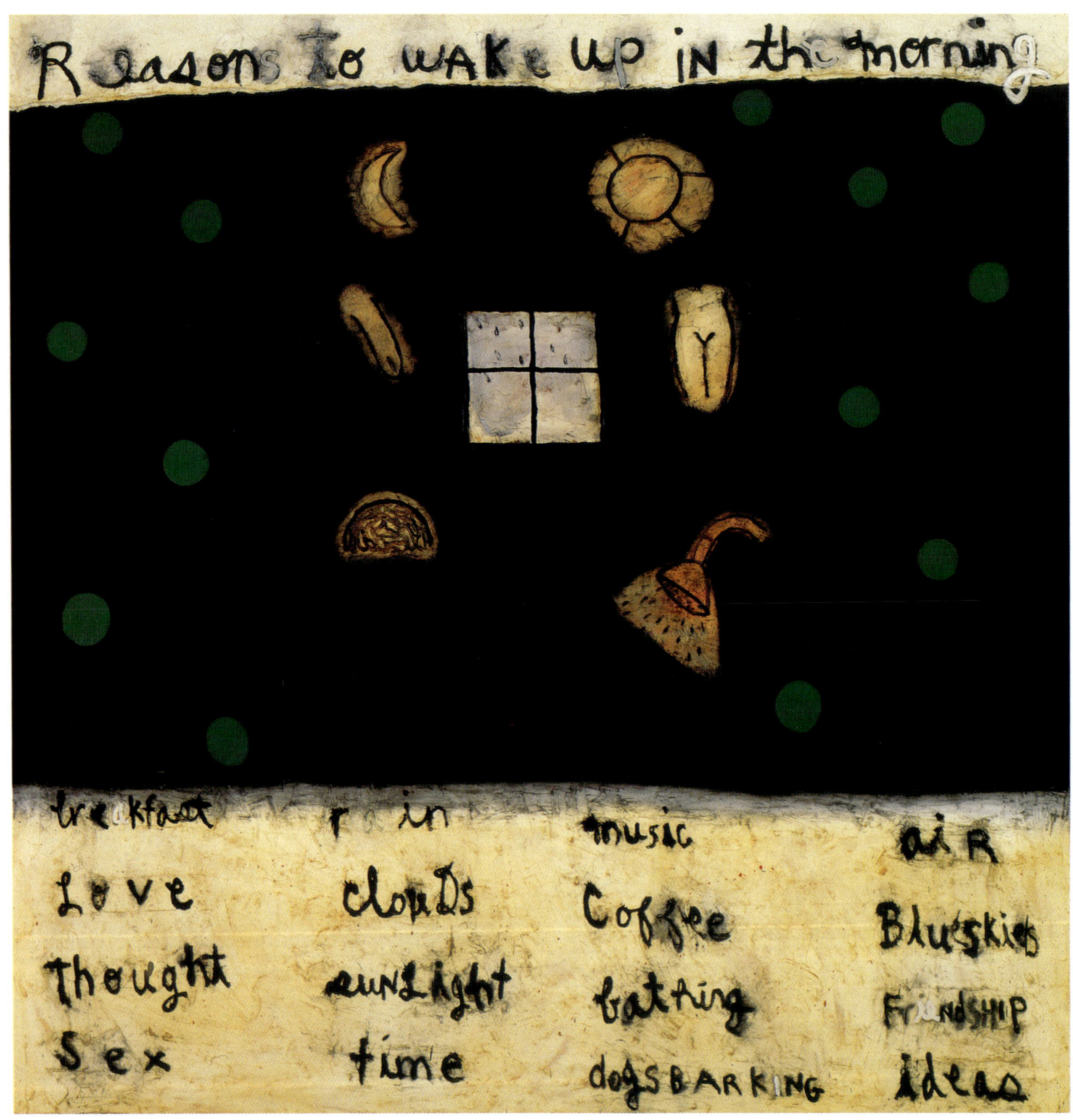

14. **Reasons,** 1991

Much has been made of painters working alone in their studios, particularly during the heyday of abstract expressionism. Carnwath's stance, though, is not a heroic, but an ethical decision. In an age that favors fabrication over the handmade, and outsourcing over individual labor, she has elected to be fully responsible for what she does. She aligns herself with manual workers rather than entrepreneurs who employ others to do their labor, refusing to side with the boss or approve of the separation of classes. The only agenda informing her decision is an ethical one, and has nothing to do with Marxism.

Recognizing that each of us is fundamentally solitary, she believes that what connects human beings across time and space is their individual labor. And, as her work makes plainly evident, paint is the medium of inclusiveness; paint alone is capable of transforming and binding together all the elements of Carnwath's eclectic, expanding, unclassifiable lexicon—lists of words, things heard and read, pictographs, handprints, polka dots and plaids, delicate linear images, roughly outlined figures—including one of an erect, humanoid bunny—stacked and interlocking blocks of color.

A subtle colorist, Carnwath evokes the natural world with her use of yellow ocher, umber, grass green, cerulean blue, deep violet, and vermilion, along with black and white, but her palette is never fixed. She runs the gamut from simple tonality to contrasting swaths of color. In paintings that are divided into discrete areas, she might juxtapose two or even three different palettes, achieving a polyphony of colors, images and layers for the mind's eye to sort out and reconfigure. The paintings are simultaneously immediate and open-ended, simple and complex; they require viewers to constantly readjust their focus, to look and to read, and to distinguish between this and that. Carnwath's unplanned but orchestrated collision between different kinds of language—written and pictographic, abstract and patterned—asserts that reality is finally irreducible, and that no one language, however extensive, can fully contain it.

At the same time that Carnwath defines herself as a painter and a laborer striving to master her craft, she grounds her practice in an intellectual curiosity that thoughtfully considers questions ranging from the most basic to the most metaphysical. For her, painting is primarily a philosophical project, an inquiry into the nature of being, a way of empirically testing what she knows. Filled with humor and pathos, both diligent and fanciful, her work becomes a place—she calls it "a guilt-free zone"—where imagination is given free rein and where the artist must be willing to follow her flights of fancy, however disquieting the trajectory might be.

In *This Is Not* (1994; p. 107), the artist has written: "How do we know? We're here? Alive?" Below this fractured, painfully stammered question, she offers a list of "ways to determine" the answer, including "pinching ourselves" and taking "a whiff." This quirky list of what can be physically experienced is only a small indication of what she tries to get into her paintings. The matter at hand in *Reasons* (1991; p. 98) is "Reasons to wake up in the morning." The list of words below includes "breakfast," "sex," "dogs barking," "bathing," and "ideas." Although this list draws on rather ordinary things, it doesn't feel mundane. Her language is flat and non-directive. And the terseness of her choices grants us permission to add our own words, to consider what we might have in common as well as what differentiates us from others. Carnwath's "reasons" subtly call attention to the fact that individual experience arises from physical sensation ("bathing"), desire ("sex"), corporeal need ("breakfast"), and thinking ("ideas")—from body and mind. In both paintings, Carnwath's lists read as if the artist is recording her thoughts as they occur. The viewer senses that these are not definitive or hierarchical judgments; they are all equally important.

While one of Carnwath's abiding subjects is domesticity, it is evident that her inquiry is actually metaphysical in scope, an exploration of assumptions about the nature of existence. Her studio becomes a kind of laboratory where perceptions and ways of thinking are tested. In *Right Now* (2003; p. 114), the artist writes "Wittgenstein or Heidegger?" Although they came to very different conclusions, both men were original, difficult, and influential thinkers who examined the relationship of language to experience and thinking. This aspect of Carnwath's inquiry, at once speculative and empirical, metaphysical and down-to-earth, philosophical and fundamental, is another reason why she works on flat square canvases. Since the format conforms to the conventions of neither landscape nor portraiture, or, put another way, to the narrative or the iconic, it is a place where inquiry and reflection can be freely opened up and revisited, where notes can be made, and where various hypotheses can be examined.

Just as no visual language dominates Carnwath's lexicon, there is no hierarchy to her subject matter: every aspect and layer of her life is equally accessible without devolving into self-obsessed narcissism or self-satisfied didacticism. She records things she has heard and read, as well as lists of "worries" in a painting of the same title. And yet, as personal as the paintings are, the viewer never feels closed out, because the details don't strike us as anecdotal. Her "worries" are disturbing and humorous, common ("bad air") and quirky ("poison mushrooms" and "lightning"); they are thoughts that could afflict anyone. Here, Carnwath's view of herself is in keeping with her definition of an artist as a manual laborer. Art equals work: there is nothing elevated about what she does or what she thinks or feels, however complex it might be. Even when dealing with abstruse issues about perception, or speculating on the meaning of existence, she most often uses a vernacular language in her work. She never singles herself out. Her remarkable ability to be at once deeply personal and coolly distanced allows the viewer to engage the work on all different levels, while inviting introspection and reflection. It's like receiving a letter from a close friend who is privy to our innermost thoughts.

Carnwath wears her seriousness lightly. She knows that painting demands that the artist negotiate subject matter (which in her case would be the relationship between the public and personal), as well as deal with all the pitfalls that are inherent to its practice (the ability to speed up production with mechanical means or the use of assistants). However direct and even confessional her painting might appear, there is nothing naïve or innocent about her approach. She isn't stricken by her state of hyperawareness and does not feel the need to escape it. In her testing of hypotheses and perceptions, Carnwath challenges the clichéd view which asserts that ideas are the province of conceptual artists, rather than painters, who are unthinking craftspeople working with their hands. In Carnwath's paintings, doing and thinking (body and mind as Wittgenstein would have put it) must always acknowledge each other's existence. In *Fragile Thoughts* (1991; p. 101), the artist writes: "Our fragility lodges itself in the body" and, below, "deep inside the flesh." Mind and body are distinct but inseparable, and Carnwath periodically focuses in her painting on their indivisible yet entangled nature.

By concentrating on the constantly changing relationship of body and mind, Carnwath can embrace a broad and diverse range of subjects; this is one way in which she has distinguished her work from that of other artists, including those who have influenced her. It has enabled her to take an extreme and challenging position, which the viewer is likely to find both disturbing and demanding. Instead of offering us answers, solutions, instructions about how to better society or ourselves, she raises questions in a quiet and indirect manner. We discover the questions on our own rather than finding ourselves confronted by them. We are witnesses, not prosecutors or judges.

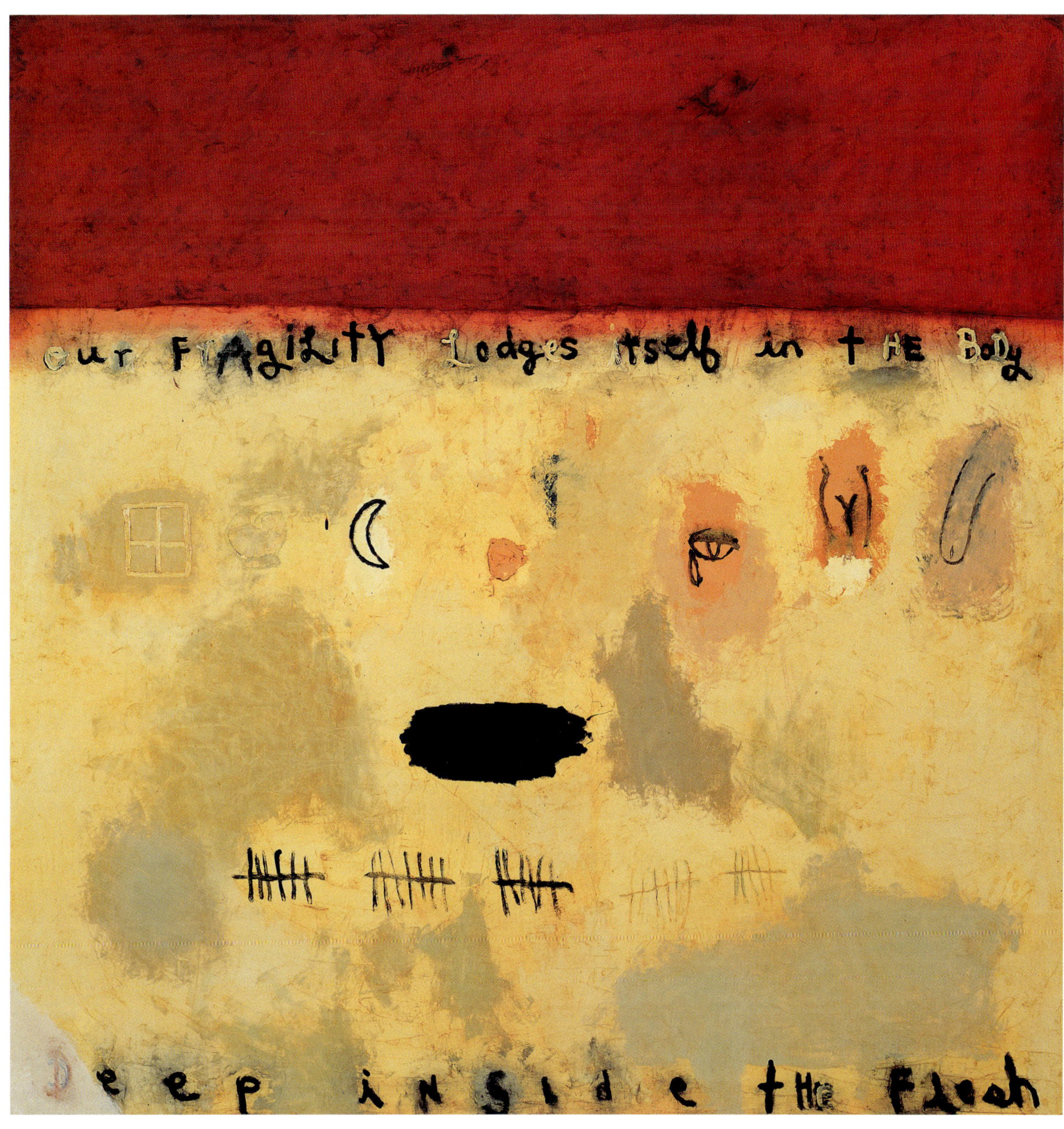

13. **Fragile Thoughts,** 1991

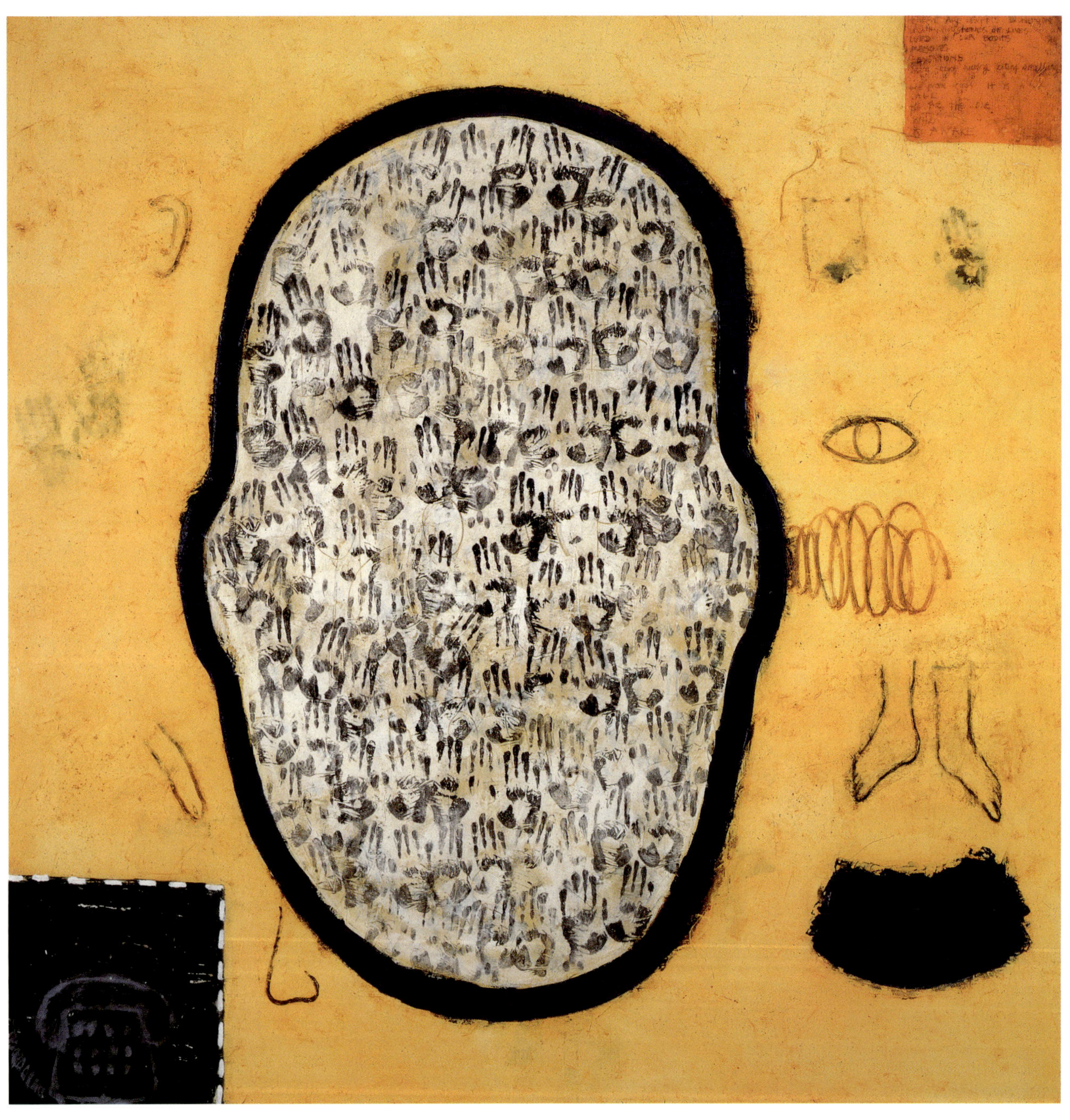

15. **A Call To Be,** 1992

In *An Inability to Remain* (1992; p. 104) Carnwath wrote, in black on a red field that takes half the canvas, "I heard a story on the radio about a joyful man who stabbed himself one hundred times. He died. Every time I see a St. Sebastian painting I am rewounded fresh." Is what she heard fact or fiction, "a story" or a news report? Is it important that we know? If so, why? Is the artist also "joyful" in being "rewounded" by art? And isn't she "rewounded" because of her belief in art's redemptive power?

Without becoming didactic, Carnwath is able to raise some painful but, I think, necessary questions in *An Inability to Remain*. Who was this man? Would knowing who he is, or at least his name, make him any more vivid to us? What should we do about feeling both compassionate and helpless? After all, the man's death does not seem to have rewounded the artist—we can't be sure—but a painting of the martyred St. Sebastian, pierced by arrows, did. Can looking at art make one more sensitive? And if it can, what does one do with such a heightened state of vulnerability? What is the relationship between art and life? Can each one teach us about the other? And what can they teach? Carnwath doesn't pose these questions in her painting. The viewer unpacks them, and others.

Through the juxtaposition of two experiences—something heard by chance on the radio and the memory of paintings of a martyrdom—Carnwath conveys the vulnerability of the mind and body circling each other, reminding us that an unpredictable external event can engender feelings of empathy and powerlessness. It is telling that she picks an event, or a "story," that seems both ordinary and fantastic, not widely known, certainly not familiar. It is not part of our collective experience, and society and the media have not influenced our response to it. By acknowledging a state in which being a witness is not enough (even when one gives testimony, as she surely does in this painting), Carnwath arrives at one of the most disquieting and common quandaries of contemporary life: What do we do with what we learn? How do we deal with the countless bits of disturbing information ("a joyful man who stabbed himself one hundred times") that otherwise have no direct effect on our lives? How do we stay open to reality? Carnwath's determination to stay open, to keep gazing directly at reality, is the driving force in all her work.

WITH ITS GRAPHIC PALETTE and crudely written words, *Black Is* (1994; p. 42) might be regarded as a contemporary riff on folk art or on an elementary school assignment. Certainly, it shares features with both. However, to see *Black Is* this way is to fail to recognize the conceptual intelligence that informs every decision the artist has made in the painting—a black ground divided by a thin white line into a rudimentary grid of similarly sized rectangles. In each rectangle the artist has written a word in red paint. The list, which includes "mustard," "hole," "belt," "panther," "walnut," "pepper," consists of word associations with "black."

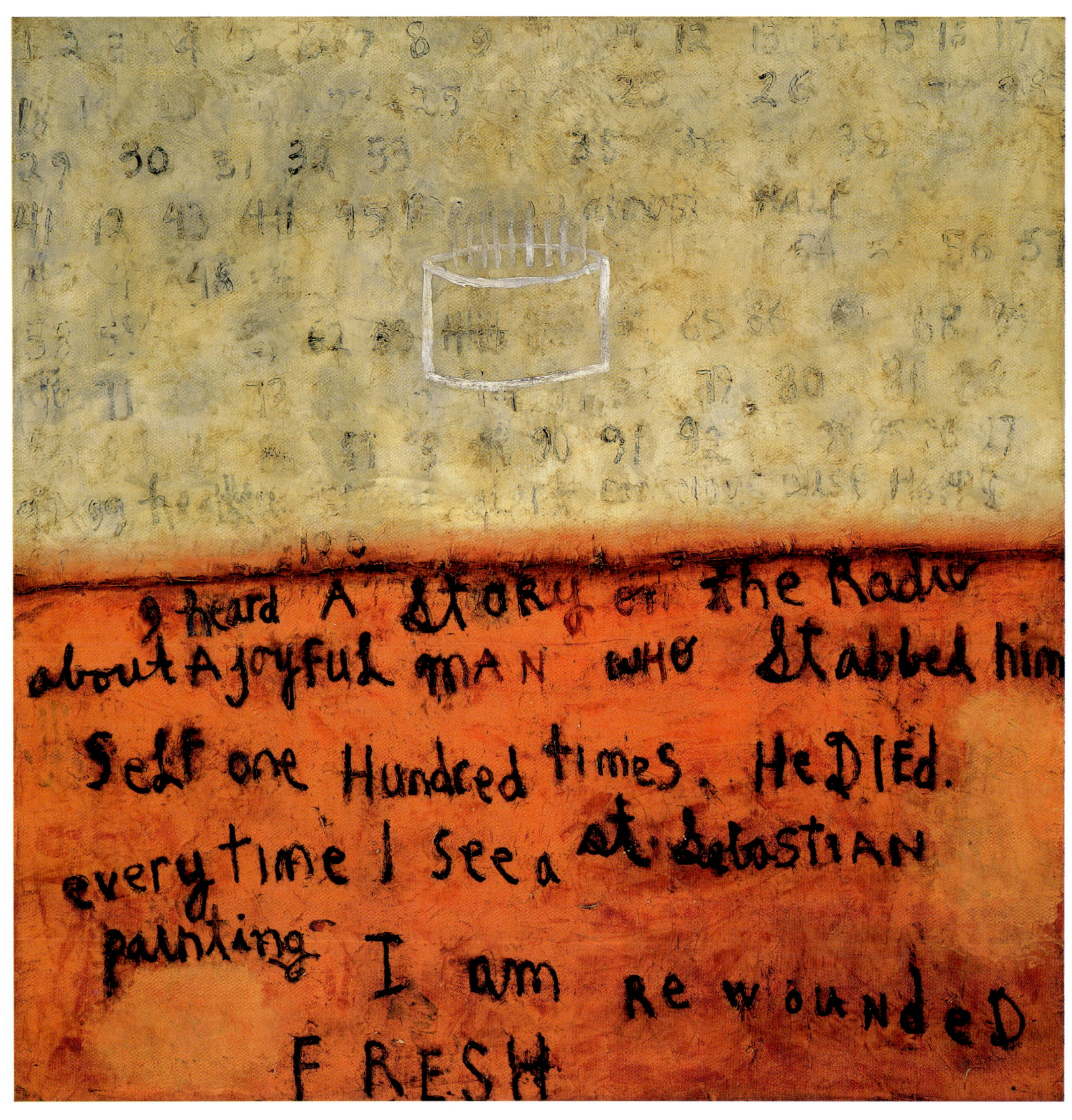

16. **An Inability to Remain,** 1992

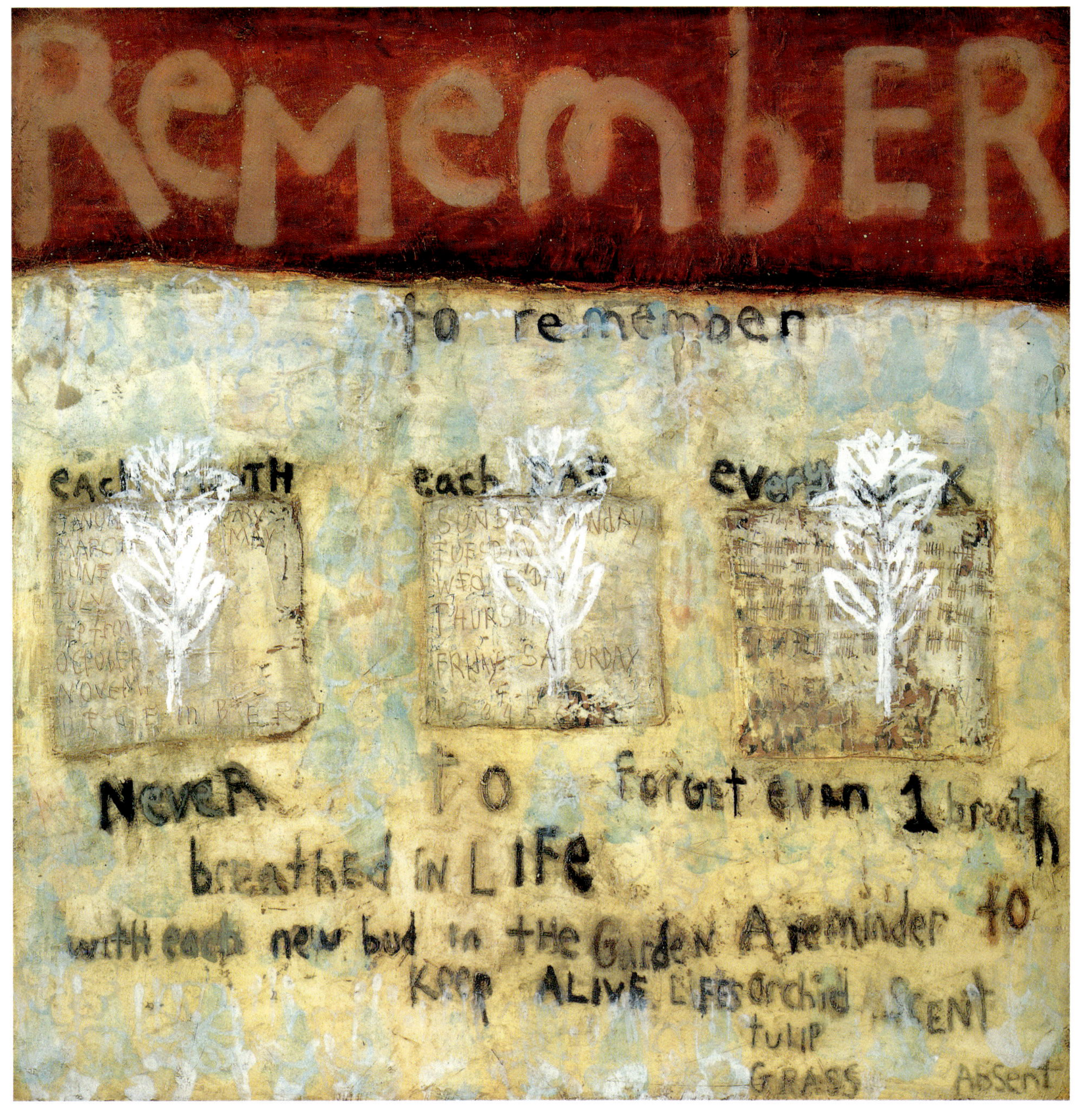

19. **Don't Forget,** 1994

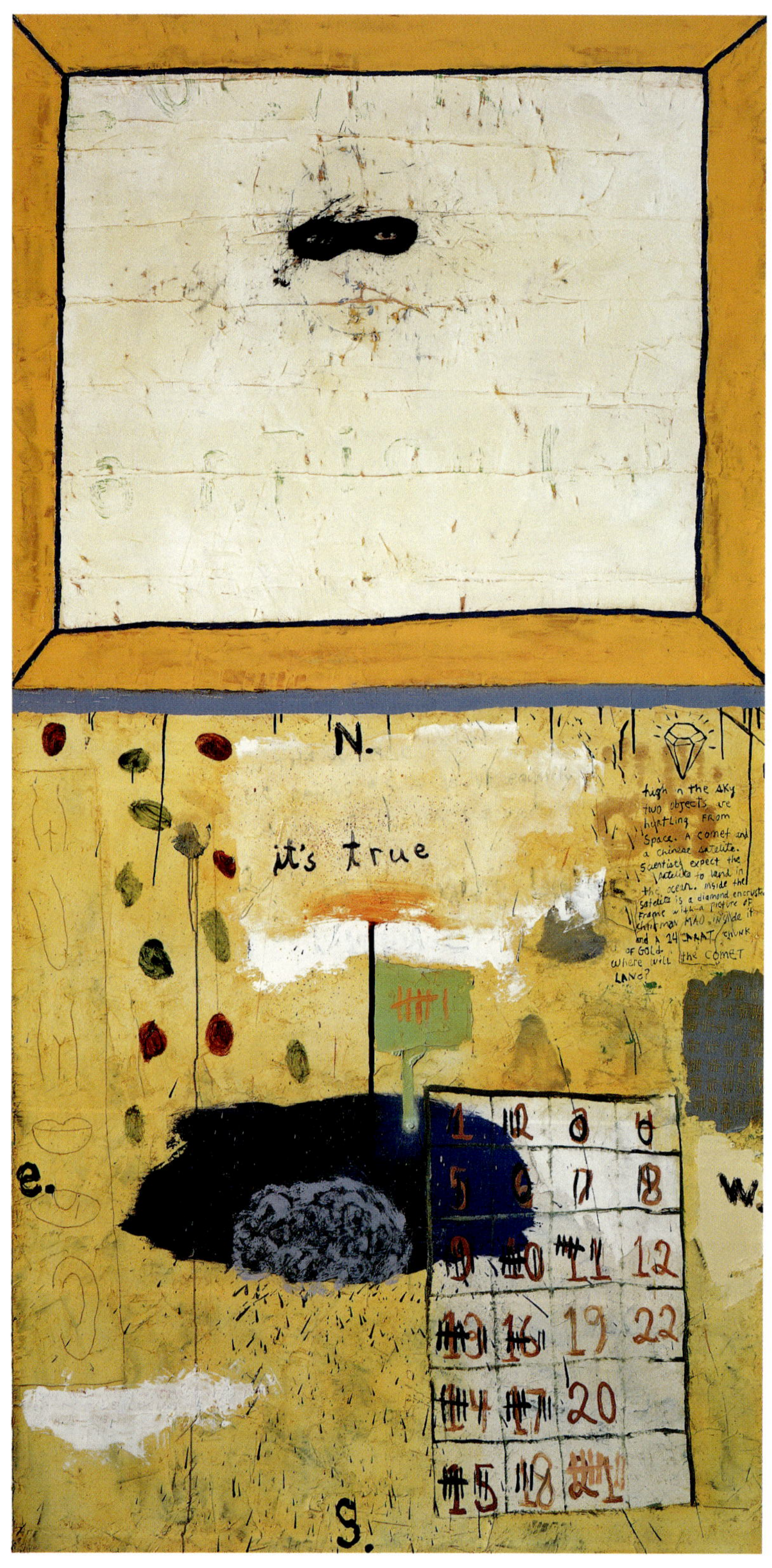

34. **Towards Earth (1995–96),** 1996

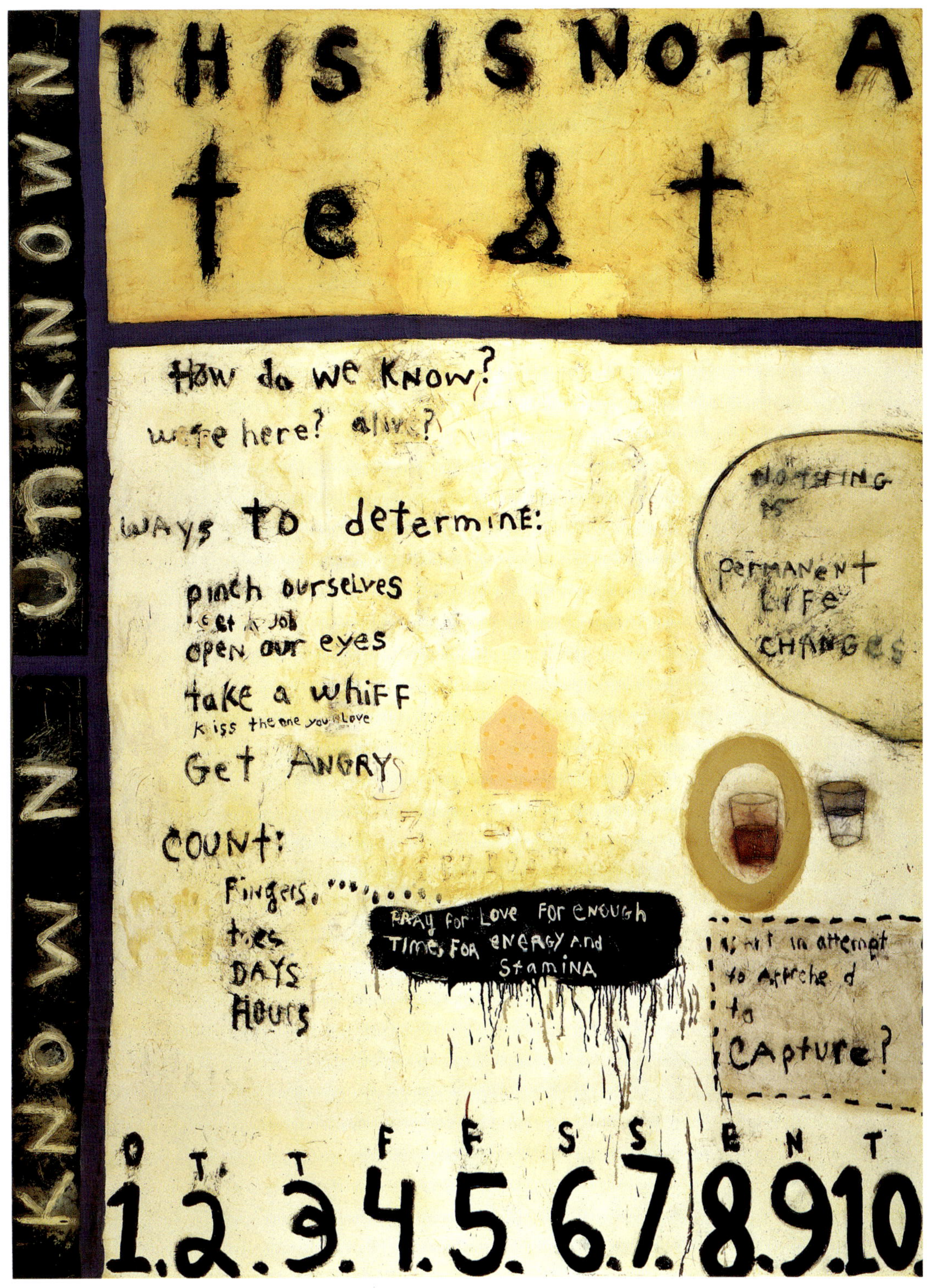

22. **This Is Not,** 1994

Some words ("studies," "power," "art") refer to social or art classifications while quietly reminding us that the artist lives and works in Oakland, which has a large African American population. Other words, like "belt," "widow," and "beard," fall outside the artist's immediate external circumstances, opening the list to include the historical ("plague" and "death") as well. What, the painting seems to be asking, is common and what is unique to our experience? What associations are we free to make, and which do we feel required to make? What are the markers that determine an individual's autonomy? These questions are basic to our self-image, but they are not necessarily ones that we reflect upon.

In this vein, it is worth noting that she also did *What White Is* (1994; pp. 44–45), a two-panel painting that includes the words, "man," "house," "pepper," and "lead." One painting often seems to lead Carnwath to another as she shifts the focus of her investigation. This openness to possibility, to not knowing in advance how the painting will turn out, is central to the artist's project, which, again, is speculative in nature. Carnwath is focused on verification, on determining what constitutes knowledge. *Black Is* isn't only a list of words, which would have made it a purely textual work. It is an optically layered painting, a small white grid superimposed on a black ground. The artist made the white grid by painting thin red lines on a white ground; in many of its vertically-oriented rectangles she laid a small daub of black. Thus the painting consists of a grid of words (textual and visual) and a grid of marks (optical and physical).

By fusing two historically antagonistic modes of representation, the textual and the visual, Carnwath directly challenges the fashionable assertion that conceptual and installation art have a lock on the written word, while painting should be confined to the optical realm. At stake is a far larger and more resonant issue than the supposed conflict between conceptual art and painting. Historically, the ocular has been a cornerstone of Western art; it is considered essential to the Platonic-Christian tradition, while the textual forms the foundation of the Hebraic tradition. By making a combination of the visual and the written central to her practice, Carnwath connects herself to the groundbreaking artist Jasper Johns, as well as to Ludwig Wittgenstein, who examined the extent to which meaning is determined by context. Wittgenstein (it should be noted) influenced Johns as well; like the philosopher's writings, Johns's art is both speculative and empirical, and concerned with verification. Carnwath's relationship to Johns, whether she is conscious of it or not, is largely one of affinity rather than influence, and not something gotten from received knowledge. Johns's breakthroughs included such formal innovations as merging a familiar flat thing—the American flag, for example—with painting's two-dimensional plane, as well as attaching three-dimensional objects to its physical surface.[2] While Carnwath's paintings are similar journeys of discovery, in which juxtaposition, layering, and placement are vital to the work's meaning, she limits herself to working on a painting's flat surface without reifying its two-dimensionality or banishing spatiality.

The words in *Black Is* might look crudely made, and the grid rudimentary, but it is wrong to associate the artist with those who place a higher value on expressiveness and innocence than on erudition and self-awareness. Her choice of words is straightforward and highly aware of the different ways in which we gain knowledge. I believe that Carnwath's ambition is to keep myriad possibilities in play, to be simultaneously impulsive and rigorous, improvisational and highly considered; her openness defines painting as a dream of freedom, an unpredictable set of possibilities. It is why she has never tried to develop a signature style, but has instead slowly expanded a lexicon that includes words, personal symbols, worldly signs, and abstract and decorative patterns, which she structures in increasingly complex ways. And this is also true of her sources, which range from the mass media to dense philosophical texts and scientific treatises, from public events to personal experiences and memories. If something (a vinyl LP, a pencil mark, a water glass, a horseshoe, a tree stump) can be turned into paint, chances are it will end up in one of Carnwath's works. The commonplace and the esoteric both have a place in the artist's work, often side by side.

If the apposition of the textual and the visual is essential to Carnwath's work, so too is the tactile. The black daubs in the white grid have a tangible presence, like fingerprints; that she didn't fill in all of the empty spaces subtly reinforces our sense of the surface as being both painted and touched by the artist. And the way she wrote in red paint, as if she were feeling her way across the black grid with her brush, echoes this tactility. In making the visual and tactile inseparable, Carnwath is again building upon Johns's work,[3] but more importantly, she formally underscores the focus of her project: the question, "How does one determine what one knows?" Seeing, reading, and touching are essential to the way we apprehend reality; they are intrinsic to experience.

In *A Call To Be* (1992; p. 102), the artist imprinted her hands over a hundred times within a large, black-lined contour of a head. Thinking, sight, and touch are placed in inextricable proximity. And while we may see the painting as "a spectacular face tattoo,"[4] we should not lose sight of the deeper intention. Carnwath wants to make a painting that is immediate and visually arresting, but that is not her final goal.

In *Plaid Lost* (1999; p. 111), Carnwath brings together the tactile, visual, and textual in a way that strikes me as logical and imaginative, necessary and surprising. On the left side of the painting, which measures two feet by two feet, there are two black handprints. Around each handprint is a faint line of paint reinforcing the contours of what they contain. On the right side, the word "lost" appears in large bold letters, and, just beneath it, "50.00 reward," presumably for the return of the bird whose image lies directly below. Once held in a cage, the bird has escaped. Underneath the bird, a phone number: "783-6855."

The size of the image and text is consistent with a sign one might see posted in a store window or on a utility pole. Running along the bottom of the painting is a plaid pattern, a decorative border such as someone might add to a flier of this sort to grab the public's attention. On a basic level, the painting memorializes a homemade poster—something that will soon be lost and forgotten—concerning something that has been lost, but will not be forgotten. By introducing a homemade poster into the space reserved for painting, Carnwath suggests there is an affinity between the two; created by an individual, both are objects that are vulnerable to external circumstances. Without a trace of irony, *Plaid Lost* evokes the transitory nature of existence and the awareness that eventually all does get covered over, forgotten, or is nowhere to be found. Additionally, and this is something the artist never comments on, the sign is somehow pathetic because it contains no description of the bird's distinguishing features. It depends on a visual image, which clearly isn't enough. The handprints—the artist's body, once removed—remind us that without physical data about the bird, all we have is a sign, an image that is twice or thrice removed. We know something (the bird) has been lost, but we have no real sense of it. We can translate this gap in our knowledge to our larger circumstances; we know that lives and possessions are constantly being lost; but we are also removed from that aspect of reality. Is this something that we find comforting or disturbing? And what can we do to know more? Or do we wish not to know more?

The conjunction of visual, textual, and tactile formally echoes Carnwath's intent to explore the mind-body relationship and the divergent ways the mind and the body apprehend reality. It also deepens her subversion of the Platonic-Christian ocular tradition. We don't just look at Carnwath's paintings; they invite us to scrutinize them, to pore over their physical surfaces and diversity of marks, all made of paint. The varying sizes of the writing—from large and bold to small and delicate—require that we constantly adjust our focus and alter our physical relationship to the painting; that we stand at a distance or move in close. By denying viewers a comfortably static vantage point, Carnwath makes them conscious of their bodies moving through space. In stark and critical contrast to artists of an earlier generation—and here I am thinking of Frank Stella, Roy Lichtenstein, and Andy Warhol—the viewer cannot see Carnwath's work all at once. Her paintings unfold in time, bit by bit. The implication is clear; knowledge does not come all at once; it is not simply a revelation.

THE LIST IS ONE WAY in which Carnwath compiles disparate pieces of information; she also observes and counts.[5] Each list is a way of verifying what information has been gathered, and of determining what is known. And yet, while the artist has used the list numerous times to organize her paintings, her compositions do not feel prearranged, but found. It is clear from her work that she doesn't think of the grid as an idealized structure or an a priori container, but simply as an effective way to display a variety of information. Effectiveness also determines the way she records what she observes and the way she counts in paint. Carnwath uses the grid because the subject demands it.

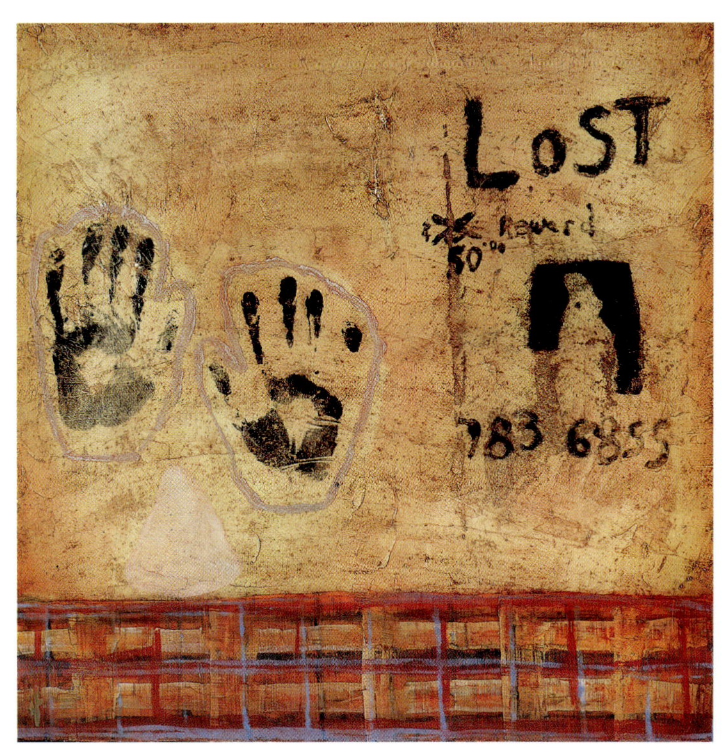

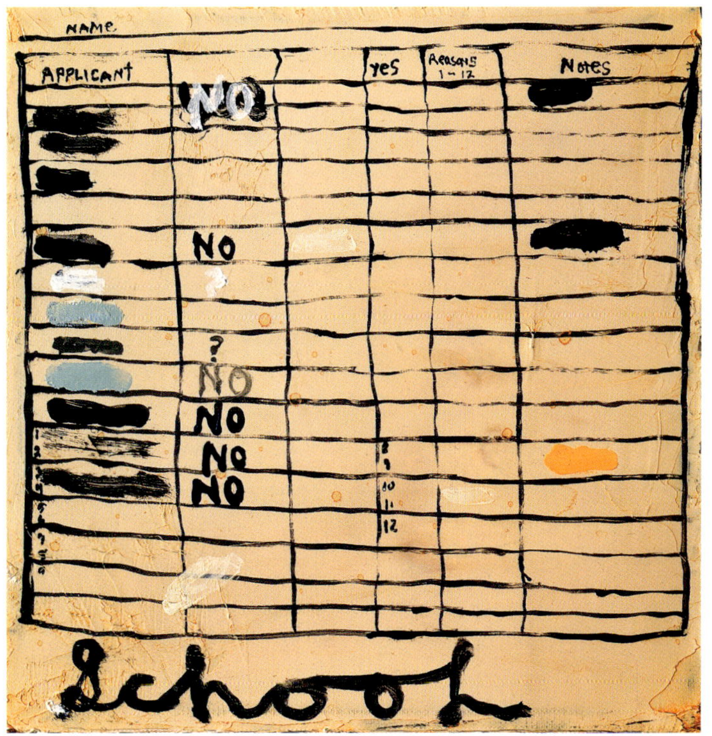

43. **Plaid Lost,** 1999 (above)

37. **Assignment,** 1998 (below)

In *Assignment* (1998; p. 111), she made a crude replica of a survey that polls applicants to a "school" (written in large letters along the bottom of the painting). Tellingly, she didn't try to make a perfect copy; emphasizing rejection, the word "no" dominates one of the columns. One of Carnwath's abiding strengths is her ability to pick out a subject that is personal and impersonal—in a larger sense, democratic. She combines aspects of a diary and a scientist's laboratory notes in a way that exceeds those categories. As *Assignment* suggests, we all endure rejection at one point or another. It was true for Mozart, for O'Keeffe, for Pollock. At bottom, however, the real issue isn't rejection, but autonomy, and what one must do to gain it. This is the subject that the artist returns to in her work. It is why she approaches her subjects in a detached, scientific manner.

While words dominate *Black Is*, stacked horizontal bands of color make up *But For Monkeys* (2003; p. 113). The words "Guilt Free Zone" appear within a circular dotted line on a trompe l'oeil sheet of lined notebook paper. Just below it, on the same sheet, Carnwath has written

> we humans are able to concept-
> ualize and understand lies,
> deceits, and secrets;
> But for monkeys, if they
> don't see it they don't
> know it.

It seems to me that the "guilt free zone" is where imagination is given free rein; it is a place where the artist is not constrained by what she knows and remembers. The dotted circle suggests a designated goal, a restricted area that one might be able to enter but not dwell in forever. Recognizing that she cannot escape her own consciousness, Carnwath posits that such a zone can and does exist, even if it must remain remote and often inaccessible.

At the same time, the viewer might identify the "monkey" as the vehicle of immediate experience. What monkeys don't know won't hurt them. This is one of the immutable divisions separating simians from human beings. Among the latter what they don't know might hurt them (or so they fear). Thus the painting juxtaposes three ways of interacting with reality (direct physical evidence, a conceptual relationship, and the ability to form ideas and images that one has not directly experienced). Concerned with facts rather than judgments, Carnwath does not claim that one is more desirable than the other, but that all three are intrinsic to our existence.

The drips skittering down the painting's surface endow the stacked abstract bands with a physical presence. We are looking not at a series of disembodied images, but at a thing made up of self-sufficient parts. The paint drips, the colored bands, the "sheet of notebook paper": each part of the painting stands on its own and yet is necessary to the whole. Carnwath recognizes that contingency is unavoidable and uses the juxtaposition of the optical, the textual, and the emblematic to frame the various ways we apprehend reality. How do we see the abstract bands of color? Does our perception of them change after we read what the artist has written? Can we imagine them to be something else? In acknowledging their own contingency, Carnwath's paintings dissolve the barrier separating art and life. Her paintings are meant to exist in rooms where life takes place, not cordoned off in some timeless zone of aesthetic appreciation, which is, finally, an artificial construct.

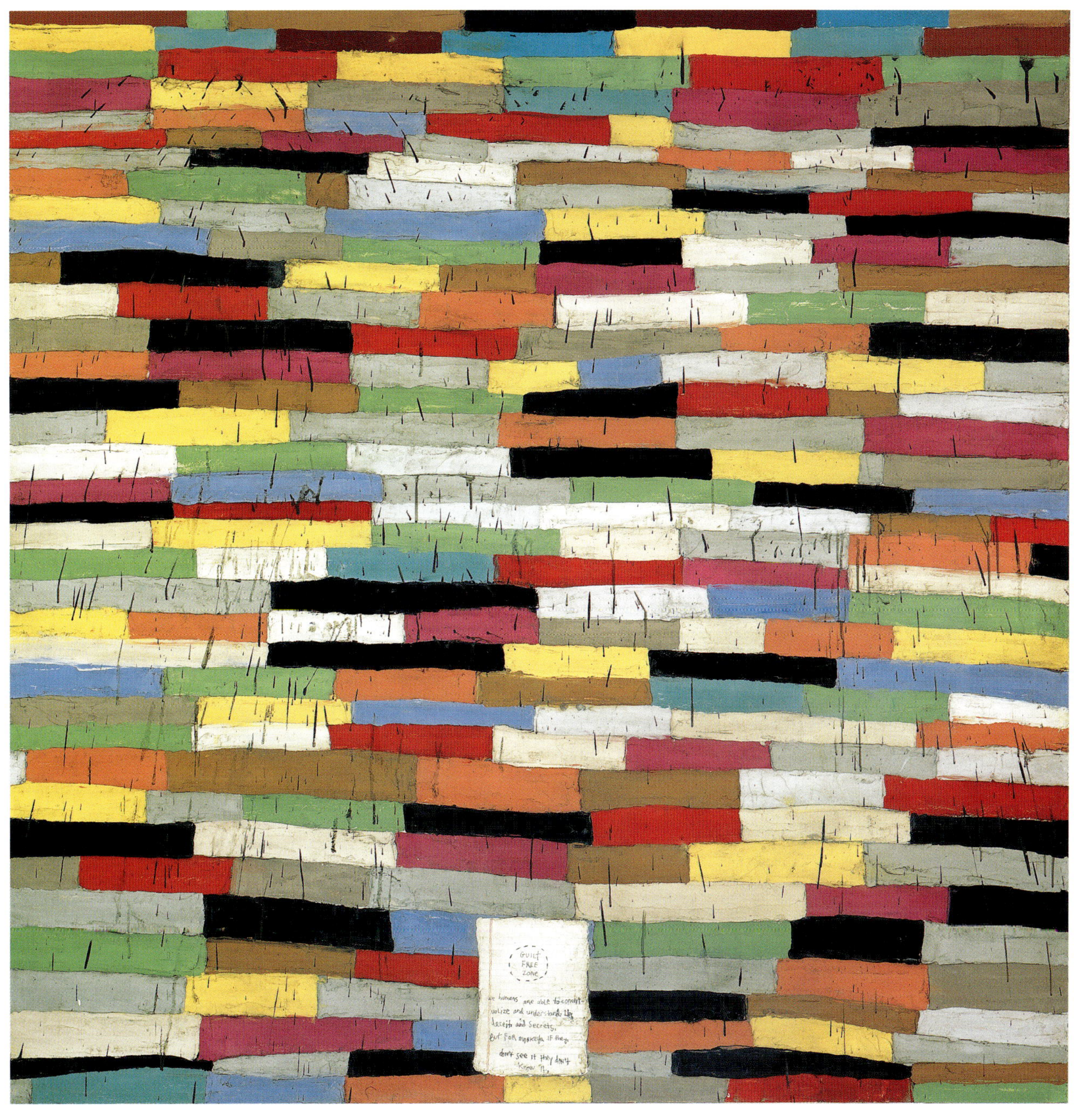

59. **But For Monkeys,** 2003

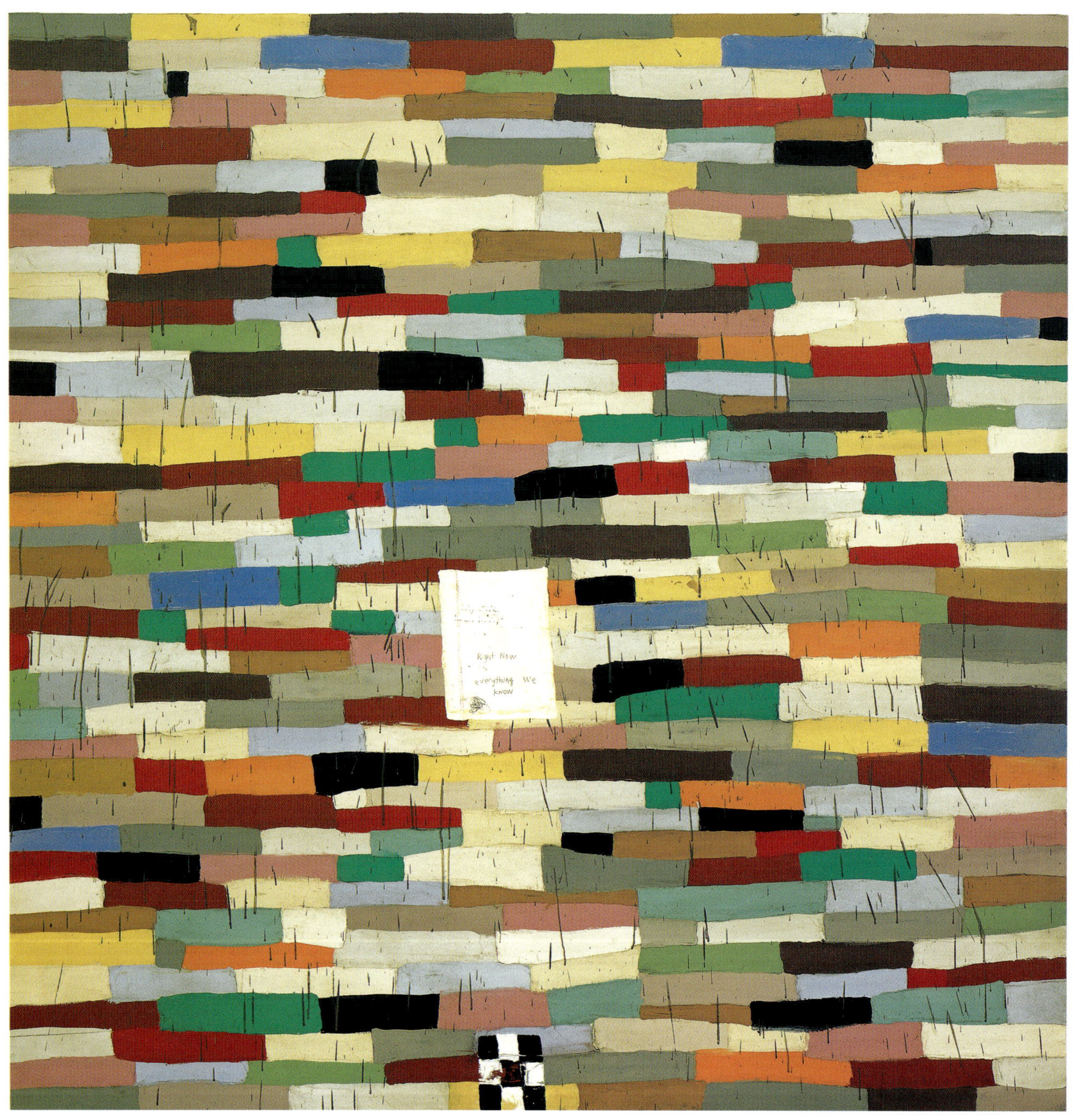

63. **Right Now,** 2003

If Carnwath finds the composition in the course of making a painting, she also finds meaning. She places an element from her lexicon into the painting, and this element calls for another element. She might later remove it or cover it over. The painting's flat, resilient surface functions as a repository of different, even contradictory observations, languages, and impulses. The layering underscores that the painting took place over time, and that the artist is conscious of time passing. This hyperawareness of time, and the feelings of mortality and vulnerability that it stirs up, is a central condition that Carnwath's paintings both define and inhabit. In *Obit* (2000; p. 116), she writes out names that she has read in the daily obituaries. The painting was done over time; the list covers its surface with the names of strangers, friends, acquaintances, and celebrities. The painting is a list, an observation, and an act of counting, and a statement that we all live in time and that our names will one day be added to this list. In picking the familiar form of the obituary as a way of organizing information, Carnwath reminds us that the universe is impersonal, that time goes on without lamenting our absence.

While this is not essential to our experience of *Obit,* it's worth noting that Carnwath needed a conceptual framework in order to bring it to completion; and this structure required that the painting be done over time without foreknowledge of the names she would have to dutifully record. Thus the painting is simultaneously a conceptual project and an act of devotion. The artist is literally a witness.[6] *Obit* isn't autobiographical; it is everyone's biography.

WORKING ALONE IN HER STUDIO, Carnwath never forgets that solitude is a fundamental condition she shares with others. In fact, her acknowledgment of isolation as inescapable suffuses the work with a depth of feeling that is rare in contemporary art. She doesn't suppress her awareness of mortality, addressing it instead with humor and registering her "worries" and fears; joy, lamentation, and vulnerability are intertwined states. And yet, her work is not overtly diaristic, and there is no pretension to a private and inaccessible language. The viewer doesn't feel as if there is a fixed "I" in Carnwath's paintings, that the events she registers in her paintings happened only to her and not to all of us. The words she employs are often impersonal and familiar; they can come from the radio or newspaper, sources that are public by definition and in that sense shared. The paintings feel democratic and inclusive. The lists and observations are ours as much as they are hers. We empathize with the impulse to count and verify, to take stock of our situation. Even when she writes "shut up" twice in big black letters across the surface of *Promise* (1999; p. 118), one feels that she is calling attention to the physical power of language—here used as a weapon—rather than confessing to something about her experience. Certainly, she is not attempting to elicit the viewer's sympathy, to single out her existence as a special case. One of Carnwath's strong points is that she can come close to painful territory and not slide into it and become maudlin.

49. **Obit**, 2000

Given to constantly testing what she knows, Carnwath is an empiricist who does not seek sanctuary in theories, belief systems, or sentimental tropes concerning painting's transcendence. She wants to stay open to reality even as she knows that time is pulling her toward chaos and oblivion. As an empiricist, she rejects the illusion that art, for all its timelessness, can protect her from time; this repudiation is an ethical decision. She will keep gazing at reality, even as she is aware that she is passing from it. Thus, beginning with *Black Is* and continuing through such recent paintings as *Reflection* (2005; p. 120) and *Real and True* (2007; p. 131), the viewer senses that despite all the changes and additions that have taken place in her work, Carnwath still regards the painting as a kind of sounding board, a place where hypotheses are tested, memories preserved, and notes are made, and a record of a life lived in time.

I have come to think of Carnwath's paintings as an imaginative transfiguration of a table, a wall, a piece of paper on which those ideas are explored, records kept, and notes compiled. And the painting becomes both a container and a surface capable of absorbing anything put there. Rather than depicting the world, which would turn the painting into a window, she uses painting to examine various perceptions of reality. In *Reflection*, which is divided into two unequal areas—a blue ground that runs across the upper part of the painting, and a larger white area that takes up the rest—she writes

> If painting is a language, is this thinking or observation? For instance, is this a picture of the sky? Or a blue-ish patch of paint? And if language represents unique ways of thinking then, painting if it is a kind of language, represents the most unique form of thinking and just to complicate things, painting is the embodiment of time: real and true.

Here, Carnwath begins with a hypothesis ("if painting is a language"), which she then tests. Is it "thinking or observation?" She goes on to dissect the capacity of painting and language to indicate meaning. I see the writing in *Reflection* as the verbal equivalent to Robert Ryman's investigations of what constitutes a painting. Both artists are intent on discovering its basic identity. Unsurprisingly, they do so in different ways and reach dissimilar conclusions.

Carnwath's lexicon doesn't give primacy to one language over the others but brings them together—images, words, signs, abstract patterns—so that each comments on the others, conveying a view of reality as a constant state of friction. Citing her acknowledgment of solitude, her interest in the mind-body relationship, and her empiricism, I have suggested that her work has affinities with Jasper Johns and Robert Ryman. Another artist who comes to mind is less well-known. Forrest Bess (1911-1977) once wrote: "I try to tell myself that only by breaking completely from society can I arrive at a reasonable existence."[7] In his oeuvre, estimated at fewer than one hundred paintings, Bess developed a highly symbolic language that includes abstract symbols, such as triangles and vertical and horizontal lines, which he derived from his study of Aboriginal art. His art was fueled by a belief in the collective unconscious—the idea that certain symbols have a universal significance and are part of the human psyche—and a desire to make himself whole. Bess believed he was a conduit, and painted what he saw on the insides of his eyelids when he was asleep; the dream was central to him. Carnwath also believes that she is a conduit. She has told me as much: "I do believe we are receivers for something."[8]

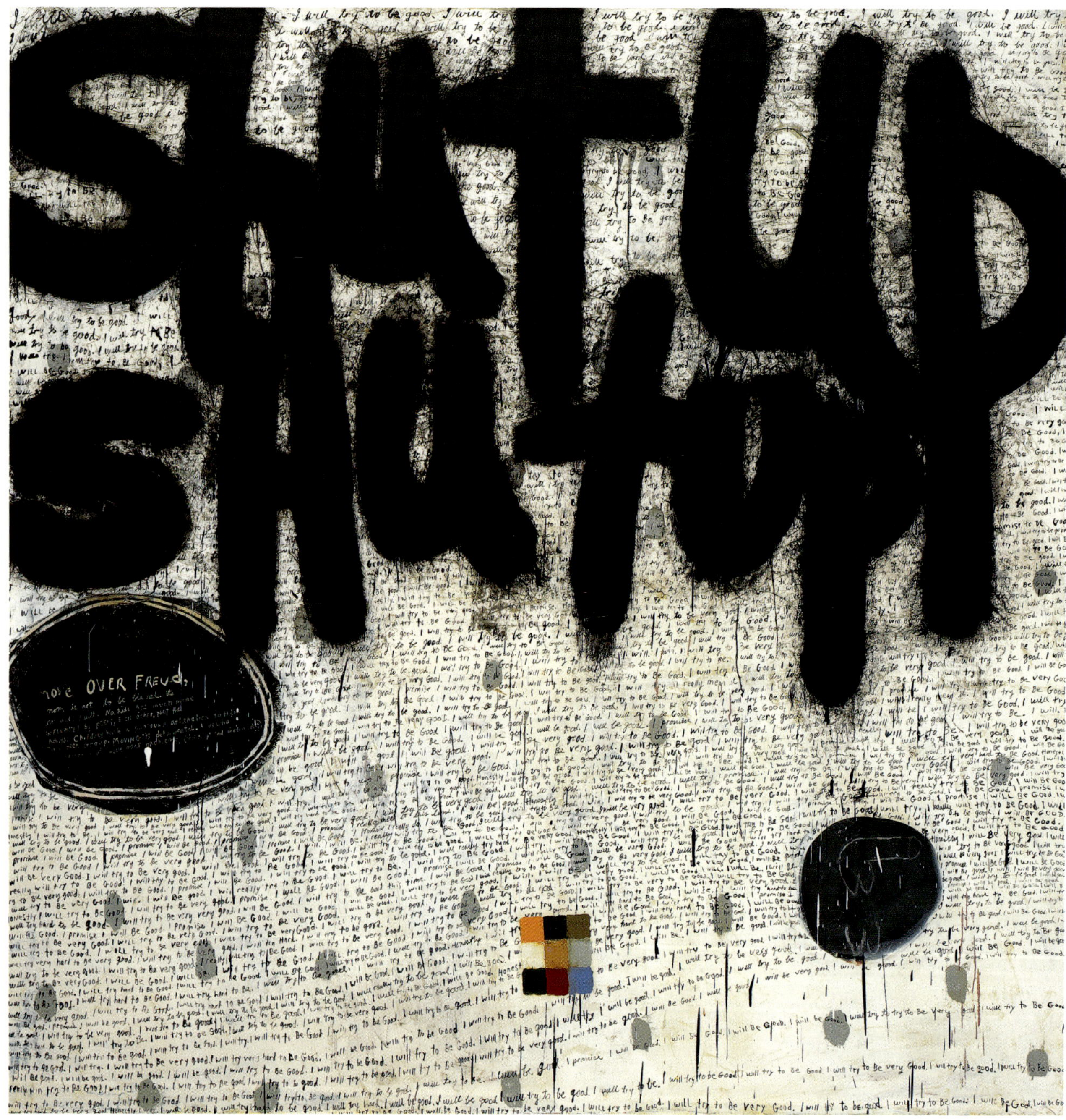

44. **Promise,** 1999

50. **Please,** 2000

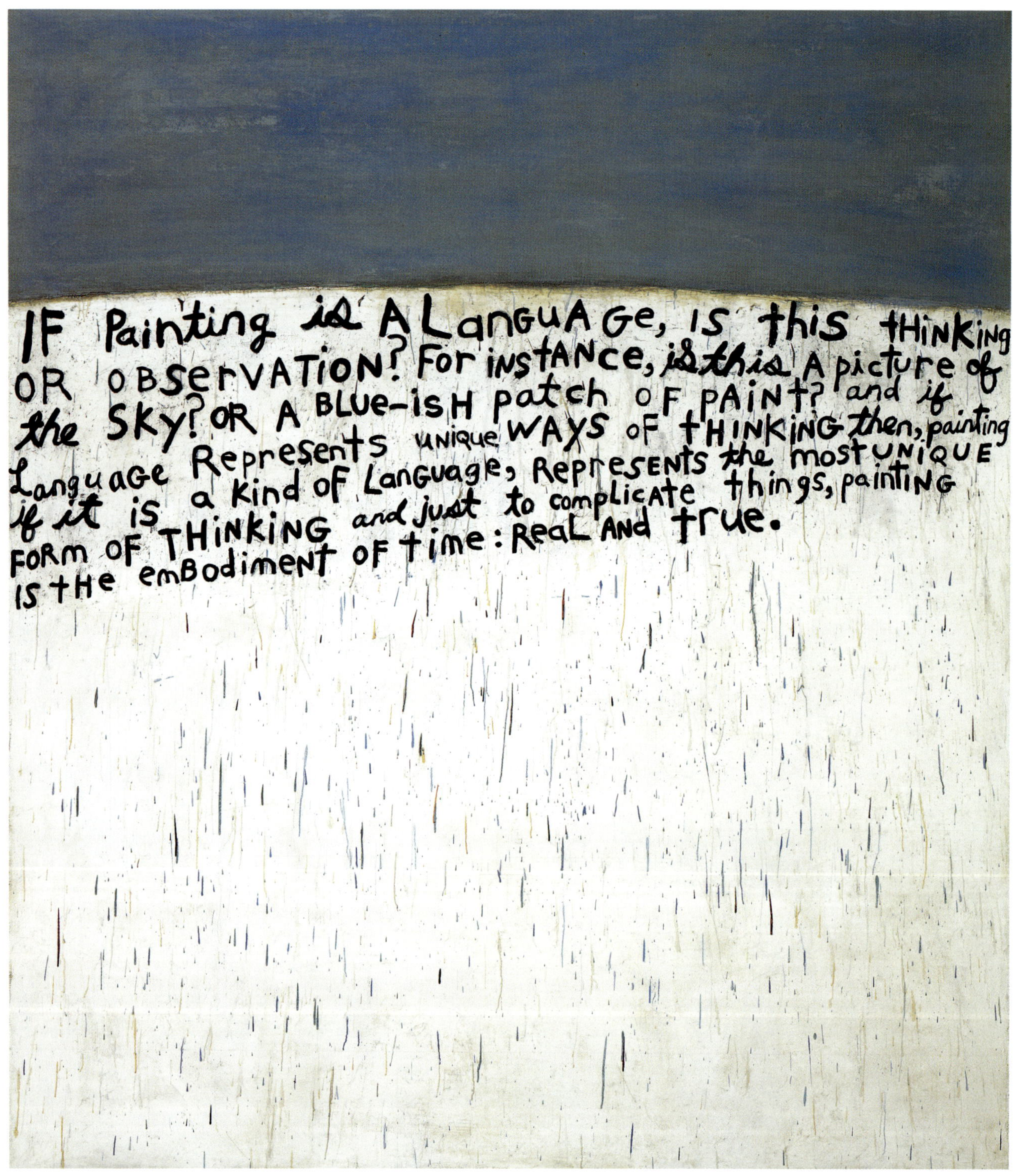

72. **Reflection,** 2005

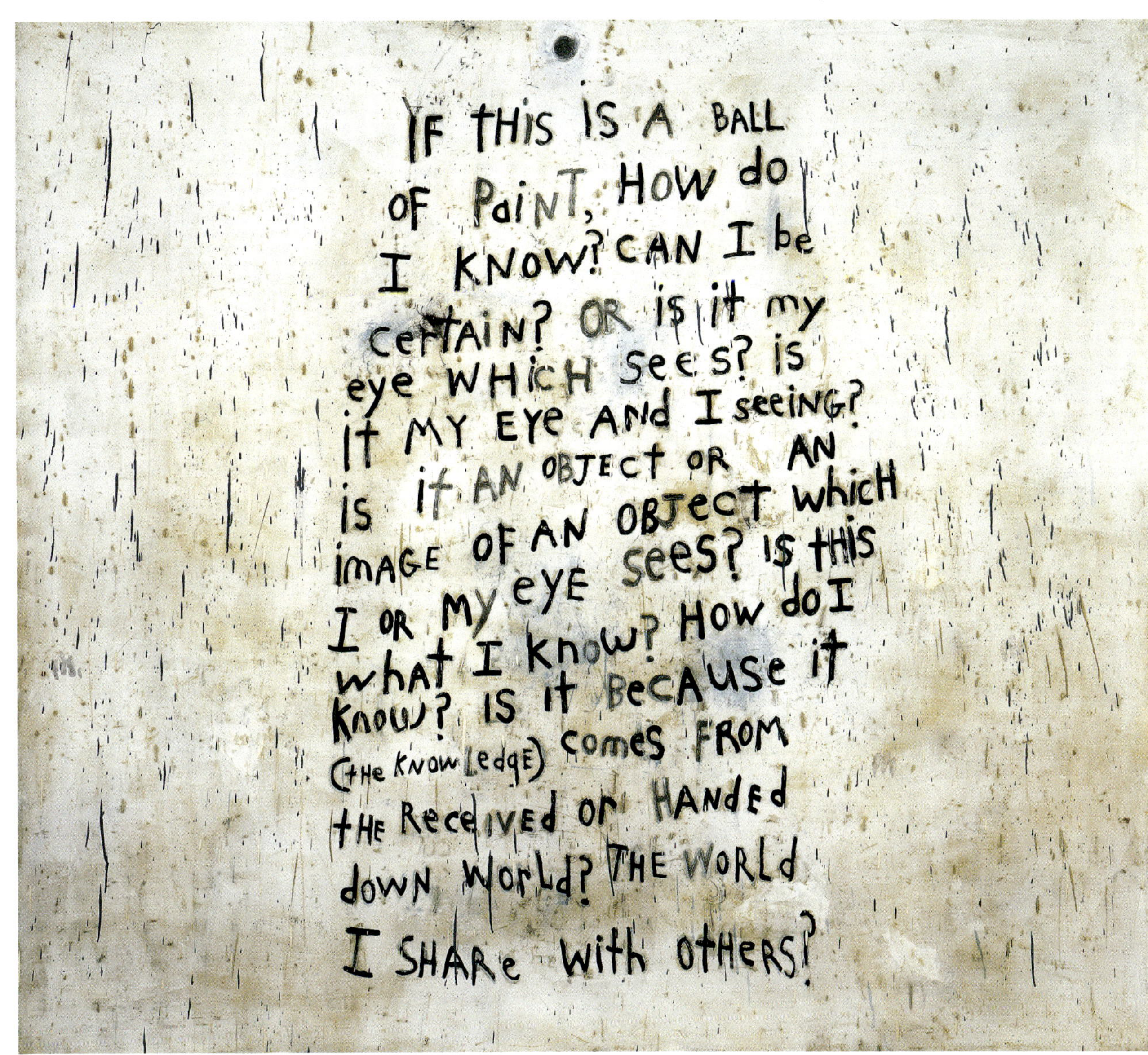

70. **Manifestation**, 2005

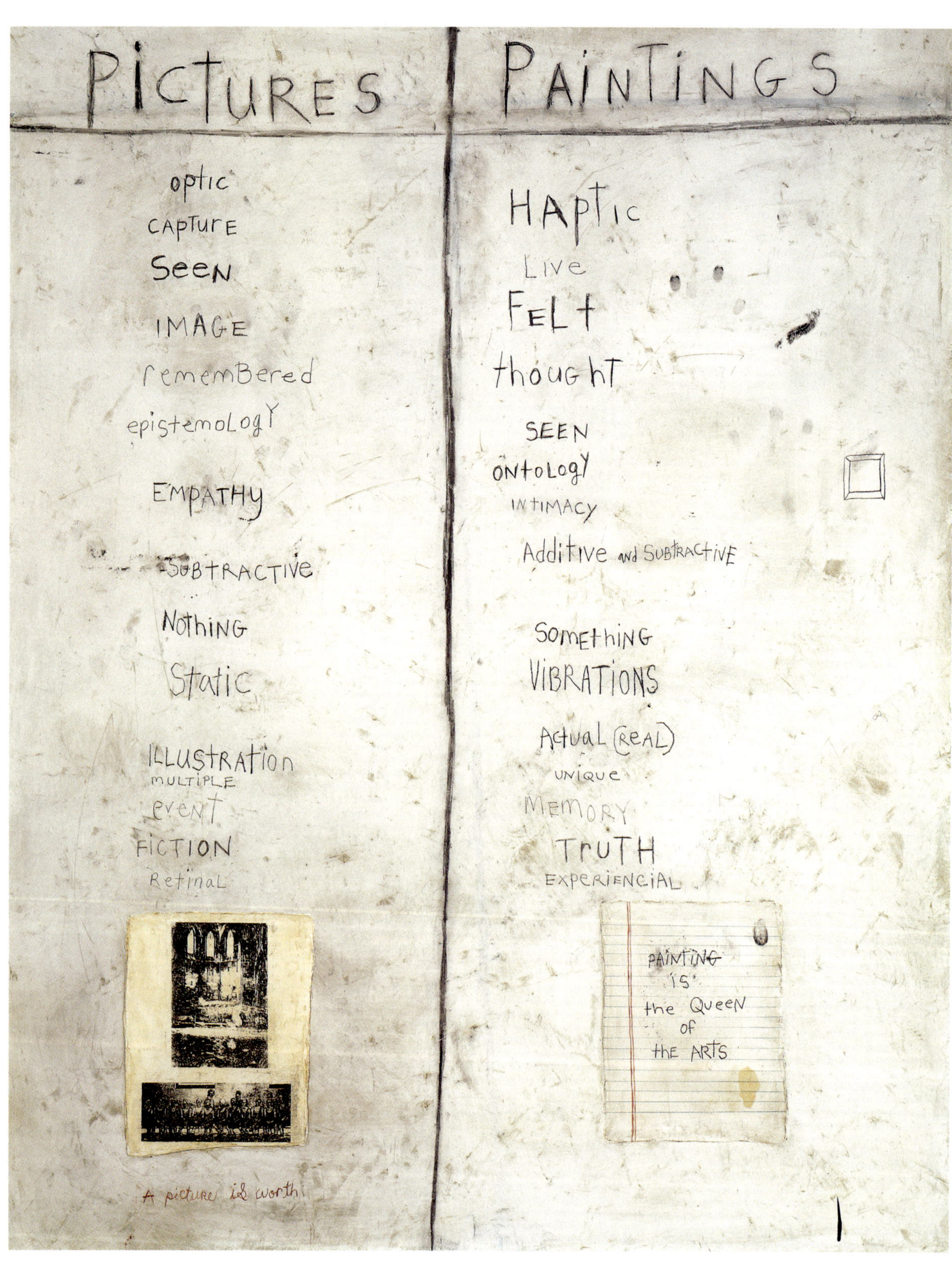

71. **Primary Research,** 2005

74. **A Painting,** 2006

I don't think that Bess influenced her so much as reinforced her. Certainly, by 1988, when Hirschl & Adler Modern, New York, exhibited a large selection of his work, Carnwath had become familiar with his work and thinking.[9] In *Stolen Borrowed* (2004; p. 128), the artist writes

> Good ideas r not made
> They are stolen

Carnwath is not appropriating the work of others (such as Bess), and her intention is not parodic. She does not accept the academic argument that in this "postmodern" era, painting's only goal is, at best, to celebrate its own death. Rather than trade in her autonomy for the acceptance of others she has set out to discover what can be verified about experience. Like other accomplished painters near her in age—I am thinking of Thomas Nozkowski, Catherine Murphy, and Mark Greenwold—Carnwath is familiar with an enormous breadth of art, ranging from the canonical to the marginalized and little known. All of these artists believe in the power of imagination and knowledge to transform into work that is authentic and felt. Additionally, all accept that painting is a craft tradition. In this regard, they share something with Manet, the belief that craft in tandem with paint's transformational powers enables one to merge ethics and the imagination.

There is a fourth artist whom I haven't mentioned, and that is Philip Guston. It seems to me that Carnwath, whose paintings bear almost no visual resemblance to Guston's late work, is his true heir. And in making this comparison, I hope it is clear that it arises from the high regard in which I hold Carnwath's work, and how much I think she has achieved.

Both Guston and Carnwath are traditionalists in the sense that they elected to work in oil paint on a flat surface, and decided that everything in their work would have to be made of paint. Both rejected the formalist injunction demanding that painters reify two-dimensionality in their work and eliminate subject matter and subjectivity, the personal. Starting in the late 1960s, Guston reintroduced spatiality and the depiction of things into his drawings; this led him to his celebrated late paintings, which burst upon the scene in 1970. For years now Carnwath has evolved a compressed and layered space in which one thing is placed directly on top of another. Thus, each artist's work involves spatiality without resorting to historical precedents such as perspective. But identifying formal affinities can take us only so far, since one can find such similarities among any number of artists.

The deeper connection between Carnwath and Guston has to do with their definition of the artist as an individual working alone in a room, and how they understand solitariness as intrinsic to human existence. In addition, each developed a language of things to which they persistently return in their paintings. Shoes, irons, and clocks appear in Guston's drawings of late 1940s, two decades before they became central symbolic presences in many of his paintings (which often allude to an artist's studio). In many of his later paintings, he makes direct reference to Piero della Francesca, as well as transforms his familiarity with works by Carlo Carra and Giorgio de Chirico—artists who had been deemed minor by many art historians—into his own compelling paintings. For nearly all of her career, Carnwath has used words and pictographs of both male and female pelvises, and other parts of the body. For more than a decade, her recurring elements have included the humanoid bunny, a delicately linear depiction of a tree stump, and the phrase "guilt-free zone" encircled by a dotted line. The difference, of course, is that Guston is largely pictorial—the obvious exception being Guston's drawings incorporating poems by Clark Coolidge, Bill Berkson, and his wife, Musa, and the many book covers he did for poets—while Carnwath combines the optical with text, signs, and words. But this dissimilarity should not blind us to their recognition of the fundamental human condition, solitude.

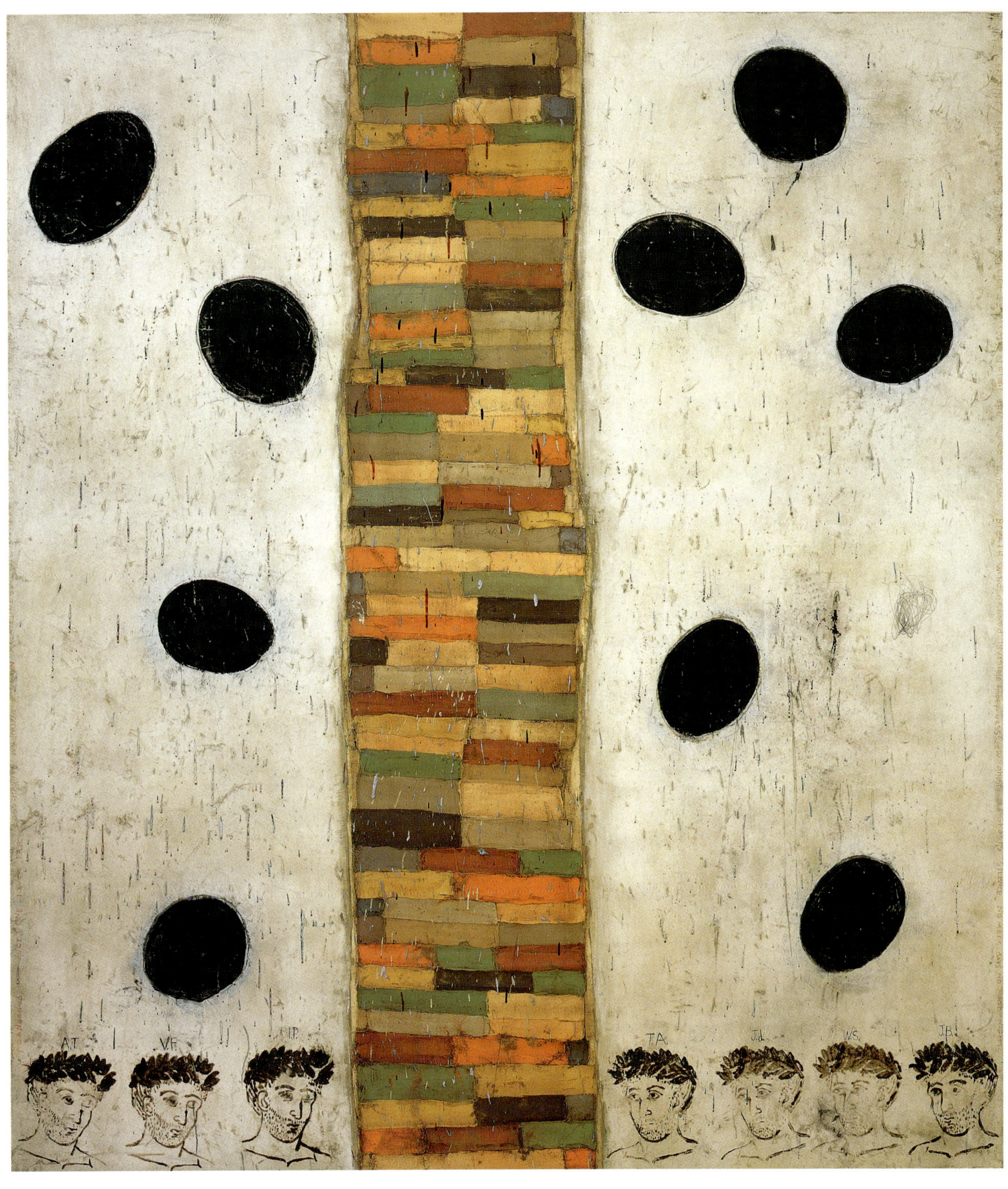

69. **Gone,** 2005

Both Carnwath and Guston accept their solitary state and do not lament it because they recognize that nothing they do can overcome it. Nor do they seek refuge in external doctrines, including the paradigms of security offered to them by theorists and critics. Rather, each defines the artist as an individual of no special merit who is capable of making out of commonly available materials an object that might cast a light on the paradoxes of existence and the artist's brief moment in it. (At its most basic, this project is both generous and antisocial.) Thus, what the two artists share is an ethic in which they are determined to be witnesses and give testimony. Guston's witness is a lumpy shape with a single eye; Carnwath's is a bedraggled, erect bunny. Both are battered, dismal beings that haven't stopped to feel sorry for themselves; they are active agents. In these surrogates, the viewer senses the artists' willingness to embrace their own awkwardness, rather than trying to cover it over. For them, being a witness means taking responsibility for all of their experiences, from the most exalted and sublime to the most commonplace and mundane.

Thus, Guston can depict a bowl piled high with cherries because they are what he likes to eat. Carnwath can make a list of reasons to get up in the morning. They celebrate ordinary life even as they knowingly face deep and disturbing issues. They recognize that domesticity offers no protection from the larger world, from time and mayhem. Guston depicts in *Head* (1975) the back of a head cut open, with stitches stretching across the open wound; Carnwath makes paintings in which she lists "worries" and "big worries." They deal with external events, personal memories, everyday occurrences, dreams, and flights of imagination, however dark or bright they may be.

And they deal with mortality. Guston painted *Tomb* (1978) two years before his death: a severely angled view of a painter's table, complete with irons, rocks, a burning cigarette, and a paintbrush thrust in a can. It's as if he left the room, with its burning cigarette, and might never return. Are the irons and rocks temporarily keeping death inside the black coffin, which is what the table resembles, and away from the artist? Tilted toward the picture plane, the objects on the table (or tomb) have been stopped in time, but one senses that they are about to come tumbling out of the painting into the world where we are standing.

Along the bottom of *Gone* (2005; p. 125), which was inspired by a news photograph of a funeral in the Middle East, Carnwath depicts a row of seven Etruscan heads that evoke Fayum portraits, in memory of woman friends, all of whom are artists. The heads are of young men; they convey a sense that their subjects died before their time. Above each head, Carnwath has painted her friend's initials: W.S., for Wendy Sussman; V.F., for Viola Frey; I.P., for Irene Pijoan; T.A., for Tre Arenz; J.D., for Jay DeFeo; J.B., for Joan Brown; A.T., for Anne Truitt. In placing the women's initials above the men's heads, she masculinizes them, a transformation that uses an image derived from history to comment on it. Black ellipses (they suggest turbaned heads) floating above the Etruscan portraits feel temporarily suspended in paint. Drips of black paint run down the white surface: gravity is inescapable. The stack of horizontal bars of muted colors running vertically down the middle of the painting is the artist's transformation of the coffins being carried through the streets, amid a throng of mourners.[10] The ellipses, Etruscan portraits, and stacked colors convey a feeling of rising, falling, and coming to rest. By connecting the deceased women to a funeral of "martyrs," essentially turning them into heroes who have made the ultimate sacrifice, Carnwath challenges a patriarchal worldview in which the male is the dominant figure.

Like Guston, Carnwath refuses to look away. In this, she continues a line going back to Leonardo, whose "Deluge" drawings are about the individual looking at chaos and immense destruction.[11] In being open to the world and its unpredictability, Carnwath devises no escape, nor does she ever fall into pretentiousness. This, I want to suggest, is a mark of her humility, and a sign of her greatness.

NOTES

1. John Yau interview with the artist, *The Brooklyn Rail* (November 2006). The interview can be found online, in the archive section, at www.brooklynrail.org.

2. For another view of Johns's art, see John Yau, *A Thing Among Things: The Art of Jasper Johns* (New York: Distributed Art Publishers, 2008).

3. Johns's innovations in this area have yet to be fully recognized. *See A Thing Among Things: The Art of Jasper Johns.*

4. Juan Rodriquez, "Body Language in Squeak Carnwath's Painting," *Squeak Carnwath: The Am-ness of Things,* exhibition brochure (Lake Worth, Fla.: Museum of Contemporary Art, Palm Beach Community College, 1999), n.p.

5. Squeak Carnwath, with Leah Levy, Ramsay Bell Breslin, and James E. B. Breslin, *Squeak Carnwath: Lists, Observations & Counting* (San Francisco: Chronicle Books, 1996). As the book's title suggests, Carnwath's paintings can be grouped in three categories.

6. While widespread, Squeak Carnwath's influence on younger artists has generally been overlooked. *Obit* anticipates Jane Hammond's *Fallen* (2005), in which "each unique handmade leaf is inscribed by the artist with the name of a U.S. soldier killed in Iraq." One difference is that Carnwath was the sole creator of *Obit,* while Hammond has help from a number of assistants in the ongoing work of *Fallen*.

7. Letter to Meyer Schapiro, in Michael Brenson, "Forrest Bess: Desire Ruled His Vision," *New York Times,* May 1, 1988.

8. *The Brooklyn Rail* (November 2006), see note 1.

9. Carnwath saw Bess's work soon after it was shown at the Whitney Museum (October 1981) in an exhibition organized by Barbara Haskell. Carnwath email to the author, June 18, 2008.

10. Carnwath summarized *Gone* in a phone conversation with the author, June 22, 2008.

11. Guston was inspired by Leonardo's "Deluge" drawings in his late paintings, such as *Night* (1977), *Deluge II* (1979), and *Group in Sea* (1979).

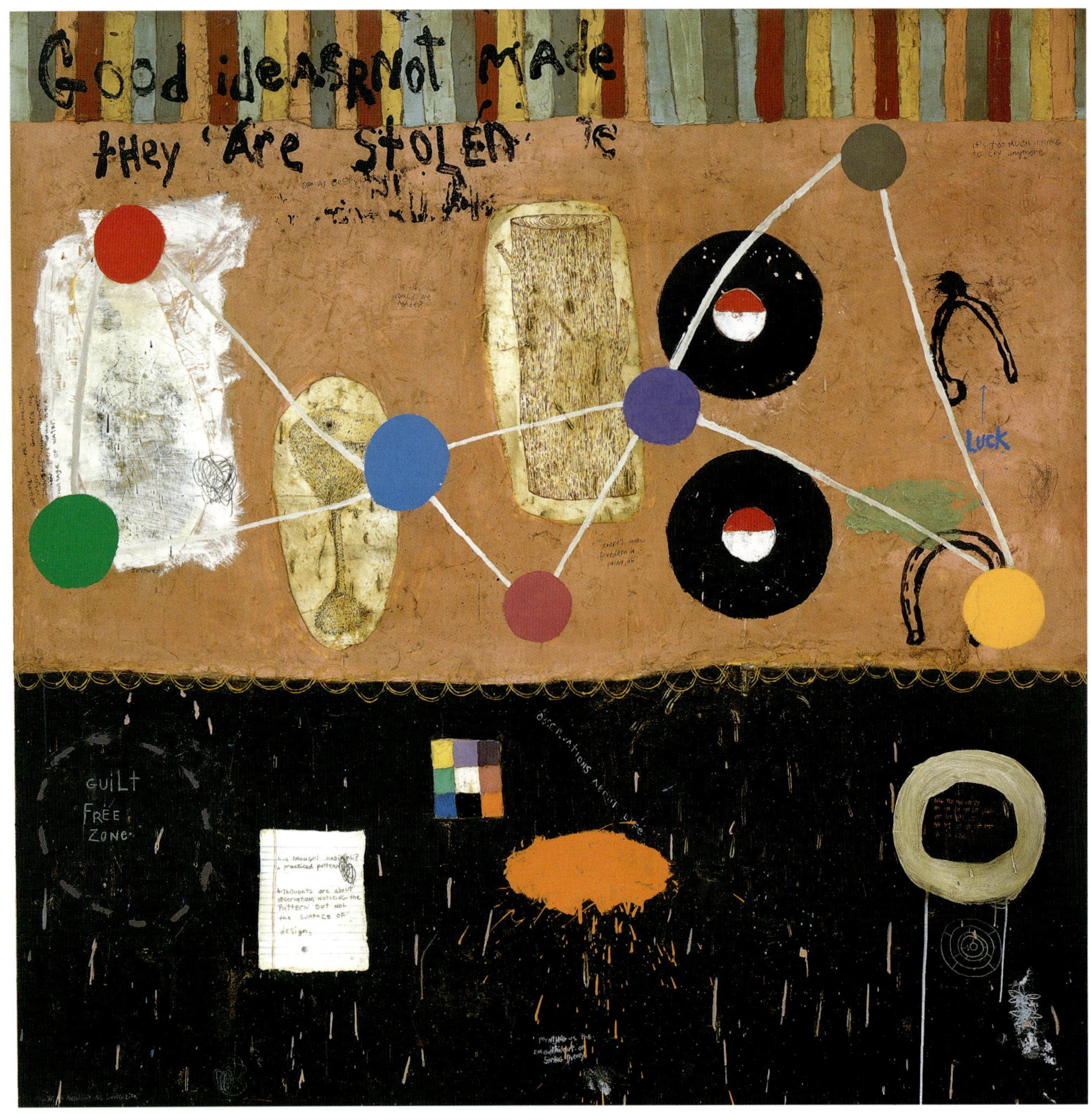

67. **Stolen Borrowed,** 2004

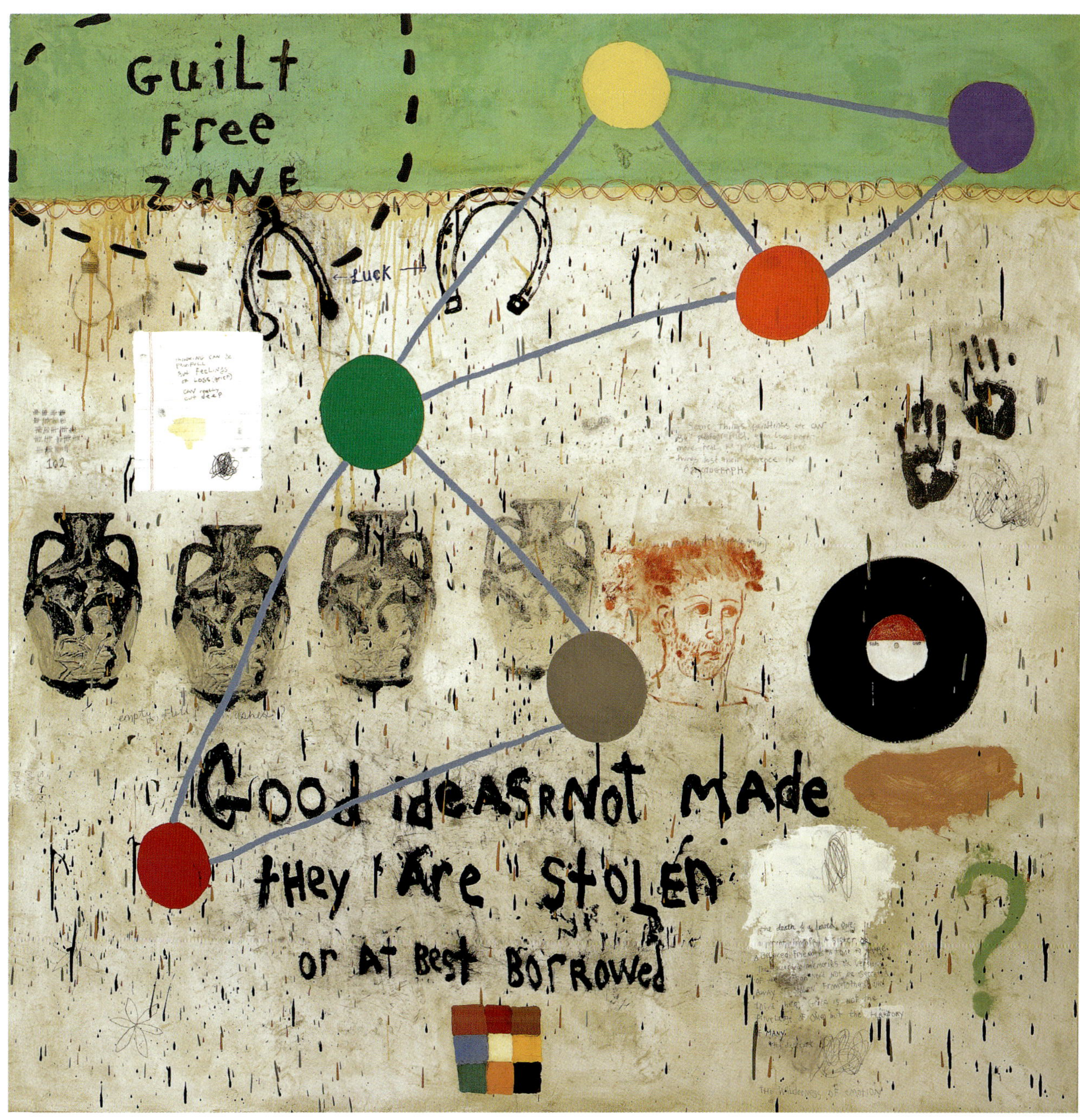

68. **Best Borrowed,** 2005

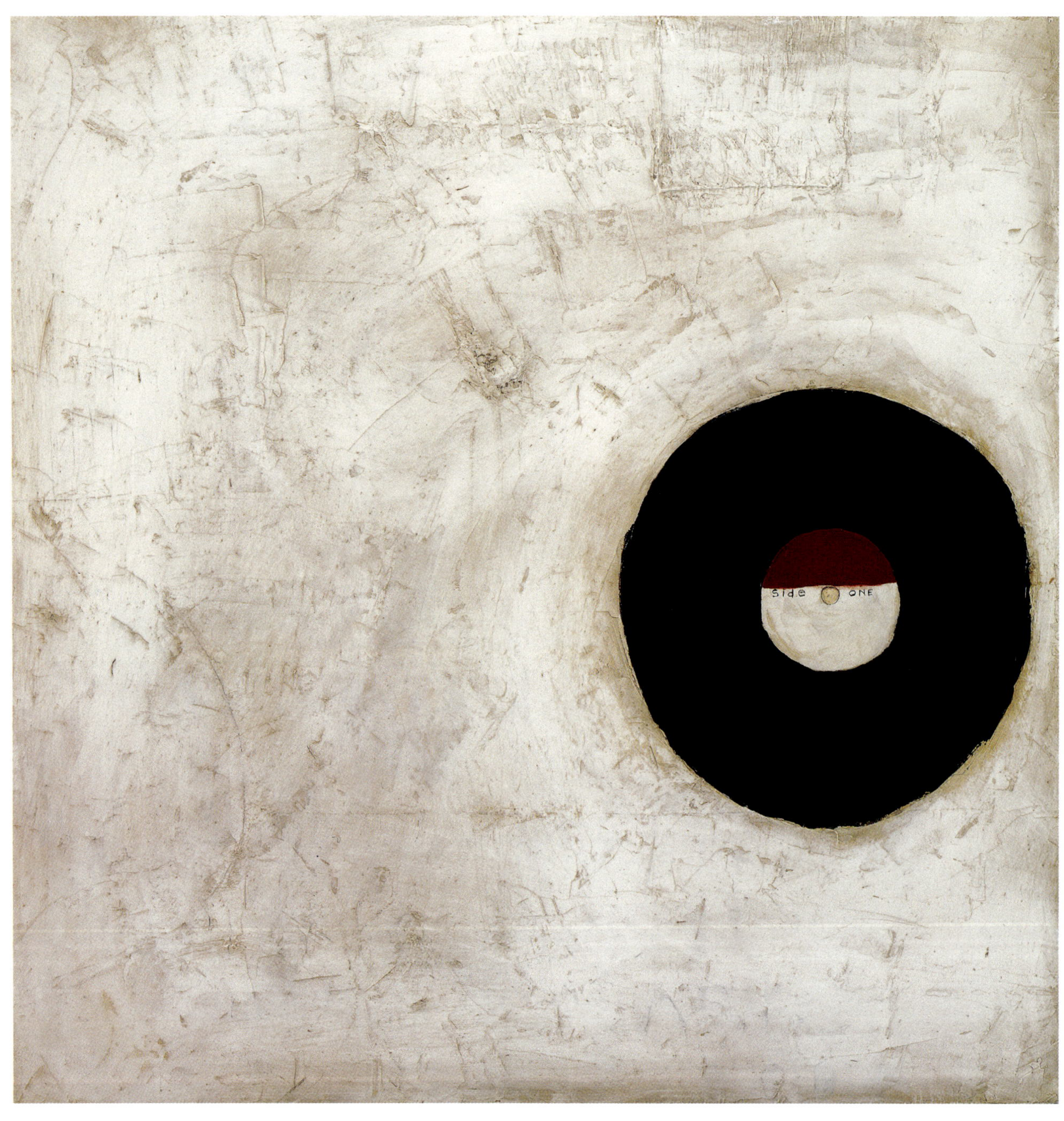

73. **Side One,** 2005

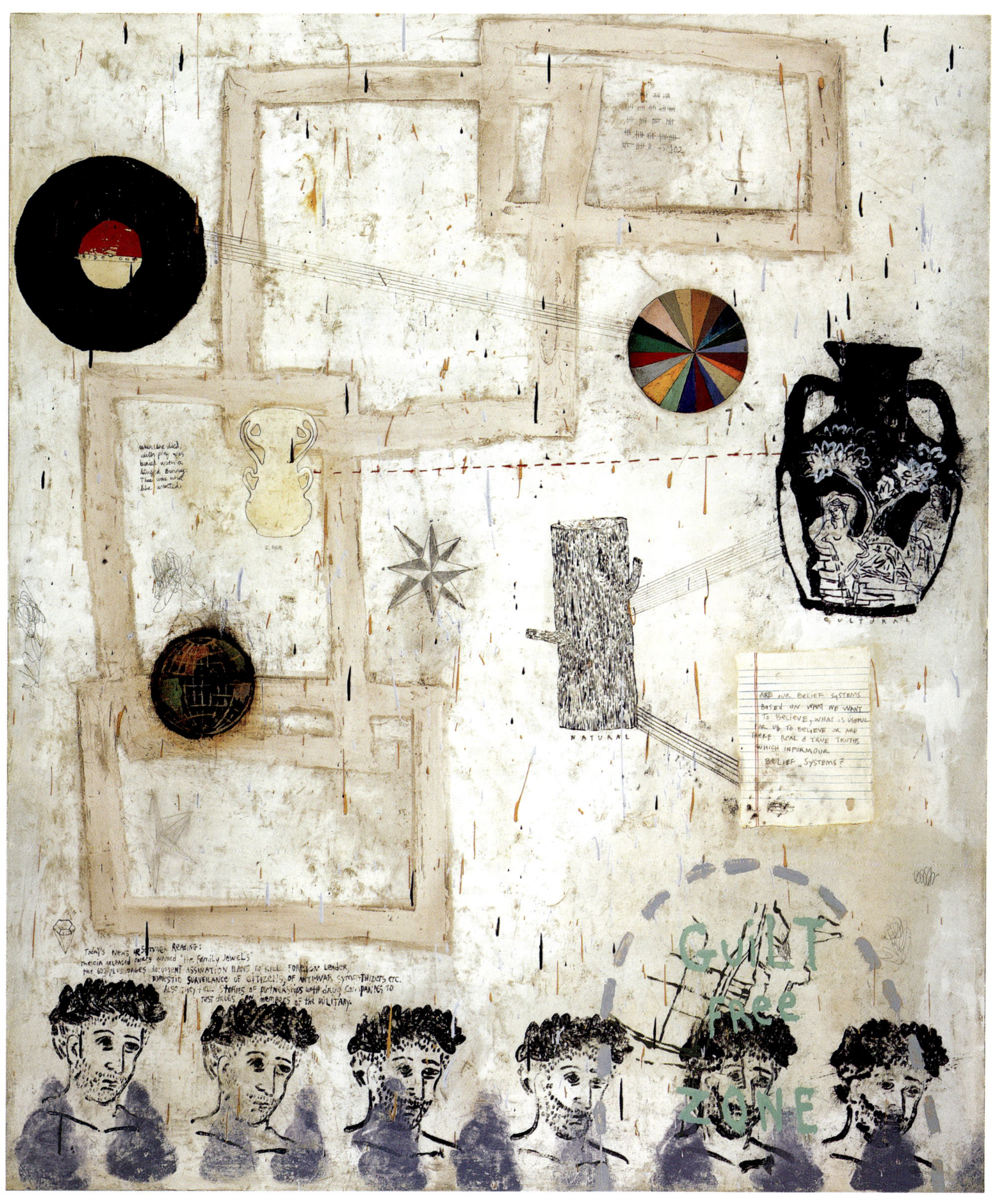

80. **Real and True**, 2007

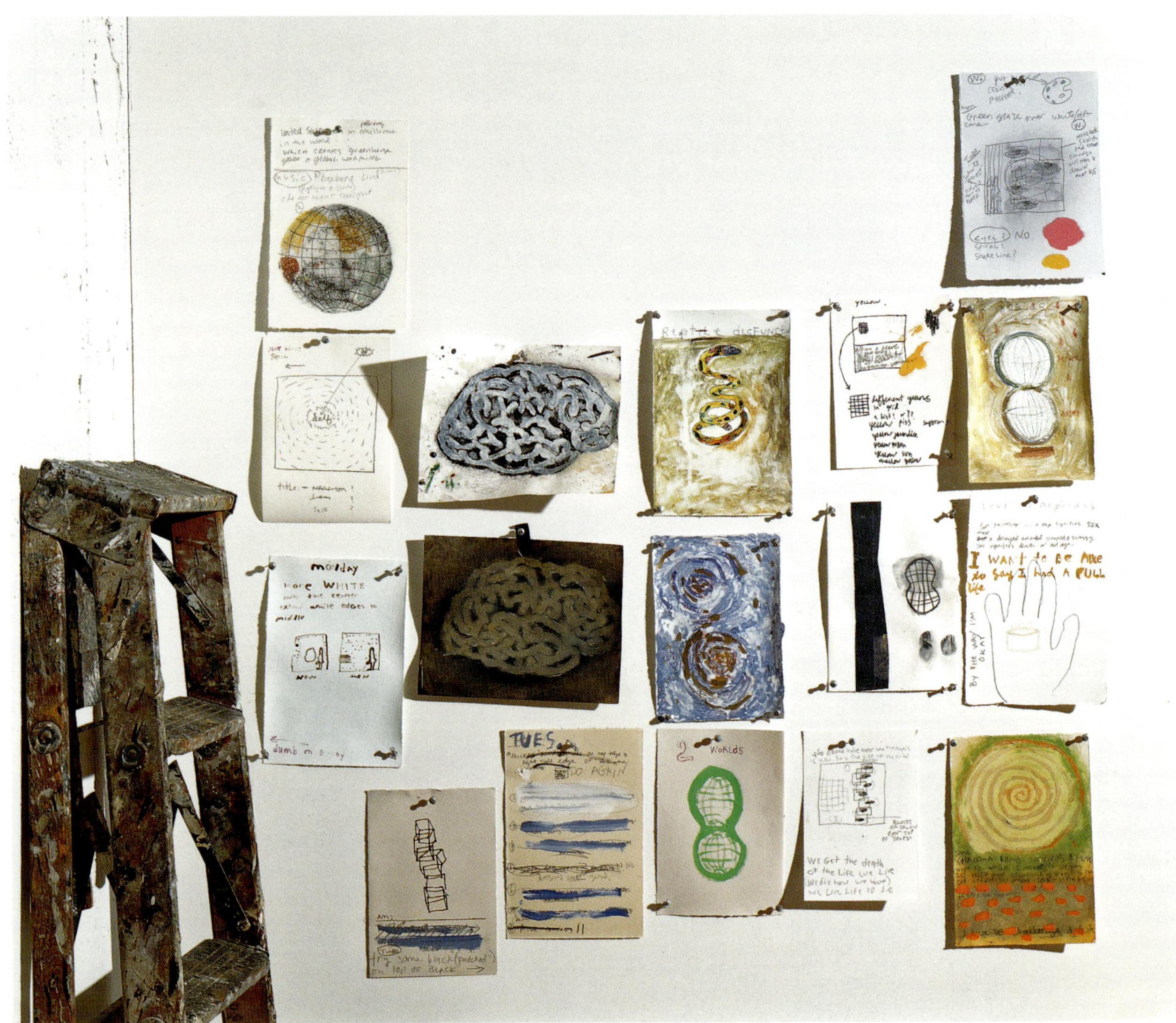

Egghouse studio, Oakland, c. 2000. © M. Lee Fatherree.

chronology

1947 Born May 24, in Abington, Pennsylvania. Shirley Carnwath Jr. (Squeak) is the first of six children born to Shirley and Samuel Carnwath.

1948–1964 Family moves frequently throughout the East Coast: Hanover, Pennsylvania; Plattsburg, Syracuse, and Port Kent, New York; Darien, Connecticut; Newton and Marblehead, Massachusetts. One year is also spent in Portland, Oregon.

1966 Graduates from Jenkintown High School, Jenkintown, Pennsylvania.

1966–1968 Attends and graduates from Monticello Junior College, Godfrey, Illinois.

1968 Attends summer program at Aegean School of Fine Arts (now Aegean Center for the Fine Arts), Paros, Greece. Meets fellow student Gary Knecht.

1968–1969 Attends Goddard College, Plainfield, Vermont.

1969 Moves to Bay Area with Knecht.

1970 Enrolls at California College of Arts and Crafts (CCAC), Oakland (now California College of the Arts). Studies with Viola Frey, Vernon Coykendall, Arthur Okamura, Charles Gill, and Ron Dahl.

1971 Stops attending classes. Works as shop master in CCAC ceramics department and as teaching assistant to ceramics instructor Vernon Coykendall.

Establishes studio in Oakland commune. Participates in the Food Conspiracy, a food-buying co-op in downtown Oakland.

Rents Oakland storefront and presents self-organized solo exhibition at Roxie & Toots' Salon d'Art.

1973 Marries Knecht.

Receives award in "Media," a juried exhibition at the Civic Arts Gallery, Walnut Creek, California.

1974–1975 Moves to Alameda, California.

Re-enrolls at CCAC; studies with Jay DeFeo, Viola Frey, and Dennis Leon.

1977 Receives MFA from CCAC, with high distinction in ceramics.

1977–1978 Works as community artist for Neighborhood Arts Program, Alameda County.

1978 Teaches at Ohlone College, Fremont, California, and is shop master in CCAC ceramics department.

1979 Teaches at CCAC as guest artist.

1980 Receives National Endowment for the Arts (NEA) Visual Artists Fellowship Grant.

One of three artists to receive San Francisco Museum of Modern Art's Society for the Encouragement of Contemporary Art (SECA) award, which includes museum exhibition of her work.

1980–1982 Returns to CCAC as shop master of ceramics department.

1982 Teaches at CCAC as guest artist.

First solo gallery exhibition in San Francisco at Hansen Fuller Goldeen Gallery.

1982–1986 Establishes studio and residence in downtown Oakland on 4th Street, near the city's produce district.

1982–1983 Teaches at University of California, Berkeley (UCB) as visiting artist. Teaching colleagues include Elmer Bischoff and Joan Brown.

1983 Creates suite of three intaglio prints, *The Elements Matter,* published by Bruce Velick Editions, San Francisco, and printed by Timothy Berry, Teaberry Press, Oakland.

Joins faculty at University of California, Davis (UCD). Teaching colleagues include Robert Arneson, Mike Henderson, Ralph Johnson, Manuel Neri, Roland Petersen, and Wayne Thiebaud.

1985 Receives second NEA Visual Artists Fellowship Grant.

1986 Etching included in print portfolio of ten artists' work, *Personal Experience,* published by Creative Growth, Oakland.

1986–1987 Relocates studio and residence to a former furniture warehouse at 5th and Adeline in Oakland.

1987 With Knecht, establishes the "Egghouse," a former egg warehouse in the produce district of Oakland. The building accommodates the artist's studio, residence, and six additional studios.

1988 Receives tenure as associate professor at UCD.

Creates first series of monoprints at Magnolia Editions, Oakland, working with Don and Era Farnsworth.

1989 First solo exhibition at John Berggruen Gallery, San Francisco, which continues to represent her work.

Produces series of etchings at Limestone Press, San Francisco, with Hank Hine.

1990 Receives grant award from the Alice Baber Art Fund, New York.

Produces series of monoprints, *The Man in Love*, at Smith Andersen, Palo Alto, California.

1991 Participates in two-week artist-in-residency program at Anderson Ranch Arts Center, Snowmass, Colorado, where she creates a series of monotypes.

Produces four lithographs at Tamarind Institute, Albuquerque.

1991–1995 Begins collaboration with Experimental Workshop, San Francisco, creating a series of monotypes, woodcuts, and etchings.

1992 Promoted to full professor at UCD.

Travels to Europe to follow the Piero della Francesca trail in Italy with Knecht and artist Maria Olivieri Quinn; to Russia, to participate in St. Petersburg group exhibition "Art Contact"; to France, to study Monet's Giverny garden and to drive, with artist Susan Martin, to Colmar to view Matthias Grünewald's Isenheim Altarpiece.

Artwork reproduced as part of artists Imagery Series wine labels for Glen Ellen Winery, Glen Ellen, California.

1993 Travels to Paris for two weeks to study art and architecture.

Participates in four-week artist-in-residency program at Djerassi Foundation, Woodside, California.

1993–1994 Takes one-year leave of absence from UCD to teach and assume associate dean position at CCAC.

1994 Solo exhibition "Squeak Carnwath" surveys seven years of painting. Organized by curator Trinkett Clark for Chrysler Museum, Norfolk, Virginia. Exhibition travels nationally.

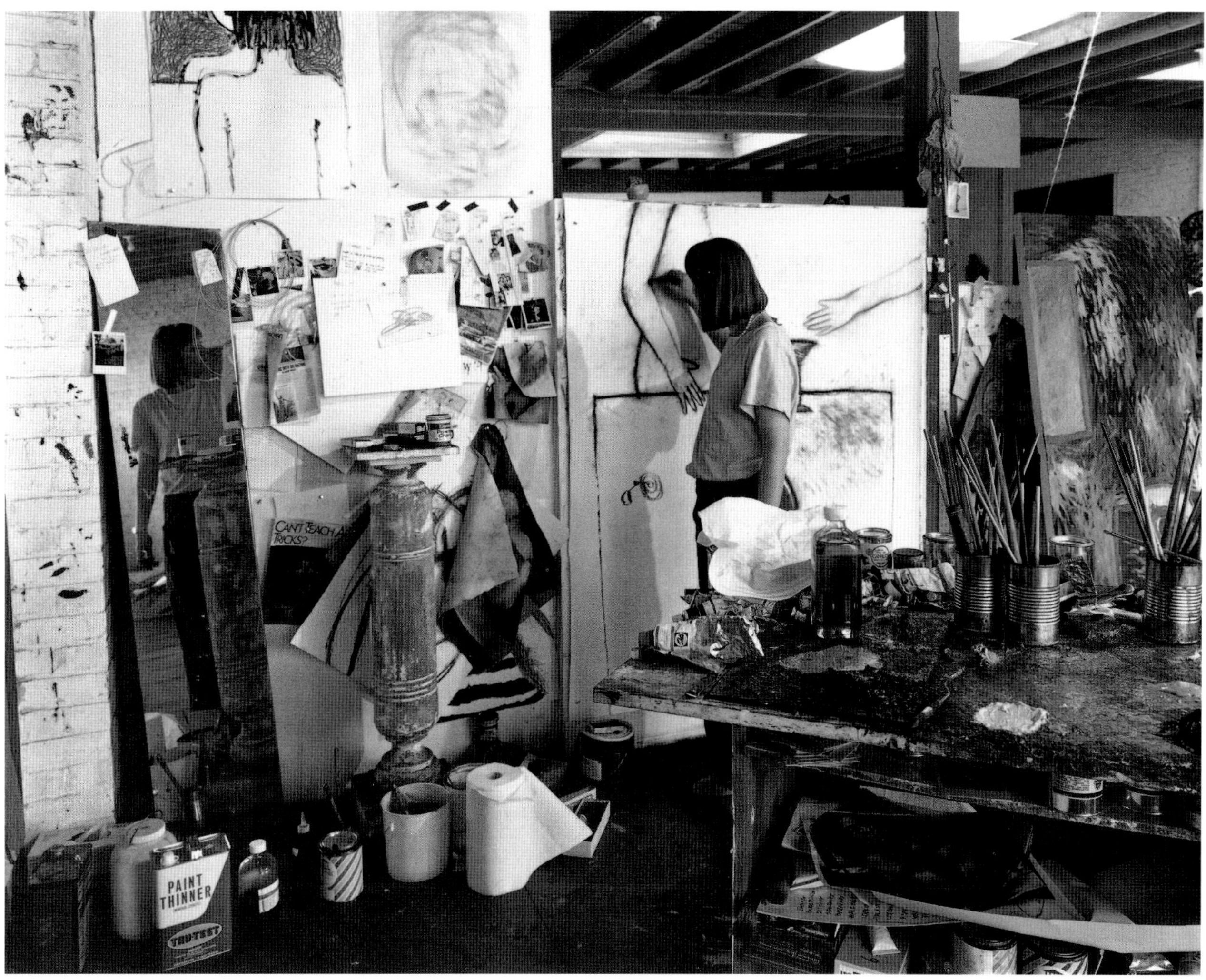

Squeak Carnwath working in 4th Street studio, Oakland, c. 1984–1985. © M. Lee Fatherree.

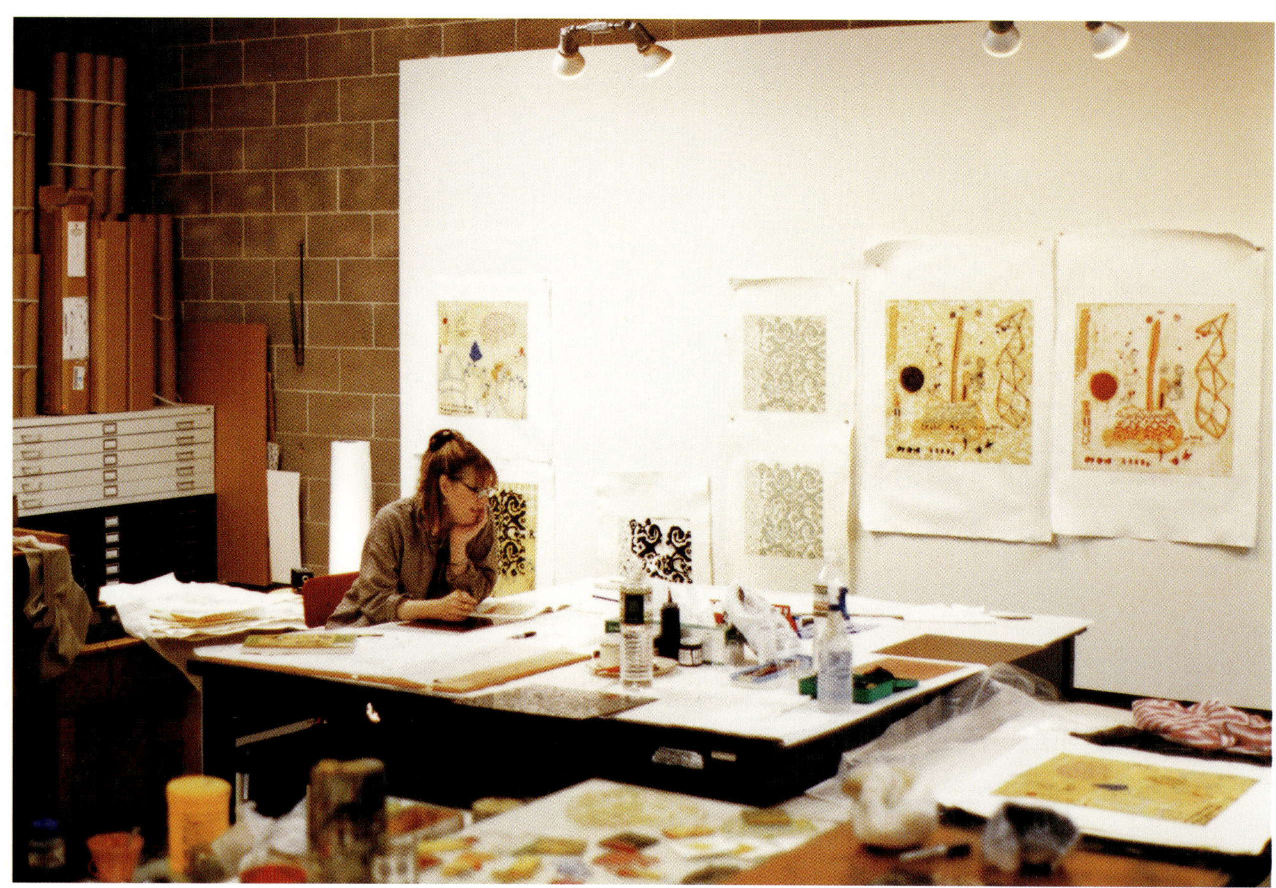

Squeak Carnwath working at Paulson Press, Emeryville, c. 1997. © Paulson Press.

Participates in artist-in-residence program at Pilchuck Glass School, Stanwood, Washington, producing glass sculpture, a series of monotypes, and egg tempera works.

Receives Guggenheim Foundation fellowship.

1994–1995 Extends leave of absence from UCD to work full-time in studio.

1995 Travels with Knecht to Paris. Continues her studies of art and architecture.

Returns to UCD; teaches and advises in graduate art program.

1996 Receives Alma B. C. Shapiro Residency for a Woman Painter at Yaddo, Saratoga Springs, New York, and spends three weeks in the artists and writers community.

1997 Creates first series of intaglio prints with Pam Paulson and Renee Bott at Paulson Press, Emeryville.

1998 Travels to Yale University, New Haven, as visiting artist at School of Art.

Joins UCB Department of Art Practice as Professor-in-Residence; continues to teach there.

Receives Modern Masters Award from Marin Museum Association, Ross, California.

1999 Travels to University of Arkansas, Little Rock, as visiting artist in Department of Art.

Travels to Vermont Studio Center, Johnson, as visiting artist.

2000 Completes *Fly, Flight, Fugit*, a seventeen-by-seventeen-foot artwork of enameled metal panels, for the San Francisco Arts Commission; it is installed at San Francisco International Airport.

2001 Receives Awards for Visual Artists 2001/2002 from Flintridge Foundation, Pasadena, California.

Receives Special Recognition Award from Precita Eyes Muralists Association, San Francisco, for San Francisco International Airport commission.

2002 Participates in Painting's Edge program, Idyllwild Arts, Idyllwild, California.

2003 Participates in workshop at Anderson Ranch Art Center, Snowmass Village, Colorado.

Begins producing tapestries at Magnolia Editions, Oakland.

2006 Works at Tandem Press, University of Wisconsin, Madison, which publishes eight editions by the artist.

Produces series of mixed-media collographs at Island Press, Washington University, St. Louis.

2008 Receives tenure as full professor at UCB.

Receives Emil & Dines Carlsen Award, "183rd Annual: An Invitational Exhibition of Contemporary American Art," National Academy Museum & School of Fine Arts, New York.

selected bibliography

Kathy Borgogno and Alexandra Franco

INTERVIEWS

Fisher, Frances Shedd. "A Conversation with Squeak Carnwath." *Nielsen Gallery News* (Boston), July 19, 2006, n.p.

Stone, Nick. "Lunch-Break: A Conversation with Squeak Carnwath." *Magnolia Editions Newsletter*, no. 9, July 2006, 3-7.

Thym, Jolene. "Squeak Carnwath." *Oakland Tribune*, May 21, 1996, CUE-2.

Van Proyen, Mark and Phyllis Shafer. "Squeak Carnwath: Excerpts from an Interview . . . " *Éxpo-See*, January/February 1984, n.p.

Walrod, Anne Gray. "Squeak Carnwath." Interview September 25, 1986, in Moira Roth, editor, *Connecting Conversations: Interviews with 28 Bay Area Women Artists* (Oakland, Calif.: Eucalyptus Press, Mills College, 1988), 22-28.

Whittaker, Richard. "A Conversation with Squeak Carnwath." *The Secret Alameda*, no. 6, 1993, 2-8.

———. "Advocate of the Unwatched Life: A Conversation with Squeak Carnwath." Interview April 2, 1993, in *Works & Conversations*, no. 1, March 1998, 18-25, 58.

———. "Squeak Carnwath." Interview December 1992, in *The Conversations: Interviews with Sixteen Contemporary Artists* (Delray Beach, Fla: Whale and Star, 2007), 36-47.

———. "Interview: Squeak Carnwath." Interview March 2, 2001. http://www.conversations.org/story.php?sid=20.

———. *Squeak Carnwath: Life Line* (San Francisco: John Berggruen Gallery, 2001). Exhibition catalogue, 2001.

Yau, John. "In Conversation: Squeak Carnwath with John Yau." *The Brooklyn Rail: Critical Perspectives on Arts, Politics and Culture*, November 2006, 48-50.

BOOKS

See also Selected Exhibition History.

Albright, Thomas. *Art in the San Francisco Bay Area, 1945-1980.* Berkeley and Los Angeles: University of California Press, 1985: 266.

Audette, Anna Held, comp. and ed. *100 Creative Drawing Ideas.* Boston and London: Shambhala, 2004: 102.

Bullis, Douglas. *100 Artists of the West Coast.* Atglen, Pa.: Schiffer Publishing Ltd., 2003: 76-77.

Byrne, Chris. *The Original Print: Understanding Technique in Contemporary Fine Printmaking.* Madison, Wisc.: Guild Publishing, 2002: 6.

Carnwath, Squeak. *Squeak Carnwath: Lists, Observations & Counting.* San Francisco: Chronicle Books, 1996.

Di Rosa, Rene. *Local Color: The di Rosa Collection of Contemporary California Art.* San Francisco: Chronicle Books, 1999: 68-69.

Gamblin, Noriko. "Squeak Carnwath," in Noriko Gamblin and Karen Jacobson, ed., *Flintridge Foundation Awards for Visual Artists.* Pasadena, Calif.: Flintridge Foundation, 2002: 12-15.

Johnstone, Mark and Leslie Aboud Holzman. *Epicenter: San Francisco Bay Area Art Now.* San Francisco: Chronicle Books, 2002: 34-39.

Landauer, Susan, ed. *Selections: The San Jose Museum of Art Permanent Collection.* San Jose, Calif.: San Jose Museum of Art, 2004: 50-51.

Moure, Nancy Dustin Wall. *California Art: 450 Years of Painting & Other Media.* Los Angeles: Dustin Publications, 1998: 517.

Nugent, Bob. *Imagery: Art for Wine.* San Francisco: Wine Appreciation Guild, 2006: 36-37.

Rosenberg, Randy Jayne, et al. *The Missing Peace: Artists & The Dalai Lama.* San Rafael, Calif.: Earth Aware, 2006: 144-145, 164.

Tsujimoto, Karen. "Artistic Harvest," in Abby Wasserman, ed., *The Spirit of Oakland.* Carlsbad, Calif.: Heritage Media Corp., 2000: 55.

SELECTED ARTICLES AND REVIEWS

Ahlander, Leslie Judd. "Abstract Ideas and Landscapes Populate the Galleries." *Miami News,* December 18, 1987, 5C.

Albright, Thomas. "Emerging, Diverging and Submerging at Oakland Museum." *San Francisco Chronicle,* October 26, 1982, 40.

———. "Imagism and a New Look." *San Francisco Chronicle*, March 8, 1982, 40.

———. "Modest Magic, Conventionalized Personalism." *San Francisco Chronicle,* September 1, 1980, 41.

Allman, Paul. "Art Who?" *New Vistas,* February 15, 1975, 14.

Armitage, Diane. "Squeak Carnwath: Selections from the Studio." *THE: Santa Fe's Monthly Magazine of the Arts*, November 2002, 38.

Artner, Alan. "Carnwath is Rare Modern Artist of Everyday." *Chicago Tribune,* October 30, 1986, 13G .

———. "Carnwath's Canvases Reflect Classic Looks at Domestic Life." *Chicago Tribune,* March 8, 1985, 38.

"Awards," *Berkeleyan* (University of California, Berkeley), January 23, 2002.

Baker, Kenneth. "Carnwath's Memories Release Rich Abstraction." *San Francisco Chronicle*, November 7, 1998, E1.

———. "Squeak Carnwath Roars at Berggruen." *San Francisco Chronicle*, September 21, 1989, E5.

———. "Squeak Carnwath's Interplay of Words and Images." *San Francisco Chronicle*, September 11, 1991, E2.

Balken, Debra Brickor. "Squeak Carnwath at LedisFlam." *Art in America*, February 1994, 103–104.

Beeler, Monique. "Word Lists, Color, Questions Mark 'Still Happy' Show." *The Argus* (Oakland), May 31, 2002, 26.

Bell, J. Bowyer, Douglas F. Maxwell, Robert M. Murdock. "Three Critical Comments: Squeak Carnwath at David Beitzel Gallery." *Review Magazine*, February 1, 1998, 26–28.

Biles, Jan. "Painting's Imagery Has Lawrence Link." *The Mag/Lawrence Journal World*, December 21, 1995.

Boettger, Suzaan. "From the Sunny Side: Six East Bay Artists." *Artforum,* January 1983, 82–83.

———. "'The Impolite Figure,' Bannam Place Exhibition Space and Southern Exposure Gallery." *Artforum*, October 2, 1983, 81.

———. "Squeak Carnwath." *Artforum,* Summer 1984, 98.

Bonetti, David. "Gallery Watch: Exhibitions Focus on Artists' Visions of '70s." *San Francisco Examiner,* September 16, 1994, D8, D9.

———. "Three S.F. Artists in Their Prime." *San Francisco Examiner*, October 29, 1998, C1.

Bourbon, Matthew. "Squeak Carnwath at David Beitzel." *NY Arts,* International edition, May 2000, 39.

Breslin, Ramsay Bell. "Those Who Forget Her Story." *Express*, February 8, 1991, 30.

Brookman, Donna. "A Bay Area Diversity." *Artweek,* October 15, 1988, 11.

Brown, Betty Ann. "Songs of the Bees." *Artweek*, March 11, 1989, 5.

Brunson, Jamie. "Squeak Carnwath: Seeing in the Dark." *Art Muse*, Summer 1998, 1–2.

Brzezinski, Jamey. "Enigmatic Extremities: Squeak Carnwath at John Berggruen Gallery." *Artweek*, September 26, 1991, 11.

Bulmer, Marge. "Squeak Carnwath." *Northern California ArtScene,* June 1994, 4.

Burkhart, Dorothy. "Promising Futures." *San Jose Mercury News,* July 17, 1988, 18–20, 27–28.

Burstein, Joanne. "From the Sunny Side: Six East Bay Artists." *Artweek*, October 23, 1982, 1.

Butterfield, David. "National Recognition for Alameda Artist." *Alameda Times-Star* (Calif.), November 10, 1980, 3.

Camper, Fred. "On Exhibit: Art Chicago 2002's Free Thinkers." *Chicago Reader*, May 10, 2002, 34.

"Carnwath Exhibition." *Ceramics Monthly,* February 1978, 83-85.

Cebulski, Frank. "Ghosts, Textures and Sound." *Artweek*, September 20, 1980, 3.

Cohn, Abby. "Bedford Gallery Goes for the Gold with the Illuminating Show 'Yellow.'" *San Francisco Chronicle,* February 18, 2000, C4.

Colby, Joy Hakanson. "Symbolism Figures Big in these Artists' Visions." *Detroit News,* May 13, 1994, 4D.

Coleman, Sarah. "Squeak Carnwath: Through November 14, John Berggruen Gallery." *San Francisco Bay Guardian*, October 28, 1998, 101.

Cook, Katherine. "Language into Image." *Artweek,* September 6, 1990, 14-15.

Corbett, William. "Squeak Carnwath: Off the Record." *Artscope Magazine*, November/December 2006, 16.

Cotter, Holland. "Squeak Carnwath at LedisFlam Gallery." *New York Times,* September 17, 1993, C18.

Curtis, Cathy. "Looking for Romance." *Artweek,* March 3, 1984, 5-6.

Cutajar, Mario. "Squeak Carnwath." *ArtScene*, December 1992, 18-19.

Da Silva, Analucia. "Squeak Carnwath and Viola Frey Have Contributed to Oakland's Art Tradition." *Oakland Tribune*, January 1, 2000, 11.

Degener, Patricia. "Exhibits at Three Galleries." *St. Louis Post-Dispatch*, June 22, 1983, 7D.

Deragon, Rick. "Artist's Day." *Monterey County Herald* (Calif.), September 25, 1992, 3D.

Diehl, Carol. "Squeak Carnwath at LedisFlam." *ARTnews*, December 1993, 132-133.

Dietsch, Deborah. "Works with Words." *Sun Sentinel* (South Florida), April 11, 1999, 3D.

Downs, David, Brady Kahn. "On the Wall" (review of "Guilt Free Zone"). *East Bay Express*, July 6-12, 2005, 33.

Edelstein, Wendy. "Bunnies, Boring Objects, and the Guilt-Free Zone." *Berkeleyan* (University of California, Berkeley). October 31, 2007, 8.

Engelfried, Sally. "Squeak Roars." *510 Magazine: East Bay Arts and Culture,* December 1994, 35-36.

Farr, Sheila. "Bold Paintings by Bay Area Artist." *Seattle Times*, June 10, 2005.

———. "Fall Shows Liven Up Pioneer Square Galleries." *Seattle Times,* September 14, 2001.

Frankel, David. "Squeak Carnwath at David Beitzel Gallery." *Artforum International*, October 1996, 116.

Frankenstein, Alfred. "Serene and Mystic Art Work." *San Francisco Chronicle,* November 17, 1978, 68.

Goodman, Jonathan. "Squeak Carnwath at David Beitzel." *Art in America*, December 2000, 125.

Henry, Gerrit. "Squeak Carnwath at Shea & Beker." *Art in America,* October 1990, 211-212.

Iannaccone, Carmine. "Squeak Carnwath at Dorothy Goldeen." *Art Issues*, January/February 1996, 43.

Jordan, Jim. "Drawn to Richmond," *East Bay Express,* July 10, 1987, 17.

Kandel, Susan. "Squeak Carnwath." *Arts Magazine,* Summer 1989, 104.

Ketcham, Diane. "Squeak's Free-wheeling Style: Eastbay Painter Emerging to Semi-stardom with Solo Show." *Oakland Tribune*, September 15, 1991, 11.

King, Sarah. "Squeak Carnwath at David Beitzel." *Art in America*, September 1998, 133.

Kirsch, Elisabeth. "The Stories of Art—Tales Continued." *Kansas City Star*, May 14, 1999, 32.

Knaff, Devorah L. "Extraordinary Depictions of Ordinary Things." *Press-Enterprise* (Riverside, Calif.), November 6, 2000, C10.

Kuenstler, Emily. "Squeak Carnwath at Paulson Press." *Artweek*, July/August 2005, 17.

Lee, Anthony W. "Squeak Carnwath." *Art of California,* May 1991, 50-54.

Levy, Mark. "Squeak Carnwath: Reclaiming Lost Territory." *Artspace: A Magazine of Contemporary Art*, January/February 1990, 35–39.

Liu, Timothy. "Squeak Carnwath." *New Art Examiner*, September 2000, 60.

Lord, Roberta. "Examining the Evidence." *New Times*, February 27, 1997, 20.

Manoogian, Bridget. "Reconstructing Carnwath." *Shift X*, 1990, 16–18.

Matthews, Lydia. "Stories History Didn't Tell Us." *Artweek*, February 14, 1991, 1, 15–16.

McCloud, John. "Not Boxed In." *SF: The Magazine of Design and Style*, May 1991, 100–105, 112–114.

McCloud, Mac. "Patinae and Pentimenti: Paintings as Palimpsests in Santa Monica." *Visions Art Quarterly*, Spring 1991, 36.

McClure, Lissa. "Squeak Carnwath at David Beitzel Gallery." *Review Magazine*, June 1996, 28.

McDonald, Robert. "Art Review: Five Young Artists' View of the Human Condition." *Los Angeles Times*, San Diego County edition, February 22, 1986.

McKenna, Kristine. "The Galleries: Santa Monica." *Los Angeles Times*, February 24, 1989, 15.

McQuaid, Cate. "Minimalist Touch Makes the Most of Everyday Materials." *Boston Globe*, November 2, 2006, C9.

Miro, Marsha. "Artists' Paintings Share Childlike Vision." *Detroit Free Press*, May 24, 1994, 9.

Moyle, Marilyn. "UCD Art Professors Show Their Work in Joint Exhibit." *Davis Enterprise* (*Weekend Magazine*), October 14, 1990, 4.

Muller, Christopher. "Nelson Displays Faculty Art." *California Aggie: REVUE*, October 9, 1985, 8.

Nadaner, Dan. "What Only Painting Can Do." *Artweek*, January 25, 1986, 3-4.

Ollman, Leah. "UC Women Faculty Artists Prove Their Worth." *Los Angeles Times*, San Diego County edition, June 3, 1988.

———. "Wonder of Life Bathes Carnwath's Canvases." *Los Angeles Times*, San Diego County edition, May 11, 1990, 19B.

Panczenko, Paula McCarthy. "Squeak Carnwath's New Prints Delight the Eye." *Tandem Press*, Summer 2006, 1–3.

Peterson, Diane. "Artist's Early Drawings Offer Insight." *On Q: The Press Democrat*, (Santa Rosa, Calif.), July 26, 1998, 8.

Pincus, Robert L. "Artist Masters Mix of Visual, Literary." *San Diego Union*, May 1, 1990, E4.

Preston, Jane. "Media at Walnut Creek." *Artweek*, November 24, 1973, 5.

Raynor, Vivien. "Art: Gauguin in Brittany in Quest of Primitivism." *New York Times*, July 10, 1987.

Roder, Sylvie. "Tales Old and New." *Artweek*, June 4, 1983, 5.

Rose, Joan. "Sensuous Exhibits at Contemporary," *Honolulu Advertiser*, November 20, 1994, G10.

Roth, Charlene. "Squeak Carnwath at Sweeney Art Gallery." *Artweek*, December 2000, 19–20.

Rubin, Michael. "Two Contrasting Artists Rising in Prominence." *St. Louis Globe Democrat*, June 25, 1983, 6F.

Sardar, Zahid. "A Lightness of Being: Artist Squeak Carnwath Commands Light and Shade in her Oakland Loftspace." *San Francisco Examiner Magazine*, June 2, 1996, 16–19.

———. "Squeak Carnwath." *Western Interiors and Design*, July/August, 2005, 33-38.

Scarborough, James. "Emotive Color and Line." *Artweek*, March 20, 1982, 4.

Schwan, Gary. "California Artist's Works Engender New Appreciation of Painted Word." *Palm Beach Post*, March 26, 1999, 36.

Schwellenbach, Ashley. "Thou Shalt Remain, in Midst of Other Woe." *New Times*, February 21–28, 2008, 18.

Shere, Charles. "Born Innocent: Artist's Style Matures." *Oakland Tribune*, January 21, 1986, C1–C2.

———. "A Handsome Showing in Various Media at S.F. Galleries." *Oakland Tribune*, September 30, 1980, C-9.

———. "Painting Worth Looking At." *Oakland Tribune*, October 10, 1982, H6.

Smith, Roberta. "Squeak Carnwath at David Beitzel Gallery." *New York Times*, May 31, 1996, C22.

"Sorry World." *Magnolia Editions Newsletter,* no. 5, Winter 2004, 1, 3.

"Squeak Carnwath at Cohen Berkowitz Gallery." *Art Now Gallery Guide,* January 1997, 8.

"Squeak Carnwath at Shea & Beker." *Cover,* April 1990, 17.

"Squeak Carnwath at Sweeney Art Gallery, Riverside." *Art Now Gallery Guide*, November 2000, 8.

Steinberg, Aaron. "Eye Candy, 'Kid Stuff.'" *C-Ville: Charlottesville's News and Arts Weekly*, January 2001, 26.

Stutzin, Leo. "Puzzling Squeak at Stan State." *Modesto Bee*, November 19, 1995, G7.

Tamblyn, Christine. "Reviews: Squeak Carnwath." *ARTnews,* December 1989, 174.

Thym, Jolene. "Artport Takes Off: SFO Clears the Way for More Artwork." *Oakland Tribune,* CUE-1, CUE-2.

———. "You Can't Ignore Her Playful Works of Art." *Oakland Tribune*, April 22, 1994, CUE-8.

Van Proyen, Mark. "Perceptions of the Self and Native." *Artweek*, January 30, 1988, 3.

Welsh, Carol Ann. "Get Your Squeak On!" *Student Life* (Washington University, St. Louis), September 29, 2003.

Winn, Steven. "California Reviews: Ramps and Ghosts." *ARTnews*, January 1981, 77–78.

Wojtas, Thomas. "Squeak Carnwath at David Klein Gallery." *New Art Examiner,* April 1995

"Working Proof." *The Journal of Prints, Drawings, and Photography*, November–December 1997, 38.

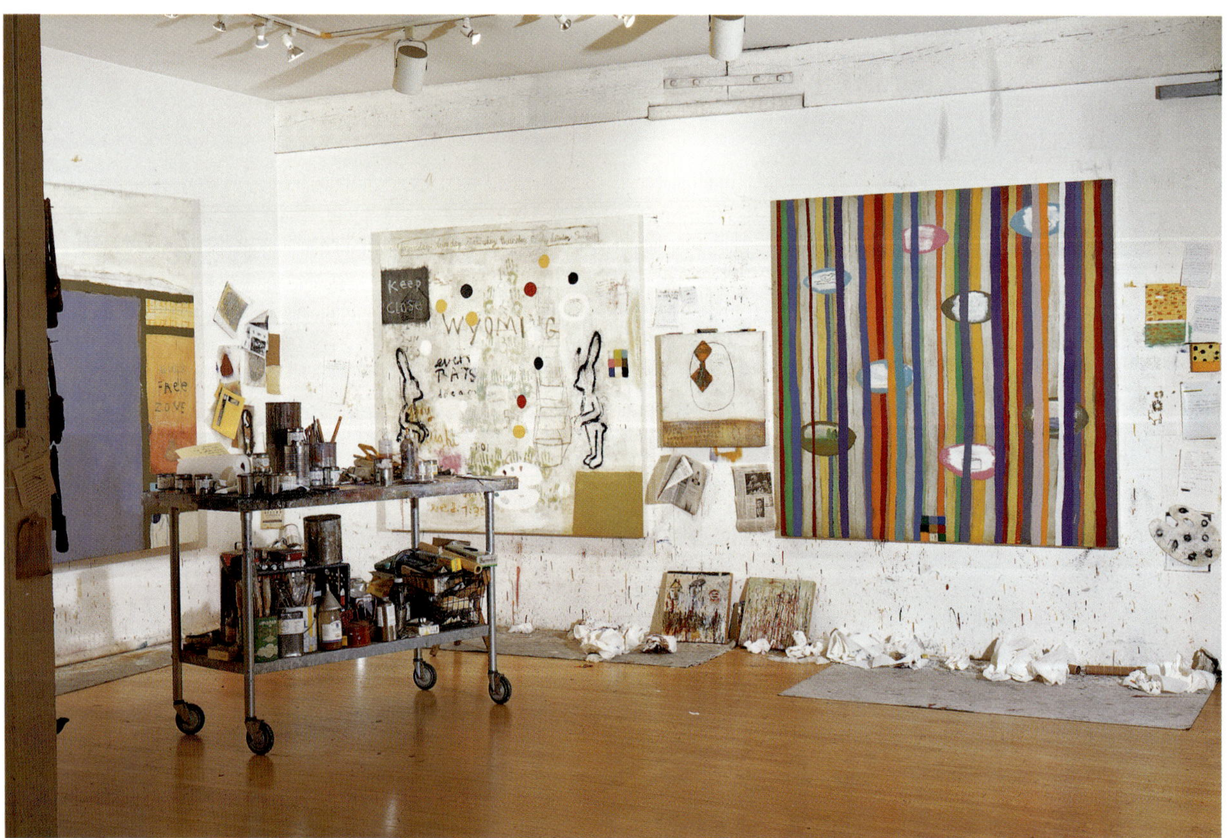

Egghouse studio, Oakland, c. 2001–2002. © M. Lee Fatherree.

selected exhibition history

Kathy Borgogno

SOLO AND TWO-PERSON EXHIBITIONS

1982 Hansen Fuller Goldeen, San Francisco. "Squeak Carnwath." March 3-27.

1983 Brentwood Gallery, St. Louis. "Squeak Carnwath." June 3-July 7.

Palo Alto Cultural Center, California. June 7-August 28.

1984 Fuller Goldeen Gallery, San Francisco. "Squeak Carnwath." March 14-April 7.

Getler/Pall/Saper, New York. "Squeak Carnwath: Paintings." April 3-28.

1985 Van Straaten Gallery, Chicago. "Squeak Carnwath." February 15-March 18.

Richard L. Nelson Gallery, University of California, Davis. "New Works/New Faculty: Squeak Carnwath Paintings and Drawings." September 29-November 1.

1986 Fuller Goldeen Gallery, San Francisco. "Squeak Carnwath." January 7-February 1.

Van Straaten Gallery, Chicago. "Squeak Carnwath." October 17-November 15.

1987 Marilyn Butler Fine Art, Scottsdale, Arizona. "Squeak Carnwath." October 8-24.

Davis Art Center, California. "Squeak Carnwath." October 9-November 6.

Gloria Luria Gallery, Miami. "Squeak Carnwath: New Paintings." December 4-24.

1988 Fuller Gross Gallery, San Francisco. "Squeak Carnwath: Boundaries." January 12-February 6.

Creative Growth Art Center, Oakland. "Making Marks." October 21-November 23.

1989 Dorothy Goldeen Gallery, Santa Monica, California. "Squeak Carnwath." February 18-March 18.

John Berggruen Gallery, San Francisco. "Squeak Carnwath." September 7- October 7.

Marilyn Butler Fine Art, Scottsdale, Arizona. "Squeak Carnwath." October 19-November 11.

1990 Shea & Beker, New York. "Squeak Carnwath." March 7-31.

University Art Gallery, San Diego State University. "Squeak Carnwath: Nature's Alchemy." April 21-May 16.

Shea & Beker, New York. "Squeak Carnwath: Words and Pictures." September 8-October 13.

Natsoulas Novelozo Gallery, Davis, California. October 5-31.

1991 Dorothy Goldeen Gallery, Santa Monica, California. "Squeak Carnwath." February 16-March 23. Brochure; essay by Mark Levy.

John Berggruen Gallery, San Francisco. "Squeak Carnwath." September 5-28. Catalogue.

1992 Monterey Peninsula Museum of Art, Monterey, California. "Squeak Carnwath: Recent Work." September 5-January 17, 1993.

Dorothy Goldeen Gallery, Santa Monica, California. "Squeak Carnwath, Daniel Wiener." November 21-December 31.

1993 LedisFlam, New York. "Squeak Carnwath." September 9-October 2.

1994 San Marco Gallery, San Rafael, California. "Squeak Carnwath: Oil Paintings." January 20–February 26.

The Chrysler Museum, Norfolk, Virginia. "Parameters: Squeak Carnwath." January 23–March 20. Traveled to San Jose Museum of Art, California, April 23–July 4; Contemporary Museum, Honolulu, November 16–January 15, 1995. Brochure; essay by Trinkett Clark.

Dorothy Goldeen Gallery, Marina Del Rey, California. "Squeak Carnwath: The Phantom Lover: Prints and Monotypes." April 15–May 28.

John Berggruen Gallery, San Francisco. "Squeak Carnwath: Recent Paintings." September 8–October 8. Catalogue; statement by the artist.

Cohen Berkowitz Gallery for Contemporary Art, Kansas City, Missouri. "Squeak Carnwath: Observations." October 14–November 12.

1995 Plaza Gallery, Bank of America World Headquarters, San Francisco. "Equations: The Paintings of Squeak Carnwath." September 18–November 17. Brochure; essay by Leah Levy.

Seigfred Gallery, Ohio University, Athens. "Squeak Carnwath: Paintings and Prints." September 25–October 18.

Dorothy Goldeen Gallery, Santa Monica, California. "Squeak Carnwath: Inside Thought." October 20–December 2. Brochure; essay by Leah Levy.

University Art Gallery, California State University, Stanislaus, Turlock. "Squeak Carnwath: Eden in the Studio." November 6–December 14. Brochure; essay by Nina Zagaris.

1996 David Beitzel Gallery, New York. "Squeak Carnwath." May 2–June 15.

John Berggruen Gallery, San Francisco. "Squeak Carnwath: Relative." November 22–January 4, 1997. Catalogue; essay by Jamie Brunson.

1997 Cohen, Berkowitz, Kansas City, Missouri. "Squeak Carnwath: Recent Paintings and Works on Paper." January 17–March 8.

1998 David Beitzel Gallery, New York. "Squeak Carnwath." January 7–February 14. Catalogue; essay by Maria Porges.

California Museum of Art, Luther Burbank Center for the Arts, Santa Rosa. "Squeak Carnwath: Seeing in the Dark." July 29–September 20. Brochure; essay by Gay Shelton.

John Berggruen Gallery, San Francisco. "Squeak Carnwath: Undraped Human Being." October 14–November 14. Catalogue; essay by Pauline Shaver.

1999 Museum of Contemporary Art, Palm Beach Community College, Lake Worth, Florida. "Squeak Carnwath: The Am-ness of Things." March 13–May 2. Brochure; text by Juan Rodriguez.

Gallery A, Chicago. "Squeak Carnwath: Paintings." March 26–April 24.

Byron Cohen Gallery, Kansas City, Missouri. "Squeak Carnwath: Stories." April 23–May 29.

Allene Lapides, Santa Fe, New Mexico. "Squeak Carnwath." September 17–October 30.

2000 David Beitzel Gallery, New York. "Squeak Carnwath." April 27–June 3.

Milwaukee Institute of Art & Design. "Marks and Conversions: The Graphic Works of Judy Pfaff and Squeak Carnwath." August 15–September 16. Brochure.

Sweeney Art Gallery, University of California, Riverside. "Squeak Carnwath: Selected Works." September 27–December 10. Brochure; essay by Karen Rapp.

2001 Fayerweather Gallery, University of Virginia, Charlottesville. "Squeak Carnwath/Selected Paintings." January 22-February 24. Brochure; text by R. Young.

John Berggruen Gallery, San Francisco. "Squeak Carnwath: Life Line." April 30-June 2. Catalogue; interview with Richard Whittaker.

James Harris Gallery, Seattle. "Squeak Carnwath." September 6-October 13.

Byron Cohen Gallery, Kansas City, Missouri. "Squeak Carnwath/Peregrine Honig." November 9-December 29.

2002 City of Oakland Craft and Cultural Arts Gallery. "Still Happy." May 13-June 21.

Allene Lapides Gallery, Santa Fe, New Mexico. "Squeak Carnwath: Selections from the Studio." October 4-December 31. Catalogue; essay by Douglas Maxwell.

2003 John Berggruen Gallery, San Francisco. "Squeak Carnwath: Paper Trail." October 22-November 22. Brochure.

2004 Oakland Art Gallery. "Squeak Carnwath." October 14-November 20.

Olin Art Gallery, Kenyon College, Gambier, Ohio. "Being Human: Paintings and Prints, 1998-2004." November 4-December 11. Brochure; essay by Dan Younger.

2005 Paulson Press, Berkeley, California. "Squeak Carnwath: Guilt Free Zone." May 6-July 16.

James Harris Gallery, Seattle. "Squeak Carnwath: Primary Research." May 19-June 25.

2006 Mendenhall Sobieski Gallery, Pasadena, California. "What Goes Around . . . " March 30-May 2.

Byron C. Cohen Gallery for Contemporary Art, Kansas City, Missouri. "Squeak Carnwath, Mette Tommerup." April 7-May 27.

Muse Gallery, Jackson, Wyoming. "Squeak Carnwath: A Dog Cannot Lie." August 11-September 18.

Nielsen Gallery, Boston. "Squeak Carnwath: Off the Record." October 21-November 25.

B. Sakato Garo, Sacramento, California. "Squeak Carnwath Paintings and Tapestries." November 1-December 2.

2007 Gail Severn Gallery, Ketchum, Idaho. "A Matter of Record." August 1-26.

The Townsend Center, University of California, Berkeley. "Squeak Carnwath." August 30-November 2.

JCM Art Gallery, Texas State University, San Marcos. "Squeak Carnwath: Short Stories." September 18-October 20.

2008 Cuesta College Art Gallery, San Luis Obispo, California. "Squeak Carnwath: New Paintings and Prints." February 8-March 5.

James Harris Gallery, Seattle. "Squeak Carnwath." May 15-June 28.

Slugfest Gallery, Austin, Texas. "Squeak Carnwath: Mixing It Up." November 1-30, 2008.

GROUP EXHIBITIONS

1971 Richmond Art Center, California. "Designer/Craftsman '71." March 26-April 25. Catalogue.

1972 Laguna Beach Museum of Art, California. "Women U.S.A." June 2-25.

1973 Richmond Art Center, California. "Designer-Craftsman '73." Dates not available. Catalogue.

Civic Arts Gallery, Walnut Creek, California. "Media." November 7-December 29. Catalogue.

1974 The Oakland Museum. "1974 California Ceramics & Glass." March 2-April 28. Catalogue.

1977 Isabelle Percy West Gallery, California College of Arts and Crafts, Oakland. "Squeak Carnwath, John Stascak, Peggy Vanbianchi: M.F.A. Exhibit." August 2-August 23.

1978 Berkeley Art Center, California. "Mixed Media on Paper: Thirty East Bay Women Artists." June 2-July 9.

Capricorn Asunder, San Francisco Art Commission Gallery. "Three Installations." November 6-December 1.

1980 Leah Levy, San Francisco. "Group Exhibition." January 10-February 10.

San Francisco Museum of Modern Art. "Society for the Encouragement of Contemporary Art (SECA) Art Award 1980." August 28-October 5. Brochure; essay by Suzanne Foley.

1981 Art Museum of South Texas, Corpus Christi. "The Figure: A Celebration." September 4-October 18. Traveled to University of North Dakota Art Galleries, Grand Forks, November 5-25.

University Galleries, California State University, Hayward. "Paintings." November 13-December 11.

1982 Richmond Art Center, California. "California College of Arts and Crafts: 75th Anniversary." September 14-October 28.

The Oakland Museum. "From the Sunny Side: Six East Bay Artists." October 2-31. Brochure.

1983 Fuller Goldeen Gallery, San Francisco. "Selections." May 4-June 4.

San Jose Institute of Contemporary Art, California. "*De te Fabula Narratur.*" May 14-June 11.

Southern Exposure Gallery, San Francisco. "The Impolite Figure." June 28-July 31. Catalogue.

De Saisset Museum, University of Santa Clara, California. "*Bon à tirer*: Selected Prints from East Bay Fine Arts Presses." September 27-December 11.

1984 Reese Bullen Gallery, Humboldt State University, Arcata, California. "Modern Romances: The Portrayal of Couples in New Bay Area Painting." January 10-February 4. Traveled to San Jose Institute of Contemporary Art, California, February 9-March 16, 1985.

Hearst Art Gallery, Saint Mary's College, Moraga, California. "The Subject is Objects: Contemporary Bay Area Still Life Paintings." March 10-April 22.

Fuller Goldeen Gallery, San Francisco. "Current Expressions: Paintings and Drawings." June 6-July 7.

Sheldon Memorial Art Gallery, University of Nebraska, Lincoln. "San Francisco Bay Area Painting." September 9-October 29. Catalogue; introduction by George W. Neubert.

Bank of America World Headquarters, San Francisco. "Highlights: Selections from the BankAmerica Corporation Art Collection." October 11-November 27.

Gloria Luria Gallery, Bay Harbor Islands, Florida. "California Deluxe: New Works by California Artists." Opening November 8.*

1985 Jane Voorhees Zimmerli Art Museum, Rutgers, The State University of New Jersey, New Brunswick. "Selections from the Rutgers Archives for Printmaking Studios." July 18-31.

Visual Arts Center of Alaska, Anchorage. "New Directions/California Painting 1985." September 16-October 12. Traveled to Fairbanks Art Association, November 1-30; Alaska State Museum, Juneau, January 18-March 2, 1986. Catalogue; essay by Pamela Hammond.

1986 Mandeville Gallery, University of California, San Diego, La Jolla. "Young American Artists IV." February 8-March 2.

University Art Museum, University of California, Berkeley. "Cal Collects 1." April 2-May 18. Brochure.

Allan Frumkin Gallery, New York. "Eccentric Drawings." June-July.*

The Brooklyn Museum, New York. "Third Western States Exhibition." June 6–August 5. Traveled nationally through April 3, 1988. Catalogue; essay by Charlotta Kotik.

Museum of Fine Arts, Boston. "70s into 80s: Printmaking Now." October 22–February 8, 1987. Catalogue; text by Clifford S. Ackley.

1987 Portland Center for the Visual Arts, Oregon. "Under Currents." February 27–March 29. Catalogue; essay by Peter Frank.

Fresno Arts Center and Museum, California. "Present Perspectives: 1975–1985." March 28–May 31.

Richmond Art Center, California. "Bay Area Drawing." May 15–July 16. Catalogue; text by Robert Tomlinson.

Nancy Hoffman Gallery, New York. "Four Bay Area Artists." June 6–July 24.

Prichard Art Gallery, University of Idaho, Moscow. "Viewing the Figure/Reflecting on the Self." September 11–October 18.

Monterey Peninsula Museum of Art, Monterey, California. "The Artist and the Myth." September 12–November 29. Brochure; text by Jo Farb Hernandez.

University Art Gallery, University of California, Riverside. "Diversity and Presence: Women Faculty Artists of the University of California." November 1–December 13. Traveled throughout California through January 27, 1989. Catalogue; essay by Melinda Wortz.

University Art Gallery, California State University, Stanislaus, Turlock. "The House in Contemporary Art." November 3–December 22. Catalogue; text by Dr. Hope B. Werness.

1988 University Art Gallery, California State University, Hayward. "Art: Not Narrative." February 22–March 16. Brochure; essay by Charles Shere.

American Academy and Institute of Arts and Letters, New York. "Paintings and Sculpture by Candidates for Art Awards." February 29–March 27.

Natsoulas Novelozo Gallery, Davis, California. "New Work '88." August 12–October 1.

Montgomery Gallery, Pomona College/Lang Gallery, Scripps College, Claremont, California. "Professors' Choice III." August 27–October 16.

John Berggruen Gallery, San Francisco. "Works on Paper: A Comprehensive Survey of Drawings and Watercolors." September 8–October 8. Catalogue.

Triton Museum of Art, Santa Clara, California. "Twelve Artists." September 22–November 13.

Hearst Art Gallery, Saint Mary's College, Moraga, California. "Contra Costa Contemporary Collections." October 29–December 11.

Dorothy Goldeen Gallery, Santa Monica, California. "Private Reserve." December 1–31.

Bernice Steinbaum Gallery, New York. "Alice and Look Who Else Through the Looking Glass." December 10–January 7, 1989. Traveled nationally and to Canada through June 15, 1991. Catalogue.

1989 Fay Gold Gallery, Atlanta. "Four California Artists." March 31–April 24.

Richard L. Nelson Gallery and the Fine Arts Collection, University of California, Davis. "A.C.D.H.H.H.J.N.P.P.S.T." April 23–May 24.

Robert Else Gallery, California State University, Sacramento. "Substance/Surface." April 25–May 25.

Rasmussen Art Gallery, Pacific Union College, Angwin, California. "Here's Looking at Us: A Selection of Figurative Works from the Rene and Veronica di Rosa Foundation." November 4–December 10.

1990 The Oakland Museum. "Oakland's Artists '90." March 24-July 1. Brochure; introduction by Harvey Jones.

John Berggruen Gallery, San Francisco. "Selected Paintings, Drawings and Sculpture." July 5-September 8.

Shea & Beker, New York. "Summer Group Show: Prints and Works on Paper." July 10-September 8.

Richmond Art Center, California. "The Painted Word." July 14-September 2.

Michael Dunev Gallery, San Francisco. "The Painted Monotype." Part I, October 4-31; Part II, November 1-30.

Bayfront Gallery, Pier 2, Fort Mason Center, San Francisco. "Lines of Force." October 5-December 21.

Dorothy Goldeen Gallery, Santa Monica. "Woodblocks, Etchings, Lithographs." October 13-November 10.

Ewing Gallery of Art and Architecture, University of Tennessee, Knoxville. "The Intimate Collaboration: Prints from the Teaberry Press." October 19-November 11. Traveled nationally through November 11, 2001; resumed national tour February 20, 2003 through December 7, 2004. Catalogue.

Jane Voorhees Zimmerli Art Museum, Rutgers, The State University of New Jersey, New Brunswick. "Intaglio Printing in the 1980s: Prints, Plates, and Proofs from the Rutgers Archives for Printmaking Studios." December 9-February 24, 1991. Catalogue; Trudy V. Hansen.

1991 Helander Gallery, New York. "Inaugural Awards to Women in the Fine Arts by The Alice Baber Art Fund, Inc." January 9-12.

Redding Museum of Art and History, California. "Selections from the Rene and Veronica di Rosa Foundation Collection of Northern California Art." January 10-February 14. Catalogue.

Sewall Art Gallery, Rice University, Houston. "California Monoprints." January 11-February 16.

The Oakland Museum. "Her Story: Narrative Art by Contemporary California Artists." January 12-March 24. Catalogue; essay by Therese Heyman.

Riverside Art Museum, California. "One Over One." February 15-April 28. Brochure; text by Jim Reed.

Dorothy Goldeen Gallery, Santa Monica, California. "Monochrome." March 31-May 11.

Berkeley Art Center, California. "Behind the Scenes: The Collaborative Process." April 28-June 2.

Shea & Bornstein Gallery, Santa Monica, California. August 1-September 7.

The National Museum of Women in the Arts, Washington, DC. "Presswork: The Art of Women Printmakers." Organized by Lang Communications Corporate Collection. September 24-December 1. Traveled nationally through October 9, 1994. Catalogue and brochure. Catalogue by Trudy Victoria Hansen and Eleanor Heartney.

Euphrat Gallery, De Anza College, Cupertino, California. "Freehand: Drawing Loosely Defined." October 15-November 26.

Bentley/Tomlinson Gallery, Scottsdale, Arizona. "Group Exhibition." December 5-29.

1992 Palo Alto Cultural Center, California. "Contemporary Uses of Wax and Encaustic." March 1-May 3.

Ellen Miller/Katie Block Fine Art, Boston. "West Comes East." March 7-April 4.

Central Exhibition Hall, St. Petersburg, Russia. "Art Contact." March 18-April 15. Catalogue.

Shea & Bornstein, Santa Monica, California. "Voices." June 6-July 30.

Modernism, San Francisco. "Beyond Just Words: I." September 10-October 31.

Syntex Gallery, Palo Alto, California. "Bay Area Greats." September 18-November 4.

Palo Alto Cultural Center, California. "Directions in Bay Area Printmaking: 3 Decades." September 20-January 3, 1993.

John Berggruen Gallery, San Francisco. "Objects of Affection." December 8-January 2, 1993.

Champion Gallery, Stamford, Connecticut. "All That Glitters." December 16-March 16, 1993.

1993 California Museum of Art, Santa Rosa, California. "Ten Years of Printmaking: Works from Magnolia Editions." February 26-April 10.

Montgomery Glasoe Fine Art, Minneapolis. "Rewriting History: The Salon of 1993." March 25-May 28.

Palo Alto Cultural Center, California. "Six Easy Pieces." June 17-July 18.

Joan Roebuck Gallery, Lafayette, California. "Fine-Art Prints." September 7-October 2.

1994 John Berggruen Gallery, San Francisco. "Twenty-Six Artists: A Selection of Works from John Berggruen Gallery." February 8-March 20.

The Oakland Museum. "Here and Now: Bay Area Masterworks from the di Rosa Collection." March 11-May 8. Catalogue; essay by Philip E. Linhares.

The Art Museum at Florida International University, Miami. "American Art Today: Heads Only." April 8-May 6. Catalogue; essay by Carol Damian.

The San Francisco Arts Commission Gallery. "The Women's Mentor Show." May 5-June 11. Catalogue; text by Beth Goldberg.

Friesen Gallery, Seattle. "Twenty-Six Artists: A Selection of Works from John Berggruen Gallery." May 7-July 13.

John Berggruen Gallery, San Francisco. "Points of Interest: Points of Departure." July 27-September 3.

Capp Street Project, San Francisco. "Old Glory, New Story: Flagging the 21st Century." December 1-February 2, 1995. Traveled to Santa Monica Museum of Art, California, July 1-30, 1995.

1995 Stephen Haller Gallery, New York. "Small Works." June 8-July 7.

Cohen, Berkowitz, Kansas City, Missouri. "Paper View: A Summer Salon." June 16-August 11.

International Centre of Graphic Arts (MGLC), Ljubljana, Slovenia. "Mednarodni Graficni Bienale (International Biennial of Graphic Art)." June 16-September 30. Catalogue.

Joan Roebuck Gallery, Lafayette, California. "Contemporary Masters' Prints." July 19-September 9.

John Berggruen Gallery, San Francisco. "XXV Years." September 7-October 11. Catalogue.

John Berggruen Gallery, San Francisco. "Objects of Desire." December 6-January 7, 1996. Brochure.

1996 Friesen Gallery, Ketchum, Idaho. "A Collaboration: John Berggruen Gallery at Friesen Gallery." August 2-September.*

California College of Arts and Crafts, Oakland. "CCAC: Past, Present and Future." September 4-October 26.

Richmond Art Center, California. "Generations: The Lineage of Influence in Bay Area Art." September 21-November 16. Catalogue; text by Jeff Nathanson.

Shasta College Gallery, Redding, California. "Art at UC Davis." October 30-December 12.

The American Academy of Arts and Letters, New York. "48th Annual American Academy Purchase Exhibition." November 4-December 1.

1997 University Art Gallery, University of California, San Diego, La Jolla. "Seduced by Surface: Eight Bay Area Painters." January 31-March 22.

Staatsgalerie Stuttgart. "The Magic of Numbers." February 1-May 19.

Bedford Gallery, Dean Lesher Regional Center for the Arts, Walnut Creek, California. "Anatomy of a Print." April 24-June 15.

California Museum of Art, Luther Burbank Center for the Arts, Santa Rosa. "A Thought Intercepted." May 7-July 13.

San Jose Museum of Art, California. "The Permanent Collection 1997: Recent Acquisitions." May 17-August 24.

Samuel P. Harn Museum of Art, Gainesville, Florida. "Evolving Forms/Emerging Faces." Organized by Jane Voorhees Zimmerli Art Museum, Rutgers, The State University of New Jersey, New Brunswick. September 12-March 6, 1998. Catalogue.

Fine Arts Museums of San Francisco, M. H. de Young Memorial Museum. "Bay Area Art from the Morgan Flagg Collection." October 18-January 4, 1998. Catalogue; essay by Timothy Anglin Burgard.

1998 David Beitzel Gallery, New York. "Knowing Children." June 19-July 31.

John Berggruen Gallery, San Francisco. "Wild Things: Artists' Views of the Animal World." July 23-September 4.

Traywick Gallery, Berkeley, California. "Prints from Paulson Press." August 12-September 13.

Nevada Museum of Art, Reno. "The Art of Collaborative Printmaking: Smith Andersen Editions." August 13-October 4. Catalogue; essay by Hilarie Faberman.

Richmond Art Center, California. "More Than Clay: The Toki Collection of Ceramics." September 2-November 14.

Cumberland Gallery, Nashville. "The Written Word: Text in Art." October 24-November 17.

1999 Meridian International Center, Washington, DC. "American Art at the Brink of the Twenty-First Century." May 20-July 11. Traveled to Museum of Fine Arts, Hanoi, August 25-September 23; Painting Institute, Shanghai, October 23-November 20; Working People's Cultural Palace, Beijing, December 8-December 28; CIPTA Gallery, Jakarta Arts Center, February 2000; Metropolitan Museum, Manila, April; Singapore Art Museum, July-September.*

San Jose Museum of Art, California. "Into the 21st Century: Selections from the Permanent Collection." May 23-September 12. Catalogue; text by Cathy Kimball, Patricia Hicks, and Karen Kienzle.

International Centre of Graphic Art (Tivoli Gallery, Modern Gallery, Jakopic Gallery, Cankarjev dom), Ljubljana, Slovenia. "23rd International Biennial of Graphic Art." June 19-September 30. Catalogue.

Palo Alto Art Center, California. "Artists' Pages." Organized by the Djerassi Resident Artists Program, Woodside, California. July 18-September 12. Traveled to Club Office Headquarters of the Commonwealth Club, San Francisco, November 1-30; San Francisco Arts Commission Gallery, June 27-August 4, 2001.

John Berggruen Gallery, San Francisco. "The Painted Canvas." September 14-October 23.

Bemis Center for Contemporary Arts, Omaha. "Sudden Incandescence." December 4-February 27, 2000.

2000 National Institute of Art and Disabilities Art Center, Richmond, California. "Presence." February 1-May 5.

Bedford Gallery, Dean Lesher Regional Center for the Arts, Walnut Creek, California. "Yellow: the First Color." February 6-April 9.

Worth Ryder Gallery, University of California, Berkeley. "Boom Boom: University of California Art Faculty." February 8-March 3.

John Berggruen Gallery, San Francisco. "Summer in the City: Major Paintings, Drawings and Sculpture." July 12-September 9.

David Beitzel Gallery, New York. "Summer Group Exhibition." July 20–August 31.

University Art Gallery, Sonoma State University, Rohnert Park, California. "Six Painters." November 2–December 17.

2001 Jane Voorhees Zimmerli Art Museum, Rutgers, The State University of New Jersey, New Brunswick. "Confrontations: Selections from the Rutgers Archives for Printmaking Studios." March 4–June 15.

John Berggruen Gallery, San Francisco. "Summer in the City." June 7–July 14.

Triton Museum of Art, Santa Clara, California. "Winter Work 2001." August 7–October 21. Brochure; text by Susan Hillhouse.

Bolinas Museum, California. "In Search of Form: Chairs by Artists, Architects and Designers." September 15–November 18.

Palo Alto Art Center, California. "Current Holdings: Bay Area Drawing/Bay Area Collections." September 23–January 2002.

Fine Arts Museums of San Francisco, California Palace of the Legion of Honor. "Recent Acquisitions of Contemporary California Works on Paper." October 27–February 10, 2002.

The Contemporary Museum, Honolulu. "Pay Attention . . . I Hope You Learned Your Lesson: Works from the Collection of Laila Twigg-Smith." November 2–January 6, 2002.

San Jose Museum of Art, California. "First Impressions: Paulson Press." December 1–March 17, 2002. Catalogue; text by Susan Landauer.

2002 Worth Ryder Gallery, University of California, Berkeley. "Fresh 02 Faculty Exhibition." February 12–March 8.

John Berggruen Gallery, San Francisco. "Spring Forward: New Work from the Studio." April 18–May 25.

Allene Lapides, Santa Fe, New Mexico. "Now in Residence." May 24–June.*

Berkeley Art Museum, University of California, Berkeley. "Fast Forward II." June 19–February 9, 2003.

Idyllwild Arts, Idyllwild, California. "Painting's Edge: The Exhibition." June 22–July 3. Brochure; text by David Wells.

Key Tower Gallery, Key Tower Building, Seattle Arts Commission, Washington. "Printworks 2002." July 29–August 25.

San Jose Museum of Art, California. "Collection Highlights." November 2–September 12, 2004.

2003 Worth Ryder Gallery, University of California, Berkeley. "Sprung." February 5–28.

Winston Wächter Mayer Fine Art, New York. "Rotations: An Alternating Exhibition of 20th–21st Century Work." May 21–September 27.

Sears-Peyton Gallery, New York. "Drawings." May 29–August 15.

John Berggruen Gallery, San Francisco. "A Way with Words." June 5–July 12.

Andrea Schwartz Gallery, San Francisco. "CCAC Alumni Exhibition Series." July 9–25.

Nathan Larramendy Gallery, Ojai, California. "Road Trip." September 5–October 31.

San Luis Obispo Art Gallery, California. "Drawings and Works on Paper: San Francisco/New York/Los Angeles." October 11–November 17. Brochure; text by Tim Anderson.

John Berggruen Gallery, San Francisco. "Color Form & Figure." November 25–January 3, 2004.

2004 Worth Ryder Gallery, University of California, Berkeley. "UCB Faculty Show." February 10–March 5.

The Kreeger Museum, Washington, DC. "The True Artist Is an Amazing Luminous Fountain." April 23–July 31. Catalogue.

DFN Gallery, New York. "Innocence Found." June 9–August 27.

Creative Growth, Oakland. "I Love Music." June 24–July 30.

San Jose Institute of Contemporary Art, California. "Weaving Weft and Warp: Tapestries from Magnolia Editions." July 23–September 17.

Bryon C. Cohen Gallery for Contemporary Art, Kansas City, Missouri. "Ten: Celebrating Our First Decade of Contemporary Art." September 11–October 30.

San Jose Museum of Art, California. "It's About Time: Celebrating 35 Years." October 3–February 13, 2005.

Winston Wächter Fine Art, Seattle. "Expansion." October 8–November 13.

Ruth Chandler Williamson Gallery, Scripps College, Claremont, California. "Reading Meaning: Word and Symbol in the Art of Squeak Carnwath, Lesley Dill, Leslie Enders Lee, and Anne Siems." October 30–December 19. Catalogue; essay by Margaret Mathews-Berenson.

Mendenhall-Sobieski Gallery, Pasadena, California. "Magnolia Tapestry Project: John Nava, Squeak Carnwath, Guy Diehl, and Don & Era Farnsworth." December 16–January 12, 2005.

2005 JayJay Gallery, Sacramento, California. "Magnolia Editions: Tapestries." January 5–February 19.

John Berggruen Gallery, San Francisco. "Paintings." January 12–February 12.

Sonoma Valley Museum of Art, Sonoma, California. "Artist/Teacher/Artist." January 22–February 27.

Worth Ryder Gallery, University of California, Berkeley. "Faculty Show." February 8–March 4.

Dwight Hackett Projects, Santa Fe, New Mexico. "Draw." April 2–May 14.

Di Rosa Preserve: Art and Nature, Napa, California. "Squeak Carnwath, Mildred Howard, Catherine Wagner: New Works." June 25–August 13.

The Judson Gallery, Los Angeles. "Tapestries by Contemporary Artists." September 17–January 6, 2006.

San Francisco Museum of Craft and Design. "Beyond the Pour: Pairing Art and Wine Label Design." October 21–January 29, 2006. Catalogue; introduction by Bob Nugent.

Bedford Gallery, Dean Lesher Regional Center for the Arts, Walnut Creek, California. "Majestic Tapestries of Magnolia Editions." November 30–January 29, 2006. Brochure; text by Carrie Lederer.

2006 Gail Severn Gallery, Ketchum, Idaho. "Surface." February 6–March 6.

Worth Ryder Gallery, University of California, Berkeley. "Faculty Exhibition." February 8–24.

Gail Severn Gallery, Ketchum, Idaho. "Painting as Object." March 8–April 21.

Muse Gallery, Jackson, Wyoming. "Limited Editions, Intaglio Prints." May 8–31.

Muse Gallery, Jackson, Wyoming. "A Feminine Approach: Women's Art Exhibition." June 2–July 6.

"The Missing Peace: Artists Consider the Dalai Lama." Organized by the Committee of 100 for Tibet and The Dalai Lama Foundation; Fowler Museum, University of California, Los Angeles, June 11–September 10; Loyola University Museum of Art, Chicago, October 28–January 14, 2007; Rubin Museum of Art, New York, March 16–September 3; Yerba Buena Center for the Arts, San Francisco, December 1–March 16, 2008; and continues to travel. Book.

2007 Nielsen Gallery, Boston. "Parallel Visions." January 20-February 24.

Worth Ryder Gallery, University of California, Berkeley. "Faculty Show 2007." February 7-23.

Richard L. Nelson Gallery, University of California, Davis. "Ten Tapestries from Magnolia Editions." March 29-May 20.

Di Rosa Preserve: Art and Nature, Napa, California. "CCA[C]@di Rosa Preserve." May 26-July 14.

Fine Arts Museums of San Francisco, M. H. de Young Memorial Museum. "Celebrating a Centennial: Contemporary Printmakers at CCA." September 29-January 6, 2008. Brochure.

Oakland Museum of California. "Artists of Invention: A Century of CCA." October 13-March 16, 2008. Brochure; essay by Philip E. Linhares. Catalogue; California College of the Arts.

Hallie Ford Museum of Art, Willamette University, Salem, Oregon. "Women's Work: Contemporary Women Printmakers from the Collection of Jordan D. Schnitzer and his Family Foundation." October 27-January 20, 2008. Traveled to Art Gym, Marylhurst University, Oregon, February 25-April 2. Brochure; essay by Robin Reisenfeld.

San Jose Museum of Art, California. "SJMA Collects CCA: Works on Paper from the Permanent Collection." November 10-February 3, 2008.

2008 Maier Museum of Art, Randolph College, Lynchburg, Virginia. "Prints from Tandem Press: Collaboration as Education." January 20-April 13.

Worth Ryder Gallery, University of California, Berkeley. "Make the Art You Need." February 6-22.

Di Rosa Preserve: Art and Nature, Napa, California. "Bay Area Ceramic Sculpture: Collection in Context." March 29-May 17.

The Heckscher Museum of Art, Huntington, New York. "To Infinity and Beyond: Mathematics in Contemporary Art." April 19-June 22.

Peter Mendenhall Gallery, Los Angeles. "Inaugural Group Exhibition." April 26-May 24.

Fort Collins Museum of Contemporary Art, Colorado. "Magnolia Tapestry Project." May 20-September 20.

National Academy Museum & School of Fine Arts, New York. "183rd Annual: An Invitational Exhibition of Contemporary American Art." May 29-September 7. Brochure.

Turner Carroll Gallery, Santa Fe, New Mexico. "The Tapestry Show." June 8-30.

* Dates not confirmed.

list of works illustrated

Titles marked with an asterisk (*) indicate artworks included in the exhibition. In the listing of dimensions, height precedes width precedes depth. Except as noted, all artworks photographed by M. Lee Fatherree.

1 *Her Room*, 1979
Mixed media installation, artist's Carleton Street studio, Berkeley, 1979
Approximately 213.4 x 457.2 x 914.4 cm (84 x 180 x 360 in.)
No longer extant

2 *My Own Ghost #9*, 1979
Mixed media on paper
157.5 x 132.1 cm (62 x 52 in.)
Location/existence unknown

3 *My Old House*, 1980
Acrylic on paper
106.7 x 76.2 cm (42 x 30 in.)
Location/existence unknown

4 *My Own Ghost*, 1980
Mixed media installation, San Francisco Museum of Modern Art, 1980
281.9 x 609.6 x 548.6 cm (111 x 240 x 216 in.)
No longer extant

5 *Sum Equations*, 1980
Acrylic on paper
106.7 x 76.2 cm (42 x 30 in.)
Collection of the artist

6 *I Must Try Harder To Believe*, 1981
Oil and acrylic on canvas
243.8 x 182.9 cm (96 x 72 in.)
Collection of Oakland Museum of California; acquired through funds provided by the Collectors Gallery

7 *Keepers of Our Culture*, 1981
Mixed media
147.3 x 33 x 33 cm (58 x 13 x 13 in.)
Collection of the artist

8 *Head Ache*, 1983
Oil on canvas
137.2 x 121.9 cm (54 x 48 in.)
Collection of the artist

9 *Companion*, 1984
Charcoal on paper
166.2 x 179.1 cm (65 7/16 x 70½ in.)
Collection of Nancy and Steven H. Oliver, San Francisco

10 *Between*, 1987
Oil and alkyd on canvas
152.4 x 152.4 cm (60 x 60 in.)
Collection of the artist

11 *Boundaries*, 1987
Oil and alkyd on canvas
208.3 x 233.7 cm (82 x 92 in.)
Collection of Art Berliner, San Francisco

12 *Grace*, 1989
Oil and alkyd on canvas
195.6 x 195.6 cm (77 x 77 in.)
Collection of Christopher Hest, San Francisco

13 *Fragile Thoughts*, 1991
Oil and alkyd on canvas
177.8 x 177.8 cm (70 x 70 in.)
Private collection

14 *Reasons*, 1991
Oil on alkyd on canvas
208.3 x 208.3 cm (82 x 82 in.)
Private collection

15 *A Call To Be*, 1992
Oil and alkyd on canvas
208.3 x 208.3 cm (82 x 82 in.)
Collection of Squeak Carnwath and Gary Knecht

16 *An Inability to Remain*, 1992
Oil and alkyd on linen
177.8 x 177.8 cm (70 x 70 in.)
Private collection

17 *Miracle*, 1992
Oil and alkyd on canvas
208.3 x 208.3 cm (82 x 82 in.)
Collection of the artist

18 *Black Is*, 1994*
Oil and alkyd on canvas
208.3 x 208.3 cm (82 x 82 in.)
Private collection

19 *Don't Forget*, 1994
Oil and alkyd on canvas
121.9 x 121.9 cm (48 x 48 in.)
Private collection, San Francisco

20 *Four Months*, 1994*
Oil and alkyd on canvas
203.2 x 203.2 cm (80 x 80 in.)
Collection of Sandra and Gerald Eskin, Chicago

21 *Some Same,* 1994*
Egg tempera on birch wood
38.1 x 38.1 cm (15 x 15 in.)
Collection of Maribelle and Stephen Leavitt, San Francisco

22 *This Is Not,* 1994
Oil and alkyd on canvas
259.1 x 193 cm (102 x 76 in.)
Collection of Bill Fromm, Mission Hills, Kansas

23 *Water Cake Lily,* 1994*
Oil and alkyd on board
22.9 x 22.9 cm (9 x 9 in.)
Collection of Natasha Beery and William B. McCoy, Berkeley, California

24 *What Is Red,* 1994
Oil and alkyd on canvas
203.2 x 203.2 cm (80 x 80 in.)
Private collection

25 *What White Is,* 1994*
Oil and alkyd on canvas
203.2 x 406.4 cm (80 x 160 in.) (two panels)
Collection of Oakland Museum of California; gift of the Art Guild of the Oakland Museum of California and friends and family in memory of Anne Gray Walrod

26 *All That I Know,* 1995*
Oil and alkyd on linen
121.9 x 121.9 cm (48 x 48 in.)
Collection of Wynn and Lauren Hanson Kapit, Santa Barbara, California

27 *Imprint,* 1995
Oil and alkyd on linen
121.9 x 121.9 cm (48 x 48 in.)
Collection of the artist

28 *Purple is Purple,* 1995*
Oil and alkyd on canvas
208.3 x 208.3 cm (82 x 82 in.)
Collection of Squeak Carnwath and Gary Knecht

29 *Things Green,* 1995
Oil and alkyd on canvas
193 x 259.1 cm (76 x 102 in.)
Collection of Squeak Carnwath and Gary Knecht

30 *Yellow Stuff,* 1995
Oil and alkyd on canvas
208.3 x 208.3 cm (82 x 82 in.)
Private collection

31 *Green Floor,* 1996*
Oil and alkyd on canvas
195.6 x 195.6 cm (77 x 77 in.)
Collection of Squeak Carnwath and Gary Knecht

32 *No More, No More,* 1996
Oil and alkyd on canvas
208.3 x 208.3 cm (82 x 82 in.)
Collection of Lynn and John Pleshette, Los Angeles

33 *Red Occupation,* 1996
Oil and alkyd on canvas
195.6 x 195.6 cm (77 x 77 in.)
Collection of Phil Schlein, San Francisco

34 *Towards Earth (1995-96),* 1996
Oil and alkyd on canvas
208.3 x 105.4 cm (82 x 41½ in.)
Collection of Francie Bishop Good and David Horvitz, Fort Lauderdale, Florida

35 *Two Minds,* 1996
Oil and alkyd on linen
139.7 x 139.7 cm (55 x 55 in.)
Collection of Justine and Steve Noonan, Alamo, California

36 *Trying To Know Lost,* 1997*
Oil and alkyd on canvas
203.2 x 279.4 cm (80 x 110 in.)
Collection of Katherine Ruttenberg, Bearsville, New York

37 *Assignment,* 1998*
Oil and alkyd on canvas
25.4 x 25.4 cm (10 x 10 in.)
Collection of Ann Hatch, San Francisco

38 *Lost Small,* 1998*
Oil and alkyd on canvas
50.8 x 50.8 cm (20 x 20 in.)
Collection of Bonney Goldstein, New Castle, New Hampshire

39 *Memory Structure,* 1998*
Oil and alkyd on canvas
76.2 x 76.2 cm (30 x 30 in.)
Collection of Katie and Amnon Rodan

40 *Nursery Wall,* 1998
Oil and alkyd on canvas
121.9 x 121.9 cm (48 x 48 in.)
Collection of Paul Babikow, Baltimore

41 *Things I've Heard or Seen in Person*, 1998*
Oil and alkyd on canvas
195.6 x 195.6 cm (77 x 77 in.)
Collection of the artist

42 *True Life*, 1998
Oil and alkyd on canvas
195.6 x 195.6 cm (77 x 77 in.)
Collection of Mr. and Mrs. Paul Stephens, Tiburon, California

43 *Plaid Lost*, 1999*
Oil and alkyd on canvas over wood panel
61 x 61 cm (24 x 24 in.)
Collection of Michael Polenske, Napa, California

44 *Promise*, 1999*
Oil and alkyd on canvas
203.2 x 203.2 cm (80 x 80 in.)
Collection of Joan Warren-Grady, La Jolla, California

45 *Resident Drawing N.M.*, 1999
Oil, alkyd, and graphite on sized paper over panel
38.1 x 38.1 cm (15 x 15 in.)
Collection of the artist

46 *The Story Of Painting*, 1999*
Oil and alkyd on canvas
195.6 x 259.1 cm (77 x 102 in.)
Private collection, Kansas City, Missouri
Photograph by E. G. Schempf

47 *Think About It*, 1999*
Oil and alkyd on canvas
195.6 x 259.1 cm (77 x 102 in.)
Collection of University of California, Berkeley Art Museum and Pacific Film Archives; purchase made possible through a gift from Phoebe Apperson Hearst

48 *In Pursuit of Happiness*, 2000*
Oil and alkyd on canvas
195.6 x 195.6 cm (77 x 77 in.)
Collection of Squeak Carnwath and Gary Knecht

49 *Obit*, 2000
Oil and alkyd on canvas
203.2 x 203.2 cm (80 x 80 in.)
Collection of the artist

50 *Please*, 2000*
Oil and alkyd on canvas
203.2 x 203.2 cm (80 x 80 in.)
Collection of Squeak Carnwath and Gary Knecht

51 *Trying Simply To Be Happy*, 2000*
Oil and alkyd on canvas
177.8 x 177.8 cm (70 x 70 in.)
Collection of Halsey Minor, San Francisco

52 *What We Cannot Control*, 2000*
Oil and alkyd on linen over panel
91.4 x 91.4 cm (36 x 36 in.)
Collection of Myrna and Stuart Aronoff, San Francisco

53 *World Upside Down*, 2000*
Oil and alkyd on canvas over panel
38.1 x 38.1 cm (15 x 15 in.)
Collection of Stephanie and Andrew Douglass, New York

54 *Anymore*, 2001*
Oil and alkyd on canvas over panel
177.8 x 177.8 cm (70 x 70 in.)
Private collection

55 *Numbered Moments*, 2001*
Oil and alkyd on canvas over panel
61 x 61 cm (24 x 24 in.)
Collection of Tracy Bosworth Bosche, Berkeley, California

56 *You Call This Happy*, 2001
Oil and alkyd on canvas
195.6 x 195.6 cm (77 x 77 in.)
Private collection

57 *Everything (2)*, 2002*
Oil and alkyd on canvas over panel
195.6 x 391.2 cm (77 x 154 in.) (two panels)
Collection of the artist, courtesy John Berggruen Gallery, San Francisco

58 *Long Happy Life*, 2002*
Oil and alkyd on canvas over panel
195.6 x 195.6 cm (77 x 77 in.)
Santiago Collection, Atherton, California

59 *But For Monkeys*, 2003
Oil and alkyd on canvas over panel
188 x 188 cm (74 x 74 in.)
Private collection

60 *Good Luck*, 2003*
Oil and alkyd on canvas over panel
195.6 x 195.6 cm (77 x 77 in.)
Collection of the artist

61 *Lucky*, 2003*
Oil and alkyd on canvas over panel
182.9 x 182.9 cm (72 x 72 in.)
Collection of Elizabeth and Frederick Crockett

62 *Mind's Freedom*, 2003*
Oil and alkyd on paper over panel
25.4 x 22.9 cm (10 x 9 in.)
Collection of Beth and Hank Holland, Ross, California

63 *Right Now,* 2003*
Oil and alkyd on canvas over panel
195.6 x 195.6 cm (77 x 77 in.)
Collection of Sally and Tim Howard, Atherton, California

64 *2 Things,* 2003*
Oil and alkyd on canvas over panel
195.6 x 195.6 cm (77 x 77 in.)
Collection of Jon and Sonja Hoel Perkins, San Francisco

65 *Last Frontier,* 2004
Oil and alkyd on canvas over panel
195.6 x 195.6 cm (77 x 77 in.)
Private collection

66 *School Demo Tree,* 2004*
Oil and alkyd on canvas
25.4 x 20.3 cm (10 x 8 in.)
Collection of Squeak Carnwath and Gary Knecht

67 *Stolen Borrowed,* 2004*
Oil and alkyd on canvas over panel
195.6 x 195.6 cm (77 x 77 in.)
Collection of the artist, courtesy Nielsen Gallery, Boston

68 *Best Borrowed,* 2005
Oil and alkyd on canvas over panel
177.8 x 177.8 cm (70 x 70 in.)
Collection of Martha Angus, San Francisco

69 *Gone,* 2005*
Oil and alkyd on canvas over panel
228.6 x 203.2 cm (90 x 80 in.)
Collection of the artist, courtesy Gail Severn Gallery, Ketchum, Idaho

70 *Manifestation,* 2005
Oil and alkyd on canvas over panel
203.2 x 228.6 cm (80 x 90 in.)
Collection of the artist

71 *Primary Research,* 2005
Oil and alkyd on canvas over panel
127 x 101.6 cm (50 x 40 in.)
Collection of Lucinda O'Connell, St. Thomas, Virgin Islands

72 *Reflection,* 2005*
Oil and alkyd on canvas over panel
228.6 x 203.2 cm (90 x 80 in.)
Collection of the artist

73 *Side One,* 2005*
Oil and alkyd on canvas over panel
76.2 x 76.2 cm (30 x 30 in.)
Private collection, Hunts Point, Washington, courtesy James Harris Gallery, Seattle

74 *A Painting,* 2006*
Oil and alkyd on canvas over panel
139.7 x 114.3 cm (55 x 45 in.)
Collection of the artist, courtesy James Harris Gallery, Seattle

75 *First Water,* 2006*
Oil and alkyd on canvas over panel
182.9 x 177.8 cm (72 x 70 in.)
Private collection, San Francisco
Photograph by Almac Camera, Donald Felton

76 *Gone Is Forever,* 2006
Oil and alkyd on canvas over panel
177.8 x 177.8 cm (70 x 70 in.)
Collection of the artist
Photograph by Art Works

77 *The Whole Truth,* 2006*
Oil and alkyd on canvas over panel
228.6 x 203.2 cm (90 x 80 in.)
Collection of the artist, courtesy James Harris Gallery, Seattle

78 *Will or Won't,* 2006*
Oil and alkyd on canvas over panel
152.4 x 177.8 cm (60 x 70 in.)
Collection of Arlene and Harold Schnitzer, Portland, Oregon

79 *Lessons Benefit,* 2007*
Oil on alkyd on canvas over panel
203.2 x 228.6 cm (80 x 90 in.)
Collection of the artist, courtesy James Harris Gallery, Seattle

80 *Real and True,* 2007*
Oil and alkyd on canvas over panel
177.8 x 152.4 cm (70 x 60 in.)
Collection of Linden Rhoads, Seattle

81 *Gateway,* 2008
Oil and alkyd on canvas over panel
139.7 x 127 cm (55 x 50 in.)
Collection of the artist

index

Page numbers in *italics* refer to illustrations.